Frontispiece **Ridley Scott,** *Blade Runner* **(1982).** Rutger Hauer and Daryl Hannah seeking J.F. Sebastian. See the chapter on Performance for a discussion of this movie.

Source: Warner Bros. Copyright © 1982 The Ladd Company (Courtesy of the Kobal Collection)

Mary Shelley's
Frankenstein

Mary Shelley's *Frankenstein* (1818) is one of the most widely studied and enjoyed works of English literature, and Frankenstein's creature has become a key figure in the popular imagination.

Taking the form of a sourcebook, this guide to Shelley's troubling novel offers:

- extensive introductory comment on the contexts and many interpretations of the text, from publication to the present
- annotated extracts from key contextual documents, reviews, critical works and the text itself
- cross-references between documents and sections of the guide, in order to suggest links between texts, contexts and criticism
- suggestions for further reading.

Part of the *Routledge Guides to Literature* series, this volume is essential reading for all those beginning detailed study of *Frankenstein* and seeking not only a guide to the novel, but a way through the wealth of contextual and critical material that surrounds Shelley's text.

Timothy Morton teaches English at the University of Colorado at Boulder, USA and has published widely on Romantic Literature.

Routledge Guides to Literature*

Editorial Advisory Board: Richard Bradford (University of Ulster at Coleraine), Jan Jedrzejewski (University of Ulster at Coleraine), Duncan Wu (St. Catherine's College, University of Oxford)

Routledge Guides to Literature offer clear introductions to the most widely studied authors and literary texts.

Each book engages with texts, contexts and criticism, highlighting the range of critical views and contextual factors that need to be taken into consideration in advanced studies of literary works. The series encourages informed but independent readings of texts by ranging as widely as possible across the contextual and critical issues relevant to the works examined and highlighting areas of debate as well as those of critical consensus. Alongside general guides to texts and authors, the series includes "sourcebooks", which allow access to reprinted contextual and critical materials as well as annotated extracts of primary text.

Available in this series:

* Some books in this series were originally published in the Routledge Literary Sourcebooks series, edited by Duncan Wu, or the Complete Critical Guide to English Literature series, edited by Richard Bradford and Jan Jedrzejewski.

Mary Shelley's
Frankenstein
A Sourcebook

Edited by Timothy Morton

Routledge
Taylor & Francis Group

LONDON AND NEW YORK

First published 2002 by Routledge
11 New Fetter Lane, London EC4P 4EE

Simultaneously published in the USA and Canada
by Routledge
29 West 35th Street, New York, NY 10001

Routledge is an imprint of the Taylor & Francis Group

This volume first published as *A Routledge Literary Sourcebook on Mary Shelley's Frankenstein*

Typeset in Sabon and Gill Sans by RefineCatch Limited, Bungay, Suffolk
Printed and bound in Great Britain by
TJ International Ltd, Padstow, Cornwall

British Library Cataloguing in Publication Data
A catalogue record for this book is available from the British Library

Library of Congress Cataloging in Publication Data
A catalog record for this book has been requested

ISBN 0–415–22731–3 (hbk)
ISBN 0–415–22732–1 (pbk)

Contents

2: Interpretations

Modern Criticism 80

3: Key Passages

Key Passages of *Frankenstein*   129

4: Further Reading

Illustrations

Annotation and Footnotes

Annotation is a key feature of this series. Both the original notes from reprinted texts and new annotations by the editor appear at the bottom of the relevant page. The reprinted notes are preface by the author's name in square brackets, e.g. [Robinson's note].

Acknowledgements

This book is designed principally for students, and, as a matter of fact, it could not have been written without the sterling support of my two research assistants, Daemian McGill and Terry Robinson. The reader will find ample evidence of their incredible work on this volume throughout. Our work on this volume has been almost fully collaborative; and I have been newly inspired about English literature in general, and *Frankenstein* in particular, because of their presence on the project. This has been especially valuable as they are the ideal student audience for the volume itself.

Duncan Wu very kindly helped at all stages of this sourcebook's production. I would like to thank Elizabeth Thompson and Rosie Waters at Routledge, Taylor & Francis for seeing the book through to publication.

For their help, comments and generous support, I would like to thank the following: Barbara Hill, Jeffrey Cox, Tim Fulford, Denise Gigante, Nicholas Halmi, Joe Riehl, Hugh Roberts, Kate Stephenson, John Stevenson, Mark Winokur and Katherine Whalen. I would like to thank all those who participated in a discussion of *Frankenstein* instigated by me on the email list for the North American Society for Studies in Romanticism, and especially Ian Balfour, John Isbell, Beth Lau, Alan Richardson, Charles Robinson, David Rollinson and Michele Sharp.

I dedicate this book to my undergraduate students of the past, present and future. Unlike the creation of Frankenstein's creature, the creation of my ideas about Shelley's novel has been collaborative and social. I trust that it will not be taken as a paradox to declare that without teaching the ideas that went into this book, I would not have had them.

The following publishers, institutions and individuals have kindly given permission to reprint materials:

CAMBRIDGE UNIVERSITY PRESS INC., for Alan Richardson, *Literature, Education and Romanticism: Reading as Social Practice*; Timothy Morton, *Shelley and the Revolution in Taste*. Published by Cambridge University Press, 1994.

COLUMBIA UNIVERSITY PRESS, for Eve Kosofsky Sedgwick, *Between Men:*

English Literature and Homosocial Desire. Published by Columbia University Press, 1985.

HARVARD UNIVERSITY PRESS, for Gayatri Chakravorty Spivak, *A Critique of Colonial Reason: Towards a Theory of the Vanishing Present*, pp. 132–40. Cambridge, Mass.: Harvard University Press. Copyright © 1999 by the President and Fellows of Harvard College.

JOHNS HOPKINS UNIVERSITY PRESS, for Barbara Johnson, *A World of Difference*, pp. 145–6; 150–1. Copyright © 1987. Reprinted by permission of the Johns Hopkins University Press; Mary Jacobus, 'Is there a woman in this text?' in *New Literary History*, 14:1 (1982), pp. 130–5. Copyright © The University of Virginia. Reprinted by permission of the Johns Hopkins University Press.

TIM MARSHALL, for the extract from *Murdering to Dissect*. Published by Manchester University Press, 1995.

OHIO UNIVERSITY PRESS, for Richard Brinsley Peake, *Presumption: Or the Fate of Frankenstein* in Jeffrey Cox (ed.) *Seven Gothic Dramas 1789–1825*. Published by Ohio University Press, 1992.

OXFORD UNIVERSITY PRESS, for H.L. Malchow, 'Frankenstein's Monster and Images of Race in Nineteenth-Century Britain'. Published in *Past and Present* Vol. 139, pp. 90–130 (1993); Paula Feldman and Diana Scott-Kilvert (eds) *The Journals of Mary Shelley 1814–1844* (2 Vols) by Mary Wollstonecraft Shelley. Published by the Clarendon Press, 1987. Reprinted by permission of Oxford University Press. Marilyn Butler, 'The Shelleys and Radical Science' in Marilyn Butler (ed.), *Frankenstein*. Published by Oxford University Press, 1994.

KATHLEEN SULLIVAN, for the extract from 'Sublime aspects of the monster's monstrosity . . . ' from her PhD thesis.

UNIVERSITY OF OKLAHOMA, for Michael Scrivener, '*Frankenstein*'s Ghost Story: The Last Jacobin Novel' in *Genre: Forms of Discourse and Culture*.

VERSO, for Franco Moretti, *Signs Taken for Wonders: Essays in the Sociology of Literary Forms*, translated by Susan Fischer, David Forgacs and David Miller, pp. 83–90.

The publishers have made every effort to contact copyright holders. Any omissions brought to our attention will be rectified in future editions.

Introduction

There is a long tradition of comparing one's own work on *Frankenstein* with Mary Shelley's work on the novel and especially with Dr Frankenstein's work on the two creatures; indeed the tradition was started by Shelley herself (see the Preface to the 1831 edition in this volume). I say 'creatures', though to be honest no one I have read has so far compared their own work with the disjointed, unfinished *female* creature that Victor Frankenstein leaves unfinished 'among the deserts of Scotland', salient as that image is to a feminist reading of the text. So let me be the first in making this analogy explicit. Far from even pretending to be an organic whole, this sourcebook is designed to be the companion to a decent edition of *Frankenstein*, such as Marilyn Butler's (Oxford, 1994). And unlike the analogy, in which Frankenstein fears his creatures' putative progeny, I look forward to seeing what new species of reading this companionship will bring.

In an age of genetic research, genetic engineering, biotechnology and cloning, the most total industrialisation of life forms to date, Shelley's novel has if anything become even more potent than before. *Frankenstein* has received many different treatments, especially in recent years, with the growing interest in Romantic-period women's writing in general and Mary Shelley in particular. The novel is fascinating to students for all the reasons literature is fascinating: questions of textual scholarship, literary interpretation, and literary, cultural and political history. This edition takes account of the recent developments in criticism and the long history of writing on Mary Shelley. It is intended to guide the student reader through the text in a constructive fashion; to present a complete, compact view of *Frankenstein*.

This book is designed to help the undergraduate student and advanced high-school student find their way around the text of Shelley's great novel, its historical and cultural context, and criticism on it. My role as editor has been quite 'hands-on': my task has been to steer the reader around the various texts collected here. I hope that if this is the first time you have looked into *Frankenstein*, you will find this a helpful and easy volume to use as a reference tool alongside a proper complete text. It may also be helpful to have within sight a copy of Anne Mellor's *Mary Shelley: Her Life, Her Fiction, Her Monsters*.

Mary Shelley was inspired to write *Frankenstein* as part of a ghost-story competition on 16 June 1816 at Byron's residence, the Villa Diodati at Cologny on the southern shore of Lac Léman in Switzerland. She, Claire Clairmont and Percy had travelled there to visit. On 15 June, Percy Shelley had a discussion about science with the assembled guests, who included Byron's doctor John William Polidori. Percy participated in the writing of the novel, suggesting, for example, that Frankenstein travel to England to assemble the female creature (*Frankenstein* ed. Rieger xviii), and correcting the proofs in 1817. On Wednesday 18 June 1817, *Frankenstein* was sent back by the publisher John Murray. On Saturday 24 August, Shelley received a letter from the firm of Lackington, Hughes, Harding, Mavor and Jones offering to publish the book. Negotiations occurred in September. The text was printed and ready for publication by Wednesday 31 December 1817 (*Journal* 189; see Contemporary Documents for further information). By December 1818 Shelley was already experimenting with revisions to the novel. In 1823, William Godwin, Shelley's father, arranged for the volume to be reprinted in two volumes. This edition is not of the significance of the 1818 and 1831 editions. Nevertheless, in the same year, Shelley presented an annotated copy of the first edition to her friend Mrs Thomas at Genoa in July 1823, with passages marked that would eventually be differently revised in the 1831 edition. The publishers Bentley and Colburn were eventually persuaded to publish this in their Standard Novels series; Shelley had begun her enquiries about this possibility in 1827.

I have chosen to use for my text the the first published version of *Frankenstein*. Why? One might object that the later Standard Novels edition, as Mary Shelley's final 'say' on the text, would be preferable. This was indeed sound editorial practice according to more traditional editing theory. Recently, however, theorists of editing have pointed out ways in which this practice is not entirely watertight. For example, an earlier version of a work might have contained material to which an author might later object. That is certainly the case with *Frankenstein*, and also with Shelley's contemporary William Wordsworth, whose long autobiographical poem *The Prelude* is significantly different in its published (1850) and pre-published forms (there are at least two of those: 1799 and 1805). Shelley thought that her novel was too radical: it could be read, for instance, as making a case against Christianity and promoting a materialist view of life (see Marilyn Butler's essay in this volume). In brief, the later edition puts more emphasis on Frankenstein as a presumptuous imitator of God. The earlier edition makes more of the contemporary scientific debate, in which Mary and Percy Shelley were both involved, between vitalist and materialist theories of life. Their friend William Lawrence was a key player in this debate, and the issue was sparking public interest around the time the original text was written. Should an apparently 'older and wiser' (and often more conservative) author be credited with changing their work in an objective, 'fair' way? All editorial decisions are to some extent political, including of course the author's editorial decisions. As the illusion of editorial objectivity disguises its basis in political decisions, the rationale that it is objectively preferable to choose a later version of the text is thus questionable.

I have included an account of later stage and film performances and adaptations of the novel. This is a very significant part of its reception history. I have, moreover, chosen to expand the notion of performance to include other cultural manifestations of the Frankenstein myth (as it has become). For example, the 'creature' (it seems more accurate not to describe him as the 'monster', which is his creator's designation) became a political archetype, the image of the gathering power of the nineteenth-century industrial working class. Chris Baldick's *In Frankenstein's Shadow* (1987) is an excellent guide to the ways in which the creature became a motif for the oppressed worker, and in this edition there will be some extracts from Baldick's argument and an exploration of some of the source materials. For example, nineteenth-century graphic satire about working-class solidarity tended to use the creature. John Tenniel executed two significant cartoons using the motif (1866, 1882), and Joseph Kenny Meadows portrayed the Irish as the creature in 1843.

The intention of this book is to give a completely digested, or at least a strongly orientated, view of the novel. In compiling the extracts from recent criticism of the novel, I have tried to select items that are not readily available in collections of essays that are currently circulating. The list of further reading at the end of this volume should point out interesting directions for future research – I have chosen not to duplicate the work that appears in other collections. I think that this book will be most helpful if you use it as a kind of hub, or bay, that will connect you with other books in the library or articles in the periodicals room.

The chapter that follows this introduction is a contextual overview, which outlines the salient features of the age in which Shelley was writing. There follows a chronology of Shelley's life, concentrating on the moment at which *Frankenstein* was conceived and written. There is an account of some of the contemporary cultural contexts in which the novel emerged, for example the debates surrounding the life sciences in which Shelley was herself engaged. A collection of extracts has been assembled from some of the early critical receptions of *Frankenstein*, while the chapter that follows explores the work in performance. The next chapter contains readings from modern criticism of the novel. *Frankenstein* itself is then presented, in the form of extracts selected for their relevance to some early and recent critical readings elsewhere in this volume. I have annotated these to hint at possible readings, especially ones that might interconnect with other texts in this sourcebook. The final chapters are a list of further reading and recommended editions of the novel, and a directory of figures, who appear throughout the sourcebook, in Shelley's immediate and more broadly ambient cultural milieux. All the figures discussed in this directory are marked in bold text on their first occurrence in the sourcebook.

1

Contexts

Contextual Overview

This part of the sourcebook is designed to help you navigate around the history of *Frankenstein*: the period in which Mary Shelley lived, and the immediate contexts connected with her authorship. It consists of a chronology of Mary Shelley's life, a selection of contemporary documents associated with the novel's writing.

Shelley's life up until the time at which she wrote *Frankenstein* was caught up in the turbulent political, scientific, cultural and literary moment often known as the Romantic period. Although recently some scholars have begun to question the efficacy of using that name (not all cultural phenomena of the period can be described as 'Romantic'), the term will serve as a useful shorthand in this overview. Shelley was born into a family pivotal in the radical thought of the period. The American and French Revolutions had established polities based on the notion that all people were equal and that all possessed certain capacities and inalienable rights. Inspired by such events, radicals from all classes were reshaping the discourses of gender, class and race. For example, Shelley's mother, **Mary Wollstonecraft** (1759–97) was the author of *A Vindication of the Rights of Woman* (1792). While working for **Joseph Johnson** as a staff writer for his *Analytical Review*, Wollstonecraft met radical thinkers and writers such as **Thomas Paine**, **William Godwin** and **William Blake**; Johnson, a publisher, was a central figure in the social world of London radicalism. Wollstonecraft was not only a feminist. Her *A Vindication of the Rights of Men* (1790) rebutted *Reflections on the Revolution in France* (1790) by **Edmund Burke** (1729–97), the principal text in opposition to the French Revolution. The republicanism apparent in descriptions of Swiss society and the English Revolution in *Frankenstein* demonstrates Shelley's own interest in political change, something she had inherited from the work of her mother and her father, William Godwin (1756–1836), the political philosopher and author of the anarchist and perfectibilist work *Enquiry Concerning Political Justice* (1793), the novels *Caleb Williams*, *Fleetwood*, *Mandeville*, *St Leon* and numerous other works.

In politics, this was a time of upheaval and change for Britain. The Act of Union with Ireland was passed in 1800, strengthening the colonial claims of England upon Ireland. The Reform Bill was passed in 1832, expanding the franchise. On the streets, food shortages (due to the Napoleonic Wars) and food riots were common, and some sectors of the population faced famine. The working class was born, as the historian E.P. Thompson has described (see Further Reading at the end of this chapter), as a result both of the enclosure of farms that had been previously subject to feudal law and were now subject to capitalist modes of production, and of the nascent Industrial Revolution. There were political clamp-downs. In the 1790s, **William Wordsworth** (1770–1850) and **Samuel Taylor Coleridge** (1772–1834) themselves were spied upon for their publication of *Lyrical Ballads*, considered radical for its putting of 'high' thoughts into the simple language of the 'low' rural working class. Shelley's husband **Percy Bysshe Shelley** (1792–1822) was spied upon for disseminating pamphlets in London and Ireland advocating reform and revolution. Habeas Corpus, a law that protects the right of citizens to bail, was periodically suspended. The feeling of living in a police state during a time of circumambient European war is palpable in the novels of Jane Austen (1775–1817), where war reports infiltrate the polite drawing rooms (for instance in *Persuasion*, 1818), and in the dense (some might say paranoid) mythographical code with which the radical artisan William Blake (1757–1827) wrote his prophetic works.

The Romantic period was a time of tremendous paradigm shifts in science. Following the generally persuasive argument of Michel Foucault (see Further Reading at the end of this chapter), one could say that this was the moment at which what used to be called 'natural history' became 'biology', a word coined in several different places at roughly the same time throughout Europe. This was to be of crucial significance to Shelley in composing *Frankenstein*. In brief, natural history concerned the classification of animals, plants and other beings according to prearranged grids. For example, consider how the Linnaean system classifies living beings according to notions of genus and species. In biology, on the other hand, the relationship between knowledge and its object has changed. Instead of being a grid of classification superimposed upon its objects, scientific knowledge 'disappears' as it were inside the object of knowledge (Foucault's idea of the 'analytic of finitude'). In other words, what makes a living being alive is a principle of life that is, so to speak, 'inside' it; and it is the job of biological science to root this out. *Biology* attempts to discover the *logos* (reason, idea) of *bios* (life). The fundamental question now became: what is the essence of life? The debate was heated. Some, the vitalists, suggested that life was the result of a sort of life force that animated the organism, such as some kind of electrical force. Others, more radical materialists, wanted to explain life from the inner workings of its organisation, without resorting to an extrinsic superadded force. The idea that living beings were 'organisms', and that this was something special that distinguished them from 'inorganic' matter, is itself a result of the new regime of knowledge called biology. Eventually, the more materialist trend won out over vitalism: the idea of the human genome, for example, is a later development of the materialist view.

Was electricity the stuff of life? Luigi Galvani (1737–98) was an Italian physicist and physician who discovered that muscle contractions could be produced with an electrical stimulus. In one experiment, he caused a muscle contraction by touching the nerves of a frog with scissors during a lightning storm. His research on animal electricity led to Alessandro Volta's development of a type of battery called the voltaic pile. Two British biologists (in the precise sense described above) directly influenced Shelley's work for *Frankenstein*. The charismatic Scottish anatomist and surgeon John Abernethy (1764–1831) (see **pp. 17–20**), who became president of the Royal College of Surgeons, was a vitalist. He might be considered an analogue for the flashy Victor Frankenstein, with his electrical theory of life. But his student and demonstrator, William Lawrence (1783–1867) (see **pp. 20–2**), became his materialist antagonist. As Percy Shelley's physician from autumn 1815, his work intimately affected Shelley's thinking.

In literature, art, music and philosophy, Romanticism swept across Europe. It took many forms: an opposition to classical order, the celebration of subjectivity, nature and life, an interest in narrative in general and in autobiography in particular, the espousal of political and social reform; the list is almost endless and certainly self-contradictory. But when one thinks, for example, of the philosophy of Georg Wilhelm Friedrich Hegel (1770–1831), certain salient features mark it as a product of the Romantic period. The idea that the world is story-shaped is one: that despite a lack of absolute authoritative external certainty, one could reason 'dialectically' from basic sense experience all the way to the realisation of what Hegel calls 'the absolute'. In the *Phenomenology of Spirit* (1807), Hegel claims that philosophy itself is the *history* of philosophy. In other words, truth takes the form of a narrative. Like a living organism as defined by biology, this kind of narrative contains its truth 'inside' it: it works itself out. In *Frankenstein*, there is no single, solid objective narrator: we are thrown upon the testimony of three witnesses. If it exists at all, the truth must emerge from the progression of the story.

One reason for the emergence of Romanticism was the new autonomy of the author from his or her audience, an effect of capitalism upon artistic production. Rather than writing for a specific audience (such as a patron), the Romantic author wrote for an abstract one, sometimes addressed as 'the people' (rather than 'the public'). Art now had a certain autonomy and freedom, and yet also a lonely separateness from immediate relationships with the public. The Romantic author was in one sense the master or mistress of all he or she surveyed, and in another, the master of nothing. Consider the paintings of the German Caspar David Friedrich, or all those images in *Frankenstein* of the lonely genius stranded on a mountain peak.

The rise of Gothic fiction in the period, as charted by scholars such as E.J. Clery, had a profound effect on Shelley. Her father was known for his politicised tales of suspense and woe, such as *Caleb Williams* (see the extract from Michael Scrivener in Modern Criticism, **pp. 105–7**). The Gothic is as nebulous as the Romantic, but tales of the supernatural, fantastic and horrific seem to be related to the rise of a consumerist society; another feature of the so-called 'long eighteenth century' (roughly from 1650 to 1850). In general, Gothic tales are interested in property and property relations amongst people; consider, for example, Austen's brilliant parody of Gothic in *Northanger Abbey* (written 1798–1803), perhaps more of a homage than a parody, in which the really terrifying secret is not an actual skeleton in the closet, but issues of class and money. Objects gained a kind of fetishistic autonomy, weirdly parallel to the autonomy of the author (noted above) and the autonomy of the subject in such idealist philosophy as that of Johann Gottlieb Fichte (1762–1814) and Immanuel Kant (1724–1804). *Frankenstein* appears different from the Gothic of **Ann Radcliffe** (1764–1823), starting a trend of biological, science-fiction horror that was obviously taken up in the many film adaptations of the twentieth century (see the section on Performance, **pp. 45–79**). Fear of the unknown, the spookiness of what lies just out of sight, is replaced by fear of the known, of the frontally horrific: we know exactly how Frankenstein's creature looks, and that is what is frightening.

Further Reading

Butler, Marilyn. *Romantics, Rebels and Reactionaries*. Oxford and New York: Oxford University Press, 1982. A useful one-volume paperback which accounts for the revolutionary energies of the period.

Clery, E.J. *The Rise of Supernatural Fiction 1762–1800*. Cambridge and New York: Cambridge University Press, 1995. A valuable account of the relationships between the Gothic and commercial society.

Foucault, Michel. *The Order of Things*. London: Tavistock Publications, 1970. Despite being painted with a very broad brush, Foucault's generalisations are often 'right on the money'. And despite claiming to break from traditional work in the history of ideas, this classic work of post-structuralist history shares more with such history than it thinks it should.

Thompson, E.P. *The Making of the English Working Class*. London: Victor Gollancz, 1963; repr. with revisions, Penguin, 1988. An indispensable guide to the social and political issues of the day as they affected ordinary people.

Chronology

Bullet points are used to denote events in Mary Shelley's life, and asterisks to denote historical and literary events.

1797
- Mary Wollstonecraft Shelley born (30 August) to William Godwin and Mary Wollstonecraft at The Polygon, Somers Town, their only daughter; Wollstonecraft dies shortly after giving birth (10 September)
* Napoleon negotiates treaty with Austria; Commons rejects abolition of slavery; tax on English newspapers to deter radical publications; Navy mutinies; Burke dies

1798–9
* Napoleon's campaigns in Egypt and Middle East; prosecution and imprisonment of Joseph Johnson the publisher; Irish Rebellion; **Thomas Malthus**, *Essay on the Principle of Population*; Wordsworth and Coleridge, *Lyrical Ballads*

1800
* Act of Union with Ireland

1801
- Godwin marries Mary Jane Clairmont; Mary and her half-sister Fanny Imlay (Wollstonecraft's child) joined by Clairmont's two children, Charles and Clara Jane; Clairmont later bears Godwin a son, William
* First census of Britain; truce between Britain and France

1802
* **William Wilberforce** postpones slavery abolition motion; Treaty of Amiens; Napoleon becomes Life Consul of France

1804
* General abolition bill passed; Napoleonic Code enacted (France); Pitt

becomes Prime Minister again; Napoleon crowns himself Emperor of France

1805
* Commons narrowly defeats abolition of slavery

1806
* End of Holy Roman Empire; Battle of Austerlitz

1807
• Family home established in Skinner Street, Holborn (also the offices of Godwin's publishing company)
* Hegel, *Phenomenology of Spirit*; Parliament passes Abolition Bill prohibiting slavery

1808
• Godwin publishes Percy Shelley's light poetry in his juvenile division (reprinted four times and also eventually illustrated)
* Convention of Cintra

1810
* **George III** recognised as insane

1811–15
* Luddite uprisings

1812
• Mary meets Percy (11 November) when he, Godwin's twenty-year-old devotee, visits Skinner Street

1812–14
• Mary stays with the Baxters in Scotland for two extended periods (possibly because of tension with her stepmother)

1813
* East India Company charter revised to allow for missionary work; Austen, *Pride and Prejudice*; Percy Shelley, *Queen Mab*

1813–15
* **Leigh Hunt** imprisoned for libel

1814
• In May Mary re-encounters Percy at the family home in Skinner Street; on 28 July, Mary and Percy elope to France accompanied by Mary's stepsister Clara, (now 'Claire'); many trials both abroad and when they return to their outraged families in England: Percy was already married to Harriet

Westbrook, (1795–1816); at the turn of the year, Percy believes he suffers from syphilis and begins treatment by William Lawrence
* Restoration of the Bourbons

1815
• Mary gives birth (22 February) to daughter Clara, a premature child who later dies (6 March); late in the year Mary and Percy live and study at Bishopsgate, near Windsor
* Restoration of Louis XVIII; Battle of Waterloo; economic depression

1816
• Mary gives birth (24 January) to son William; in the summer, Mary and Percy plan a trip to the Continent with their son and Claire, who arranges for them to meet **George Gordon Byron,** her lover, in Geneva; visiting Byron at the Villa Diodati (on the shore of Lake Léman), the group have conversations about science and decide to have a ghost-story contest: this is some of the impetus leading to initial drafting of *Frankenstein* (15–16 June); Byron's doctor, **John William Polidori,** also participates; they return to England in September; Mary's half-sister Fanny commits suicide (October); Percy's wife Harriet commits suicide; Mary marries Percy Shelley (30 December)

1817
• *Frankenstein* finished in May; Mary gives birth to a second daughter, again named Clara; *History of a Six-Weeks' Tour* (about the elopement) published
* *Blackwood's Magazine* founded; Jane Austen dies

1818
• Mary's daughter Clara dies in Venice; *Frankenstein* published
* Habeas Corpus restored

1819
• Mary's son William dies in Rome; Mary gives birth to another son (November), Percy Florence, while living in Florence
* Peterloo Massacre of civilian protesters by the Yeomanry Cavalry

1820
* Accession of **George IV**

1820–1
• The Shelleys move between Bagni di San Giuliano and Pisa

1821
* Napoleon dies

1822

- Percy dies at sea while returning from Leghorn (Livorno); Mary goes to Genoa, joining the Hunts (Percy was sailing to visit Leigh Hunt) and Byron

1823

- *Valperga* published (February); Mary returns to England (August)

1824

*   Beethoven's Ninth Symphony

1826

- *The Last Man* published (February); Mary's son Percy Florence inherits the right to his father's name and estate when Harriet and Percy's first son, Charles Bysshe, dies

1827

*   Greek independence; Blake dies

1829

*   Catholic Emancipation Act

1830

- *Perkin Warbeck* published
*   Liverpool and Manchester Railway opens; George IV dies

1831

*   National Union of Working Classes founded (helped by Robert Owen); Faraday discovers electromagnetic induction

1831–3

*   Cholera epidemic

1832

*   Reform Bill

1833

*   Oxford Movement begins; abolition of colonial slavery; New Poor Law passed

1834

*   Emancipation Act takes effect

1835

- *Lodore* published

1836
- Godwin dies

1837
- *Falkner* published
* Charles Dickens, *Oliver Twist*; **William IV** (George's brother) dies; Victoria accedes to the throne

1838
* Chartism comes into existence; National Gallery completed

1839
* War with China; Hong Kong captured

1840
- Mary and son Percy Florence tour the Continent with friends
* Introduction of Penny Postage

1841
- Percy Florence graduates from Cambridge
* Opium War (China and Britain)

1842
* Treaty of Nanking

1842–3
- Mary and son again tour the Continent

1843
* Factory safety regulations enacted; beginning of custom of sending Christmas cards

1844
- *Rambles in Germany and Italy* published; Percy Florence inherits the Shelley title and assets when Sir Timothy Shelley dies (April)

1845
* Beginning of the Irish Potato Famine

1846
* Repeal of Corn Laws; planet Neptune discovered

1847
* Marx and Engels, *Communist Manifesto* (published 1848)

1848
* Pre-Raphaelite Brotherhood founded; United States annexes California, Utah, Arizona, New Mexico

1850
* Wordsworth dies

1851
* J.M.W. Turner dies
• Mary Shelley dies in Chester Square, London (February), and is buried in the Bournemouth churchyard

Contemporary Documents

Introduction

This section contains a wealth of material from the period contemporary with Shelley's writing of *Frankenstein*. I have placed special weight on the scientific debate surrounding the novel. The debate between vitalists such as John Abernethy, **pp. 17–20**, and materialists such as William Lawrence, **pp. 20–2**, radically informs Shelley's text, setting up Victor as a bombastic scientific entrepreneur, who, for all he knows, *is* imitating God. The creature, on the other hand, comes across much more like Lawrence's sceptical materialist. (For further discussion of this, see the extract from Marilyn Butler's article in Modern Criticism, **pp. 82–5**.) Also included in these extracts is a taste of Shelley's novel *The Last Man*, **pp. 24–6**, whose protagonist, Lionel, enters into scenes reminiscent of *Frankenstein*. Some snapshots from her journal and letters concerning *Frankenstein*, **pp. 26–30** indicate the personal and cultural contexts of Shelley's work. Percy Shelley's atmospheric writing on the Alps, **pp. 30–2**, is included to give the reader an idea of the literary backgrounds of the sublime writing on nature in *Frankenstein*.

For biographical information, please consult the Directory, **pp. 183–90**. Some minor errors in the copy texts have been silently corrected. Names in bold indicate the first appearance of figures discussed in the Directory.

John Abernethy, *An Enquiry into the Probability and Rationality of Mr. Hunter's Theory of Life: Being the Subject of the First Two Anatomical Lectures Delivered before the Royal College of Surgeons, of London* (1814) London: Longman, Hurst, Rees, Orme, and Brown

In *The Order of Things*, the French historian Michel Foucault asserts that the Romantic period witnessed a moment at which biology, in the sense of the science of life, was born. Natural history, the previous incarnation of knowledge about living creatures (or 'episteme' as Foucault calls it), was content to classify animals, plants and so forth upon a predetermined grid. Biology (a word coined during Mary Shelley's day), on the other hand, seeks the very source and structure of life itself. Is the essence of life to be distinguished from its material substance? The principal goal of knowledge here disappears inside the organism, to be discovered for instance in the mapping of the human genome in the late twentieth century. The debate between Abernethy and Lawrence is pitched around the notion of 'organisation'. Does life result entirely from its material structure, or is some property or force external to it responsible in some measure? Abernethy, a vitalist who believes that the source of life is not simply its material organisation, asserts that there is something about electrical forces that contributes to the life of the organism. One can see here the kinds of argument that Dr Frankenstein himself would have employed in expressing his interest in constructing a creature.

In surveying the great chain of living beings, we find life connected with a vast variety of organization, yet exercising the same functions in each; a circumstance from which we may I think naturally conclude, that life does not depend on organization. Mr. [John] Hunter, who so patiently and accurately examined the different links of this great chain, which seems to connect even man with the common matter of the universe, was of this opinion. In speaking of the properties of life, he says, it is something that prevents the chemical decomposition, to which dead animal and vegetable matter is so prone; that regulates the temperature of the bodies it inhabits, and is the cause of the actions we observe in them. All these circumstances, though deduced from an extensive contemplation of the subjects, may however, be legitimately drawn from observations made on the egg. A living egg does not putrefy under circumstances that would rapidly cause that change in a dead one. The former resists a degree of cold that would freeze the latter. And when subjected to the genial warmth of incubation, the matter of it begins to move or to be moved so as to build up the curious structure of the young animal. [. . .]

The opinions of Mr. Hunter deserve at least to be respectfully and attentively considered. That he was a man of genius, according to the beautiful definition of that quality given by Dr. Johnson; that he possessed the power of mind that collects, combines, amplifies and animates, the energy without which judgment is cold, and knowledge is inert; cannot I think be doubted by any one who has carefully considered his writings. That he was a man of uncommon industry, by which he collected an abundance of facts, will be admitted by every one who has even beheld his museum. That he was a man of constant and deep reflection, is to me equally apparent.

(16–19)

The phænomena of electricity and of life correspond. Electricity may be attached to, or inhere, in a wire; it may be suddenly dissipated, or have its powers annulled, or it may be removed by degrees or in portions, and the wire may remain less and less strongly electrified, in proportion as it is abstracted. So life inheres in vegetables and animals; it may sometimes be suddenly dissipated, or have its powers abolished, though in general it is lost by degrees, without any apparent change taking place in the structure; and in either case putrefaction begins when life terminates.

(42)

The experiments of **Sir Humphry Davy** seem to me to form an important link in the connexion of our knowledge of dead and living matter. He has solved the great and long hidden mystery of chemical attraction, by shewing that it depends upon the electric properties which the atoms of different species of matter possess. Nay, by giving to an alkali electric properties which did not originally belong to it, he has been able to control the ordinary operations of nature, and to make potash pass through a strong acid, without any combination taking place. That electricity is something, I could never doubt, and therefore it follows as a consequence in my opinion, that it must be every where connected with those atoms of matter, which form the masses that are cognizable to our senses; and that it enters into the composition of every thing, inanimate or animate. If then it be electricity that produces all the chemical changes, we so constantly observe, in surrounding inanimate objects, analogy induces us to believe that it is electricity which also performs all the chemical operations in living bodies; that the universal chemist resides in them, and exercises in some degree peculiar powers because it possesses a peculiar apparatus.

Sir Humphry Davy's experiments also lead us to believe, that it is electricity, extricated and accumulated in ways not clearly understood, which causes those sudden and powerful motions in masses of inert matter, which we occasionally witness with wonder and dismay; that it is electricity which causes the whirlwind, and the water spout, and which 'with its sharp and sulphurous bolt splits the unwedgeable and gnarled oak',[1] and destroys our most stabile edifices; that it is electricity which by its consequences makes the firm earth tremble, and throws up subterraneous matter from volcanoes.

When therefore we perceive in the universe at large, a cause of rapid and powerful motions of masses of inert matter, may we not naturally conclude that the inert molecules of vegetable and animal matter, may be made to move in a similar manner, by a similar cause?

It is not meant to be affirmed that electricity is life. There are strong analogies between electricity and magnetism, and yet I do not know that any one has been hardy enough to assert their absolute identity. I only mean to prove, that Mr. Hunter's Theory is verifiable, by shewing that a subtle substance of a quickly and powerfully mobile nature, seems to pervade every thing, and appears to be the life of the world; and therefore it is probable that a similar substance pervades organized bodies, and produces similar effects in them.[2]

(48–51)

---

1   A quotation from William Shakespeare, *Measure for Measure* II.ii.113–16; *The Riverside Shakespeare*, ed. G. Blakemore Evans (Boston, Dallas etc: Houghton Mifflin, 1974).
2   German *Naturphilosophie*, contemporary with Hunter and Abernethy and exemplified by philosophers such as Friedrich von Schelling, asserted the existence of a primordial life substance or life force. Romantic-period authors such as Coleridge became very interested in such theories, which are poised somewhat precariously between materialism and theism.

The human mind has been the same at all periods of the world; in all ages there have been men of a sceptical disposition, disinclined to believe any thing that was not directly an object of their senses. At all periods there have been other men of a contemplative, and perhaps more credulous character, who have been disposed to believe that there were invisible causes, operating to produce the alterations which are visible, and who from much less numerous facts have drawn the same inferences that I have done. And many of these, from Pythagoras downwards, have expressed their sentiments, though with some variety, yet pretty much to the same effect. The Greek philosophers recognized in man, the Σομα, Ψυχη, and Νους,[3] the body, vital principle, and mind, whilst some used words significant of intellect, to express the energizing principle in nature, without apparently having any clear ideas of intelligence.

What was called the Anima Mundi, was, however, by many considered as a distinct and active principle, and was not confounded with intelligence of any kind. I know not how I can better exhibit to my audience the subject I am alluding to, or better acquaint them with the general tenour and tendencies of these opinions, than by quoting that portion of these philosophical notions, which Virgil is said to have put into the mouth of Anchises,

> Spiritus intus alit, totamque infusa per artus
> Mens agitat molem, & magno se corpore miscet.[4]

And please to observe, gentlemen, it is Virgil says, it is Anchises speaks, that which I also this day have been saying; –

> Inde hominum pecudumque genus, vitæque volantum
> Et quæ marmoreo fert monstra sub æquore pontus.[5]

(52–4 [end of Lecture I])

William Lawrence, *An Introduction to Comparative Anatomy and Physiology; Being the Two Introductory Lectures Delivered at the Royal College of Surgeons, on the 21st and 25th of March, 1816*
(1816) London: Printed for J. Callow

For a discussion of William Lawrence, see Contextual Overview (**p. 9**) and the introduction to this chapter (**p. 17**).

---

3   Transliterated, 'soma' (body), 'psyche' (vital principle) and 'nous' (mind).
4   'A spirit within sustains, and mind, pervading its members, sways the whole mass and mingles with its mighty frame'; Virgil, *The Aeneid* 6.726–7 (Anchises' description of the life principle of the universe).
5   'Thence the race of man and beast, the life of winged things and the strange shapes the ocean bears beneath its glassy flow'; Virgil, *The Aeneid* 6.728–9. (See the previous note for the correct citation.) My thanks to Barbara Hill for helping me with translation.

Organization means the peculiar composition, which distinguishes living bodies; in this point of view they are contrasted with inorganic, inert, or dead bodies. Vital properties, such as sensibility and irritability, are the means, by which organization is capable of executing its purposes; the vital properties of living bodies correspond to the physical properties of inorganic bodies; such as cohesion, elasticity, &c. Functions are the purposes, which any organ or system of organs executes in the animal frame; there is of course nothing corresponding to them in inorganic matter. Life is the assemblage of all these functions, and the general result of their exercise. Thus organization, vital properties, functions, and life are expressions related to each other; in which organization is the instrument, vital property the acting power, function the mode of action, and life the result.

(Lecture 2, 'On Life', 120–1)

Having thus proceeded, as far as we can, in ascertaining the nature of life by the observation of its effects, we are naturally anxious to investigate its origin, to see how it is produced, and to inquire how it is communicated to the beings in which we find it. We endeavour therefore to observe living bodies in the moment of their formation, to watch the time, when matter may be supposed to receive the stamp of life, and the inert mass to be quickened. Hitherto, however, physiologists have not been able to catch nature in the fact [. . .] All have participated in the existence of other living beings, before they exercised the functions of life themselves. Thus we find that the motion proper to living bodies, or in one word, Life, has its origin in that of their parents. From these parents they have received the vital impulse; and hence it is evident, that in the present state of things, life proceeds only from life; and there exists no other but that, which has been transmitted from one living body to another, by an uninterrupted succession.

(140–2)

The science of organized bodies should therefore be treated in a manner entirely different from those, which have inorganic matter for their object. We should employ a different language, since words transposed from the physical sciences to the animal and vegetable economy, constantly recall to us ideas of an order altogether different from those which are suggested by the phenomena last mentioned [the vital properties such as 'digestion' and 'inflammation', 151]. Although organized bodies are subjected in many respects to physical laws, their own peculiar phenomena present no analogy to those which are treated in chemistry, mechanics, and other physical sciences: the reference therefore to gravity, to attraction, to chemical affinity, to electricity or galvanism, can only serve to perpetuate false notions in physiology, and to draw us away from the proper point of view, in which the nature of living phenomena and the properties of living beings ought to be contemplated. We might just as rationally introduce the language of physiology into physical science; explain the facts of chemistry by irritability, or employ sensibility and sympathy to account for the phenomena of electricity and magnetism, or for the motions of the planetary system.[1]

(160–1)

In the science of physiology we proceed on the observation of facts, of their order and connexion; we notice the analogies between them; and deduce the general laws, to which they are subject. We are thus led to admit the vital properties, already spoken of, as causes of the various phenomena; in the same way as attraction is recognised for the cause of various physical events. We do not profess to explain *how* the living forces in one case, or attraction in the other, exert their agency. But some are not content to stop at this point; they wish to draw aside the veil from nature, to display the very essence of the vital properties, and penetrate to their first causes; to shew, independently of the phenomena, what is life, and how irritability and sensibility execute those purposes, which so justly excite our admiration. They endeavour to give a physical explanation of the contraction of a muscle, and to teach us how a nerve feels. They suppose the structure of the body to contain an invisible matter or principle, by which it is put in motion. Such is the ένορμεν [enormen] or *impetum faciens* of Hippocrates, the *Archeus* of Van Helmont, the *Anima* of Stahl, *Materia Vitæ* of Hunter, the *calidum innatum*, the vital principle, the subtle and mobile matter of others;[2] – there are many names for it, as each successive speculator seems to have fancied that he should establish his own claim to the offspring by baptizing it anew. Either of the names, and either of the explanations may be taken as a sample: they are all equally valuable, and equally illustrative.

Most of them indeed have long lain in cold obstruction amongst the rubbish of past ages; and the more modern ones are hastening after their predecessors to the vault of all the Capulets.

(164–5)

It seems to me that this hypothesis or fiction of a subtle invisible matter, animating the visible textures of animal bodies, and directing their motions, is only an example of that propensity in the human mind, which has led men at all times to account for those phenomena, of which the causes are not obvious, by the mysterious aid of higher and imaginary beings. Thus in the earlier ages of the world, and in less advanced states of civilization, all the appearances of nature, which the progress of science enables us to explain by means of natural causes, have been referred to the immediate operation of the divinity[.]

(174–5)

---

1   Lawrence is here dismissing an idea that has in some circles recently become fashionable: that which the biologist E.O. Wilson calls 'consilience', in which all phenomena can be explained in terms of the most elemental terms; for example, thought by quantum physics; *Consilience: The Unity of Knowledge* (New York: Alfred A. Knopf, 1998).

2   'Impetum faciens' literally means 'that which causes the [mental] impulse'; 'calidum innatum' means 'innate heat'.

Quarterly Review, 22 (1820): 1–34

The following is a clear example of the extent to which the media contemporary with *Frankenstein* were engaged in the debate on the life sciences. For further discussion, please refer to *Frankenstein*, ed. Butler, Appendix C.

Voltaire, it is well known, checked his company from repeating blasphemous impieties before the servants, 'lest', said he, 'they should cut all our throats'; and Mr Lawrence, we apprehend, would much sooner entrust his life and property to a person who believed that he had an immortal and accountable soul, than to one who believed, with him, that medullary matter thinks, and that the whole human being perishes with the dissolution of the body. What advantage then can he propose to himself, by endeavouring to promote the general reception of his opinions? Is it possible that he can desire to increase human vice and misery, to degrade his species by sowing the seeds of more sensuality, impiety, profligacy and worldy-mindedness than he actually finds among them? Or, when he knows that such is the tendency of his conduct, is it possible that his fancied love of truth, or the indulgence of his vanity can outweigh the feeling of what he owes to the welfare of his fellow-creatures?

We are by no means surprized to hear that Mr Lawrence has seriously injured himself in the opinion of the more respectable part of his profession by his late proceedings; and that he has already experienced from the public some of those consequences which he might have foreseen as the natural result. It has sometimes been said that sceptical opinions are prevalent to a considerable extent in the profession to which he belongs. We hope, and we believe, that this is not the case. Certain we are, that while Mr Lawrence is an almost solitary instance of a person of any consideration in that profession who has publicly maintained opinions hostile to religion, very many of the most eminent individuals in it have been distinguished for the firmness and the soundness of their religious principles; and, on the present occasion, the stand which many of them have made against his pernicious and degrading doctrines has been such as to do them infinite credit.

But something is necessary for the satisfaction of the public and the credit of the institution. It appears to us imperative on those who have the superintendence of the Royal College of Surgeons, to make it an indispensable condition of the continuance of Mr Lawrence in the office of lecturer, not only that he should strictly abstain from propagating any similar opinions in future, but that he should expunge from his lectures already published all those obnoxious passages which have given such deserved offence, and which are now circulating under the sanction of the College.

Mary Wollstonecraft Shelley, *The Last Man. By the Author of Frankenstein* (1826), ed. Hugh J. Luke, Jr. (1993) Lincoln: University of Nebraska Press; first edition London: Henry Colburn, 1826

The Last Man is arguably the second science-fiction novel in English after *Frankenstein*, a thought experiment about a global plague that wipes out the entire human race, except for one survivor. Themes of the global and the local, under intense scrutiny now because of the debate around globalisation, are legible in Shelley's novel. The novel also shares themes with *Frankenstein*, as is demonstrated below. Lionel Verney, the novel's narrator, is discovered by Adrian as if he were a savage (literally, a forest dweller), at the beginning of the narrative. Later, while studying philosophy, he eats 'scanty fare, which I sometimes robbed from the squirrels of the forest' (55–6). As the last man, he wanders around a deserted Rome, like the creature wandering around the forest, and discovers his reflection in a mirror, as the creature discovers his in a pool of water, like Milton's Eve and moreover like Frankenstein's creature. The novel's protagonists may be read as ciphers for Shelley's circle, for example Raymond (Byron) and Adrian (Percy Shelley).

It soon became known that Adrian took great delight in his park and preserves. He never sported, but spent hours in watching the tribes of lovely and almost tame animals with which it was stocked, and ordered that greater care should be taken of them than ever. Here was an opening for my plans of offence, and I made use of it with all the brute impetuosity I derived from my active mode of life. I proposed the enterprize of poaching on his demesne to my few remaining comrades, who were the most determined and lawless of the crew; but they all shrunk from the peril; so I was left to achieve my revenge myself. At first my exploits were unperceived; I increased in daring; footsteps on the dewy grass, torn boughs, and marks of slaughter, at length betrayed me to the gamekeepers. They kept better watch; I was taken, and sent to prison. I entered its gloomy walls in a fit of triumphant extasy: 'He feels me now', I cried, 'and shall, again and again!' – I passed but one day in confinement; in the evening I was liberated, as I was told, by the order of the Earl himself. This news precipitated me from my self-raised pinnacle of honour. He despises me, I thought; but he shall learn that I despise him, and hold in equal contempt his punishments and his clemency. On the second night after my release, I was taken again by the gamekeepers – again imprisoned, and again released; and again, such was my pertinacity, did the fourth night find me in the forbidden park. The gamekeepers were more enraged than their lord by my obstinacy. They had received orders that if I were to be again taken, I should be brought to the Earl; and his lenity made them expect a conclusion which they considered ill befitting my crime. One of them, who had been from the first the leader among those who had seized me, resolved to satisfy his own resentment, before he made me over to the higher powers.

The late setting of the moon, and the extreme caution I was obliged to use in this my third expedition, consumed so much time, that something like a qualm of fear came over me when I perceived dark night yield to twilight. I crept along by the fern, on my hands and knees, seeking the shadowy coverts of the underwood, while the birds awoke with unwelcome song above, and the fresh morning wind, playing among the boughs, made me suspect a footfall at each turn. My heart beat quick as I approached the palings; my hand was on one of them, a leap would take me to the other side, when two keepers sprang from an ambush upon me: one knocked me down, and proceeded to inflict a severe horse-whipping. I started up – a knife was in my grasp; I made a plunge at his raised right arm, and inflicted a deep, wide wound in his hand. The rage and yells of the wounded man, the howling execrations of his comrade, which I answered with equal bitterness and fury, echoed through the dell; morning broke more and more, ill accordant in its celestial beauty with our brute and noisy contest. I and my enemy were still struggling, when the wounded man exclaimed, 'The Earl!' I sprang out of the herculean hold of the keeper, panting from my exertions; I cast furious glances on my persecutors, and placing myself with my back to a tree, resolved to defend myself to the last. My garments were torn, and they, as well as my hands, were stained with the blood of the man I had wounded; one hand grasped the dead birds – my hard-earned prey, the other held the knife; my hair was matted; my face besmeared with the same guilty signs that bore witness against me on the dripping instrument I clenched; my whole appearance was haggard and squalid. Tall and muscular as I was in form, I must have looked like, what indeed I was, the merest ruffian that ever trod the earth.

The name of the Earl startled me, and caused all the indignant blood that warmed my heart to rush into my cheeks; I had never seen him before; I figured to myself a haughty, assuming youth, who would take me to task, if he deigned to speak to me, with all the arrogance of superiority. My reply was ready; a reproach I deemed calculated to sting his very heart. He came up the while; and his appearance blew aside, with gentle western breath, my cloudy wrath: a tall, slim, fair boy, with a physiognomy expressive of the excess of sensibility and refinement stood before me; the morning sunbeams tinged with gold his silken hair, and spread light and glory over his beaming countenance. 'How is this?' he cried. The men eagerly began their defence; he put them aside, saying, 'Two of you at once on a mere lad – for shame!' He came up to me: 'Verney', he cried, 'Lionel Verney, do we meet thus for the first time? We were both to be friends to each other; and though ill fortune has divided us, will you not acknowledge the hereditary bond of friendship which I trust will hereafter unite us?'

As he spoke, his earnest eyes, fixed on me, seemed to read my very soul: my heart, my savage revengeful heart, felt the influence of sweet benignity sink upon it; while his thrilling voice, like sweetest melody, awoke a mute echo within me, stirring to its depths the life-blood in my frame. I desired to reply, to acknowledge his goodness, accept his proffered friendship; but words, fitting words, were not afforded to the rough mountaineer; I would have held out my hand, but its guilty stain restrained me. Adrian took pity on my faltering mien: 'Come with me,' he said, 'I have much to say to you; come home with me – you know who I am?'

'Yes,' I exclaimed, 'I do believe that I now know you, and that you will pardon my mistakes – my crime.'

Adrian smiled gently; and after giving his orders to the gamekeepers, he came up to me; putting his arm in mine, we walked together to the mansion.

(16–17)

I entered one of the places, and opened the door of a magnificent saloon. I started – I looked again with renewed wonder. What wild-looking, unkempt, half-naked savage was that before me? The surprise was momentary.

I perceived that it was I myself whom I beheld in a large mirror at the end of the hall. No wonder that the lover of the princely Idris should fail to recognize himself in the miserable object there pourtrayed. My tattered dress was that in which I had crawled half alive from the tempestuous sea. My long and tangled hair hung in elf locks on my brow – my dark eyes, now hollow and wild, gleamed from under them – my cheeks were discoloured by the jaundice, which (the effect of misery and neglect) suffused my skin, and were half hid by a beard of many days' growth.

Yet why should I not remain thus, I thought; the world is dead, and this squalid attire is a fitter mourning garb than the foppery of a black suit. And thus, methinks, I should have remained, had not hope, without which I do not believe man could exist, whispered to me, that, in such a plight, I should be an object of fear and aversion to the being, preserved I knew not where, but I fondly trusted, at length, to be found by me. Will my readers scorn the vanity, that made me attire myself with some care, for the sake of this visionary being? Or will they forgive the freaks of a half crazed imagination? I can easily forgive myself – for hope, however vague, was so dear to me, and a sentiment of pleasure of so rare occurrence, that I yielded readily to any idea, that cherished the one, or promised any recurrence of the former to my sorrowing heart.

(331)

Mary Wollstonecraft Shelley, *The Journals of Mary Shelley 1814–1844*, ed. Paula R. Feldman and Diana Scott-Kilvert (1987) 2 vols, Oxford: Clarendon Press

Wednesday 24th July 1816

We ~~des~~ arrived wet to the skin – I read nouvelle nouvelles[1] and write my story – Shelley writes part of letter.

Thursday 25th

This day promises to be fine & we set out at nine for Montanvert ↑with↓ *Beaucoup de Monde* go also – we get to the top at twelve and behold *le mer de Glace*.[2] This is the most desolate place in the world – iced mountains surround it – no

---

1   '*Nouveaux contes moraux et nouvelles historiques*, by Madame de Genlis (1802)' (*Journals*, 1.118).
2   'In chapter ix of *Frankenstein* Mary was to use the Mer de Glace as the background for the dramatic confrontation between Frankenstein and the Monster' (*Journals*, 1.119).

sighn g sign of vegetation appears except on the place from which w[e] view the scene – we went on the ice – It is traversed by irregular crevices the whose sides of ice appear blue while the surface is of a dirty white – We dine on the mountain – the air is very cold yet many flowers grow here & among other the *rhododendron* or *Rose des Alps* in great profusion – We descend leisurely – Shelley goes to see the mine of Amianthe[3] but finds nothing worth seeing. We arrive at the inn at six fatigued by our days journey but pleased and astonish[ed] by the world of ice that was opened up to our view –

(1.118–19)

Monday 12 [August 1816]

Write my story and translate – Shelley goes to the town and afterwards goes out in the boat with Lord B. – after dinner I go out a little in the boat and then Shelley goes up to [the Villa] Diodati – I translate in the evening and read le vieux de la Montagne[4] – Shelley in coming down is attacked by a dog which delays him – we send up for him & Lord B. comes down – in the meantime Shelley returns.

(1.124)

Sunday 18 [August 1816]

Talk with Shelley and write – read Curtius – Shelley reads Plutarch in Greek – Lord B – comes down & stays here an hour – I read a novel in the evening – Shelley goes up to Diodati & Monck [**Matthew**] Lewis – See Apollo's Sexton,[5] who tells us many mysteries of his trade. We talk of Ghosts. – Neither Lord B. or M.G.L.[ewis] seem to believe in them, & they both agree in the very face of reason, that none could believe in Ghosts without also believing in God. – I do not think that all the persons who profess to discredit these visitations, really discredit them, or if they do in the daylight, are not admonished by the approach of th loneliness & midnight to think more respectfully of the world of Shadows.

[There then follow four ghost stories, published with revisions in Percy Shelley, *Essays, Letters from Abroad, Translations and Fragments*, ed. Mary Shelley, 2.98–102.]

(1.126)

Teusday[6] 29th [October 1816]

Draw. Read Davy's Chemistry with Shelley – read Curt. and Ides travels.[7] Shelley reads Montaigne and Don Quixote aloud in the evening.

(1.143)

---

3 'An asbestos mine' (*Journals*, 1.119).

4 '*Le Vieux de la montagne, histoire orientale, traduite de l'arabe par l'auteur de la Philosophie de la nature*, by Jean-Baptiste-Claude Izouard, dit Delisle de Sales (1799)' (*Journals*, 1.124).

5 'Byron had named Monk Lewis 'Apollo's Sexton' in *English Bards and Scotch Reviewers*' (264–82; *Journals*, 1.126).

6 Shelley habitually misspelt 'Tuesday' as 'Teusday'.

7 *Driejaarige reize naar China, te lande gedaan door den Moskovischen afgezant*, by E. Ysbrants Ides (1704), translated as *Three Years Travels from Moscow over-land to China, thro' great Ustiga, Sirianaia, Permia, Siberia, Daour, Great Tartary, etc., to Peking* (1706). Shelley had begun her reading of *Elements of Chemical Philosophy*, by Sir Humphry Davy (1812) on Monday 28.

Mary Wollstonecraft Shelley, *The Letters of Mary Wollstonecraft Shelley*, ed. Betty T. Bennett (1980) 3 vols, Baltimore and London: Johns Hopkins University Press

These letters represent the period during which *Frankenstein* was composed, and its subsequent performance and public reception (including mention of a fascinating allusion in the Houses of Parliament).

To ?Fanny Imlay

Campagne C[hapuis], near Coligny
1 June 1816

You will perceive from my date that we have changed our residence since my last letter. We now inhabit a little cottage on the opposite shore of the lake, and have exchanged the view of Mont Blanc and her snowy *aiguilles* for the dark frowning Jura, behind whose range we every evening see the sun sink, and darkness approaches our valley from behind the Alps, which are then tinged by that glowing rose-like hue which is observed in England to attend on the clouds of an autumnal sky when day-light is almost gone. The lake is at our feet, and a little harbour contains our boat, in which we still enjoy our evening excursions on the water. Unfortunately we do not now enjoy those brilliant skies that hailed us on our first arrival to this country. An almost perpetual rain confines us principally to the house; but when the sun bursts forth it is with a splendour and heat unknown in England. The thunder storms that visit us are grander and more terrific than I have eve[r] seen before. We watch them as they approach from the opposite side of the lake, observing the lightning play among the clouds in various parts of the heavens, and dart in jagged figures upon the piny heights of Jura, dark with the shadow of the overhanging cloud, while perhaps the sun is shining cheerily upon us. One night we *enjoyed* a finer storm than I had ever before beheld. The lake was lit up – the pines on Jura made visible, and all the scene illuminated for an instant, when a pitchy blackness succeeded, and the thunder came in frightful bursts over our heads amid the darkness.

(1.20)

To Sir Walter Scott

Bagni di Lucca   14 June – 1818

Sir

Having received from the publisher of Frankenstein the notice taken of that work in Blackwood's magasine [*sic*], and intelligence at the same time that it was to your kindness that I owed this favourable notice I hasten to return my acknowledgements and thanks, and at the same time to express the pleasure I receive from approbation of so high a value as yours.

Mr Shelley soon after its publication took the liberty of sending you a copy but as both he and I thought in a manner which would prevent you from supposing that he was the author we were surprised therefore to see him mentioned in the notice as the probable author, – I am anxious to prevent your continuing in the mistake of supposing Mr Shelley guilty of a juvenile attempt of mine; to which – from its being written at an early age, I abstained from putting my name – and from respect to those persons from whom I bear it. I have therefore kept it concealed except from a few friends.

I beg you will pardon the intrusion of this explanation –

Your obliged &c &c

Mary Wollst^{ft} Shelley.

(1.71)

Letter to Leigh and Marianne Hunt 14 August 1823, Paris

I have just had a visit from HS [**Horace Smith**] – who was very polite & kind – He says that there is a great outcry against the new Cantos, of DJ [*Don Juan* cantos 6–8] & that they have a limited sale – He does not know much English News, except that they brought out Frankenstein at the Lyceum[1] and vivified the Monster in such a manner as caused the ladies to faint away & a hubbub to ensue – however they diminished the horrors in the sequel, & it is having a run [. . .]

(1.369)

Letter to Leigh Hunt 18 August 1823, Paris

Going to the fountain head of all knowledge I found that it was not true that the ladies were frightened at the first appearance of Frankenstein – K. says that the first appearance of the Monster from F.'s laboratory down a dark staircase had a fine effect – but the piece fell off afterwards – though it is having a run. –

(1.374)

Letter to Leigh Hunt 9 September 1823, London

I resolved not to think of certain things, to take all as a matter of course and thus contrived to keep myself out of the gulph of melancholy, on the edge of which I was & am continually peeping. –

But lo & behold! I found myself famous! – Frankenstein had prodigious success as a drama & was to be repeated for the 23rd night at the English opera house. The play bill amused me extremely, for in the list of dramatis personæ came, ——— by Mr **T.[homas] Cooke**: this nameless mode of naming the un[n]ameable is rather good. On Friday Aug. 29th Jane My father William & I went to the theatre to see it. [James] **Wallack** looked very well at the end of the 1st Act. the stage represents a room with a staircase at the end leading to the *F* workshop – he goes to it and you see his light at a small window, through which a frightened servant

---

1 Godwin's letter of 22 July informed Mary Shelley that *Presumption, or the Fate of Frankenstein* would be produced the following Monday (Godwin to Mary Shelley, Huntington Library [HM 11634]). **Richard Brinsley Peake** was the dramatist. See the section on performance (**pp. 48–55, 59–60**).

peeps, who runs off in terror when F. exclaims 'It lives!' – Presently F himself rushes in horror & trepidation from the room and while still expressing his agony & terror —— throws down the door of the laboratory, leaps the staircase & presents his unearthly & monstrous person on the stage. The story is not well managed – but Cooke played ——'s part extremely well – his seeking as it were for support – his trying to grasp at the sounds he heard – all indeed he does was well imagined & executed. I was much amused, & it appeared to excite a breathless eagerness in the audience – it was a third piece   a scanty pit filled at half price – & all stayed till it was over. They continue to play it even now. [. . .]

One [sic] the strength of the drama my father had published *for my benefit* a new edition of F. & this seemed all I had to look to, for he despaired utterly of my doing anything with S.T.S. [Sir Timothy Shelley].

(1.378)

Letter to Edward John Trelawny, London, 22 March 1824

Parliament is met here and Canning[2] is making a figure – he does not seem at all to like the part he was forced to play with regard to Spain, & said in the House that he would not tacitly acquiesce in such another invasion as that of the French at the risk of any war. They are introducing some ammelioration [sic] in the state of the slaves in some parts of the West Indies – during the debate on the subject Canning paid a compliment to Frankenstein in a manner sufficiently pleasing to me.

(1.416–17)

Percy Bysshe Shelley, from *Letters Written in Geneva* (1817), in E.B. Murray, ed. *The Prose Works of Percy Bysshe Shelley* (1993) Oxford: Clarendon Press, 1.224–6

July 24

Yesterday morning we went to the source of the Arveiron. It is about a league

---

2   George Canning (1770–1827), a British statesman who was credited for his liberal policies while he served as Foreign Secretary, from 1822 to 1827. The Congress of Verona (October 1822) of the Quadruple Alliance gave France a mandate to suppress the Spanish Revolution begun in 1820. On 31 August 1823 the revolutionaries were defeated, and Ferdinand VII was restored to the Spanish throne. Canning, however, had refused to cooperate with the other members of the Alliance in this action, and this led to the dissolution of the Alliance. Canning alluded to *Frankenstein* on 16 March 1824 (Great Britain, *Hansard's Parliamentary Debates*, 2d ser., 10 [1824], col. 1103). The quotation from Hansard is as follows: 'To turn him [the slave] loose in the manhood of his physical strength, in the maturity of his physical passion, but in the infancy of his uninstructed reason, would be to raise up a creature resembling the splendid fiction of a recent romance.' The literary historian Chris Baldick comments in his volume *In Frankensteins's Shadow: Myth, Monstrosity and Nineteenth-Century Writing* (Oxford: The Clarendon Press, 1987; paperback, 1990) that 'Shelley felt flattered by the attention shown to her tale in such quarters, but seems not to have noticed how *Frankenstein* was being used by the nervous liberal statesmen to delay reform, nor how the monster (and worse, the slave) was being transformed by such rhetoric into a mindless brute. Canning, a former contributor to the *Anti-Jacobin Review* and a founder of the *Quarterly Review*, was clearly reclaiming the monster as a Burkean bogy figure to illustrate the danger of reform turning into rebellion.' (60)

from this village; the river rolls forth impetuously from an arch of ice, and spreads itself in many streams over a vast space of the valley, ravaged and laid bare by its inundations. The glacier by which its waters are nourished, overhangs this cavern and the plain, and its forests of pine which surround it, with terrible precipices of solid ice. On the other side rises the immense glacier of Montanvert, fifty miles in extent, occupying a chasm among mountains of inconceivable height, and of forms so pointed and abrupt, that they seem to pierce the sky. From this glacier we saw as we sat on a rock, close to one of the streams of the Aveiron, masses of ice detach themselves from on high, and rush with a loud dull noise into the vale. The violence of their fall turned them into powder, which flowed over the rocks in imitation of waterfalls, whose ravines they usurped and filled.

In the evening I went with Ducrée, my guide, the only tolerable person I have seen in this country, to visit the glacier of Bossons. This glacier, like that of Montanvert, comes close to the vale, overhanging the green meadows and the dark woods with the dazzling whiteness of its precipices and pinnacles, which are like spires of radiant crystal, covered with a net-work of frosted silver. These glaciers flow perpetually into the valley, ravaging in their slow but irresistible progress the pastures and the forests which surround them, performing a work of desolation in ages, which a river of lava might accomplish in an hour, but far more irretrievably; for where the ice has once descended, the hardiest plant refuses to grow; if even, as in some extraordinary instances, it should recede after its progress has once commenced. The glaciers perpetually move onward, at the rate of a foot each day, with a motion that commences at the spot where, on the boundaries of perpetual congelation, they are produced by the freezing of the waters which arise from the partial melting of the eternal snows. They drag with them from the regions whence they derive their origin, all the ruins of the mountain, enormous rocks, and immense accumulations of sand and stones. These are driven onwards by the irresistible stream of solid ice; and when they arrive at a declivity of the mountain, sufficiently rapid, roll down, scattering ruin. I saw one of these rocks which had descended in the spring, (winter here is the season of silence and safety) which measured forty feet in every direction.

The verge of a glacier, like that of Bossons, presents the most vivid image of desolation that it is possible to conceive. No one dares to approach it; for the enormous pinnacles of ice which perpetually fall, are perpetually reproduced. The pines of the forest, which bound it at one extremity, are overthrown and shattered to a wide extent at its base. There is something inexpressibly dreadful in the aspect of the few branchless trunks, which, nearest to the ice rifts, still stand in the uprooted soil. The meadows perish, overwhelmed with sand and stones. Within this last year, these glaciers have advanced three hundred feet into the valley. Saussure,[1] the naturalist, says, that they have their periods of increase and decay: the people of the country hold an opinion entirely different; but as I judge, more probable. It is agreed by all, that the snow on the summit of Mont Blanc and the neighbouring mountains perpetually augments, and that ice, in the form of

---

1 'Horace Bénédict de Saussure (1740–99), Swiss geologist and alpinist, who felt that the Alps provided the key to the true theory of the earth's formation' (Murray 446).

glaciers, subsists without melting in the valley of Chamouni during its transient and variable summer. If the snow which produces this glacier must augment, and the heat of the valley is no obstacle to the perpetual existence of such masses of ice as have already descended into it, the consequence is obvious; the glaciers must augment and will subsist, at least until they have overflowed this vale.

I will not pursue [Comte de Georges-Louis Leclerc] Buffon's sublime but gloomy theory – that this globe which we inhabit will at some future period be changed into a mass of frost by the encroachments of the polar ice, and of that produced on the most elevated points of the earth. Do you, who assert the supremacy of Ahriman,[2] imagine him throned among these desolating snows, among these places of death and frost, so sculptured in this their terrible magnificence by the adamantine hand of necessity, and that he casts around him, as the first essays of his final usurpation, avalanches, torrents, rocks, and thunders, and above all these deadly glaciers, at once the proof and symbols of his reign; – add to this, the degradation of the human species – who in these regions are half deformed or idiotic, and most of whom are deprived of any thing that can excite interest or admiration. This is a part of the subject more mournful and less sublime; but such as neither the poet nor the philosopher should disdain to regard.

This morning we departed, on the promise of a fine day, to visit the glacier of Montanvert. In that part where it fills a slanting valley, it is called the Sea of Ice. This valley is 950 toises,[3] or 7600 feet above the level of the sea. We had not proceeded far before the rain began to fall, but we persisted until we had accomplished more than half of our journey, when we returned, wet through.

Further Reading

Aldini, John. *An Account of the Late Improvements in Galvanism, with a Series of Curious and Interesting Experiments [in Paris and London, with] Appendix, Containing the Author's Experiments on the Body of a Malefactor Executed at Newage.* London: Cuthell and Martin and J. Murray, 1803. One of the key contemporary texts on electricity.

Darwin, Erasmus. *The Botanic Garden; a Poem, in Two Parts.* London: printed for J. Johnson, 1790–1. Part 1 is the poem called *The Temple of Nature*, referred to by Mary and Percy Shelley as the source of conversations about the creation of life.

Shelley, Percy Bysshe. 'Alastor' (1816). This is the poem Percy Shelley was writing around the time of the composition of *Frankenstein*. It shares some remarkable similarities, making a case for the Shelleys as somewhat collaborative authors.

---

2   Ahrimanes, one of the two gods of Zoroastrian religion: the evil demiurge who creates the universe of matter. The good god, Oromazes, presides over the world of spirit. Zoroastrian thought and imagery was popular among Shelley's circle, used, for instance, in the novels of Thomas Love Peacock.

3   'A French lineal measure of 6 French feet, roughly equal to 1.949 metres, or 6⅖ English feet. Chiefly in military use' (*OED*).

For example, there is a framing device in which at least one unreliable narrator is presented. The central figure is a polymath, a poet and scientist who is obsessed with pursuing what he feels are the secrets of nature. Language very similar to that used in *Frankenstein* is employed, of a necrophiliac ransacking of mother nature's body.

Volney, Constantin-François. *The Ruins: Or a Survey of the Revolutions of Empires. With Notes Historical, Geographical, and Explanatory. To Which is Annexed the Law of Nature*. London: T. Davidson, 1816. One of the texts on the creature's reading list, it invokes 'ye mouldering and silent Walls', 'mixing the dust of the proudest kings with that of the meanest slaves, you called upon us to contemplate this example of EQUALITY' (vii).

2

Interpretations

2
Interpretations

Presumption, Science and Religion: Early Receptions of *Frankenstein*

Introduction

Most early reviews and stage adaptations of Shelley's novel, with the notable exception of Percy Shelley's own essay on it, were keen naïvely to repeat the view of the second narrator of the novel: that of Victor Frankenstein himself. Victor is convinced that the wrath of God is being visited upon him for making the creature; and in return he is determined to act out his own wrath upon his creature. Of course, prior to this, he is convinced that others (perhaps the psychoanalytic Other, in relationship to which he derives his identity, according to the theory) will praise him for his magnificent achievement. On the whole, early readings of the novel tend to dismiss or underestimate the power of the creature's own side of the story, forgetting that Shelley gives pride of place to this paradoxical narrative of natural education. The question to ask when reading these extracts and descriptions is: how successfully do these early readings take account of the aesthetic form of the novel? This is the Chinese box effect of inset narratives, 'culminating' at the centre in the orientalist narrative of Safie.

I have chosen a fairly representative selection of reviews, and Percy Shelley's essay on *Frankenstein*. I have also summarised reviews that could not be reproduced because of space issues. Where strictly necessary, I have minimally edited the copy text.

Reviews

Anon., *The Belle Assemblée, or Bell's Court and Fashionable Magazine* 17 (March 1818): 139–42

The review describes the novel as 'bold' and possibly 'impious', but it also praises it for its 'originality, excellence of language, and peculiar interest'. In explaining Frankenstein's search for the origin of life, the review comments, 'how vain', thus developing the interpretative theme of the wrath of God. On the other hand, the review dismisses the central section of the novel (the creature's narrative) as 'rather prolix and unnatural'. The review duly notes that Godwin, to whom the novel is dedicated, is now, far from remaining a philosophical anarchist, 'happily converted to what he once styled ancient prejudices'.

Anon., Review of *Presumption; or The Fate of Frankenstein* (Richard Brinsley Peake's adaptation) (Tuesday 29 July and Wednesday 30 July 1823), the London *Morning Post*

Betty Bennett writes the following on Cooke's performance in Paris: 'a review of the production of *Frankenstein* at the Theatre de la Porte Saint-Martin from *Le Globe: Journal Litteraire*, 17 June 1826 . . . was generally unfavorable, particularly condemning Cooke, saying that his performance could have been equaled by an amateur. Praise was reserved for the set, particularly for the reality of the sea and storm scenes' (Shelley, *Letters* 1.522).

Tuesday, July 29, 1823

A new three act piece, described as 'a romance of a peculiar interest', was last night produced at this theatre, entitled, *Presumption, or the Fate of Frankenstein*.

The fable represents Frankenstein, a man of great science, to have succeeded in uniting the remains of dead persons, so as to form one being, which he endows with life. He has, however, little reason to exult in the triumph of his art; for the creature thus formed, hideous in aspect, and possessed of prodigious strength, spreads terror, and carries ruin wherever he goes. Though wearing the human form, he is incapable of associating with mankind, to whom he eventually becomes hostile, and having killed the mistress and brother of Frankenstein, he finally vanquishes his mortal creator, and perishes himself beneath a falling avalanche.

Such is the outline of the business of a drama more extraordinary in its plan, than remarkable for strength in its execution. There is something in the piecemeal resurrection effected by Frankenstein, which, instead of creating that awful interest intended to arise from it, gives birth to a feeling of horror. We have not that taste for the monstrous which can enable us to enjoy it in the midst of the most startling absurdities. To Lord BYRON, the late Mr. SHELLEY, and philosophers of that stamp, it might appear a very fine thing to attack the Christian faith from a masked battery, and burlesque the resurrection of the dead, by representing the fragments of departed mortals as starting into existence at the command of a man; but we would prefer the comparatively noble assaults of [Constantin-François de Chasseboeuf] VOLNEY, VOLTAIRE, and PAINE.[1] In the first scene in which —— (so the creature of Frankenstein is indicated in the bills) makes his

1   Writers who would be considered republican or radical by a reactionary press.

appearance, the effect is terrific. There are other parts in which a very powerful impression is produced on the spectators, but to have made the most of the idea a greater interest ought early in the drama to have been excited for Frankenstein and the destined victims of the non-descript, and he himself would have been an object of greater attention if speech had been vouchsafed. The efforts to relieve the serious action of the Piece by mirth and music were generally successful, and the labours of Mr. WATSON the composer we often loudly applauded.

The acting was very grand. WALLACK as Frankenstein, displayed great feeling and animation; T.P. COOKE as —— (or the made up man), was tremendously appalling. The other performers did as much as could be expected in the parts allotted to them, and the piece though it met with some opposition at the close had a large majority in its favour, and was announced for repetition.

The entertainment of the 'Rival Soldiers' followed, in which Mr. W. CHAPMAN played Nipperkin with much genuine humour. He is an actor of sterling merit and will improve as he goes on.

Wednesday, July 30, 1823 ENGLISH OPERA HOUSE

At this Theatre last night, *Presumption, or the Fate of Frankenstein*, was again performed. Whatever may be thought of *Frankenstein* as a novel, or of the principles of those who could indite such a novel, there can be but one opinion of it as a drama. The representation of this piece upon the stage is of astonishing, of enchaining, interest. In the novel the rigid moralist may feel himself constantly offended, by the modes of reasoning, principles of action, &c. – But in the Drama this is all carefully kept in the back ground. Nothing but what can please, astonish, and delight, is there suffered to appear; Frankenstein despairingly bewails his attempt as impious, and suffers for it; partial justice is rendered; and many more incidents in the novel might have been pourtrayed, of harrowing interest! though without infringing good taste. As it stands, however, as a drama, it is most effective; and T. P. COOKE well pourtrays what indeed it is a proof of his extraordinary genius so well to portray – an unhappy being without the pale of nature – a monster – a nondescript – a horror to himself and others; – yet the leaning, the bias, the nature, if one may so say, of the creature is good; he is in the beginning of his creation gentle, and disposed to be affectionate and kind, but his appearance terrifies even those to whom he has rendered the most essential service; the alarm he excites creates hostility; his miserable frame assailed by man; and revenge and the malignity are thus excited in his breast. Instead of being longer kind or gentle he becomes ferocious, sets fire to the cottage where his services had been so ungratefully requited (and this scene is admirably managed), and perceiving that Frankenstein, the author of his existence, shuns and abhors him as much as others, he becomes enraged against him, and seeks his destruction and that of all dear to him, in which he too fatally succeeds. Too much cannot be said in praise of T. P. COOKE, his development of first impressions, and naturally perceptions, is given with a fidelity to nature truly admirable. Take for instance the pourtraiture of his first sensations on hearing music, than which nothing can be finer. The acting of WALLACK, the unhappy Frankenstein, is painfully interesting; he looks, he seems to feel the very character he assumes, so abstracted, so wretched, so care-worn. Upon the whole, though from diversity of taste this Piece may meet with some opposition, it cannot fail to stand its ground in ultimate conjunction with other pieces. The applause predominated in a more marked degree last night. The pleasant Afterpiece of Where shall I Dine? followed, and kept the house in a continued laughter.

Sir Walter Scott, *Blackwood's Edinburgh Magazine* 2 (20 March/ 1 April 1818): 613–20

Walter Scott's review declares Shelley's work to be 'a novel, or more properly a romantic fiction', one of 'the class of marvellous romances' (in which the belief of the reader and characters are strongly solicited). In *The Fantastic*, Tzvetan Todorov has distinguished between the fantastic uncanny and the fantastic marvellous: the fantastic uncanny relates events that seem out of the ordinary but end up having an empirical scientific explanation. The fantastic marvellous, on the other hand, tells of things that really do impinge upon other worlds or different orders of reality (the supernatural).[1] Surely Scott is not quite correct in his assessment of the novel? *Frankenstein* seems to straddle, ambiguously, both kinds of fantastic literature. But Scott then continues by noting that unlike the work of Collins (unabashed fantasy), Shelley's work is of 'A more philosophical and refined use of the supernatural', 'in order to shew the probable effect which the supposed miracles would produce on those who witnessed them'. In **Jonathan Swift**'s *Gulliver's Travels* (a text sometimes compared with *Frankenstein*), the humour derived from Gulliver's being stuck in a giant pin, Scott notes, 'lies not so much in the comparatively pigmy size which subjected Gulliver to such a ludicrous misfortune, as in the tone of grave and dignified feeling with which he resents the disgrace of the incident'.

Scott is a little ambiguous over how he feels about the episode of the creature's education:

> This detail is not only highly improbable, but it is injudicious, as its unnecessary minuteness tends rather too much to familiarize us with the being whom it regards, and who loses, by this lengthy oration, some part of the mysterious sublimity annexed to his first appearance. The result is, this monster, who was at first, according to his own account, but a harmless monster, becomes ferocious and malignant, in consequence of finding all his approaches to human society repelled with injurious violence and offensive marks of disgust.

---

1   Tzvetan Todorov, *The Fantastic: A Structural Approach to a Literary Genre*, tr. Richard Howard (Cleveland: Case Western Reserve University Press, 1973).

Scott later declares that it would have been just as odd if the creature had learnt double-entry bookkeeping, a remark in keeping with the extent to which this part of the novel recapitulates the myth of the self-made (money-making) man. He appears, however, at least to understand the purpose of Shelley's thought experiment. While Scott has something of a tin ear for the novel's political register, as the evidence of the example above demonstrates, he does have a thought that the fictional mode of the novel is well suited to 'political satire'. Scott praises the novel's classical style, its lack of 'hyperbolical Germanisms'. Not surprisingly, as the book was published anonymously, he cannot distinguish between what was written by Shelley and what was written by Percy Shelley, praising the author's style with a quotation from Percy's ode on mutability.

The first general division of works of fiction, into such as bound the events they narrate by the actual laws of nature, and such as, passing these limits, are managed by marvellous and supernatural machinery, is sufficiently obvious and decided. But the class of marvellous romances admits of several subdivisions. In the earlier productions of imagination, the poet, or tale-teller does not, in his own opinion, transgress the laws of credibility, when he introduces into his narration the witches, goblins, and magicians, in the existence of which he himself, as well as his hearers, is a firm believer. This good faith, however, passes away, and works turning upon the marvellous are written and read merely on account of the exercise which they afford to the imagination of those who, like the poet Collins, love to riot in the luxuriance of oriental fiction, to rove through the meanders of enchantment, to gaze on the magnificence of golden palaces, and to repose by the water-falls of Elysian gardens.[2] In this species of composition, the marvellous is itself the principal and most important object both to the author and reader. To describe its effect upon the minds of the human personages engaged in its wonders, and dragged along by its machinery, is comparatively an inferior object. The hero and heroine, partakers of the supernatural character which belongs to their adventures, walk the maze of enchantment with a firm and undaunted step, and appear as much at their ease, amid the wonders around them, as the young fellow described by the *Spectator*, who was discovered taking a snuff with great composure in the midst of a stormy ocean, represented on the stage of the Opera.

A more philosophical and refined use of the supernatural in works of fiction, is proper to that class in which the laws of nature are represented as altered, not for the purpose of pampering the imagination with wonders, but in order to shew the probable effect which the supposed miracles would produce on those who witnessed them. In this case, the pleasure ordinarily derived from the marvellous incidents is secondary to that which we extract from observing how mortals like ourselves would be affected by scenes like these which, daring to depart from sober truth, are still to nature true. [. . .]

2   Scott is referring to William Collins (1721–59).

We have only to add, that this class of fiction has been sometimes applied to the purposes of political satire, and sometimes to the general illustration of the powers and workings of the human mind. Swift, Bergerac, and others, have employed it for the former purpose, and a good illustration of the latter is the well known *Saint Leon* of William Godwin. In this latter work, assuming the possibility of the transmutation of metals, and of the elixir vitae, the author has deduced, in the course of his narrative, the probable consequences of the possession of such secrets upon the fortunes and mind of him who might enjoy them. *Frankenstein* . . . is said to be written by Mr Percy Bysshe Shelley, who, if we are rightly informed, is son-in-law to Mr Godwin; and it is inscribed to that ingenious author. [. . .]

It is no slight merit in our eyes, that the tale, though wild in incident, is written in plain and forcible English, without exhibiting that mixture of hyperbolical Germanisms with which tales of wonder are usually told, as if it were necessary that the language should be as extravagant as the fiction. The ideas of the author are always clearly as well as forcibly expressed; and his descriptions of landscape have in them the choice requisites of truth, freshness, precision, and beauty. The self-education of the monster, considering the slender opportunities of acquiring knowledge that he possessed, we have already noticed as improbable and overstrained. That he should have not only learned to speak, but to read, and, for aught we know, to write – that he should have become acquainted with Werter, with *Plutarch's Lives*, and with *Paradise Lost*, by listening through a hole in a wall, seems as unlikely as that he should have acquired, in the same way, the problems of Euclid, or the art of book-keeping by single and double entry. The author has however two apologies – the first, the necessity that his monster should acquire those endowments, and the other, that his neighbours were engaged in teaching the language of the country to a young foreigner. His progress in self-knowledge, and the acquisition of information, is, after all, more wonderful than that of Hai Eben Yokhdan, or Automathes, or the hero of the little romance called *The Child of Nature*, one of which works might perhaps suggest the train of ideas followed by the author of *Frankenstein*. We should also be disposed, in support of the principles with which we set out, to question whether the monster, how tall, agile, and strong however, could have perpetrated so much mischief undiscovered, or passed through so many countries without being secured, either on account of his crimes, or for the benefit of some such speculator as **Mr. Polito**, who would have been happy to have added to his museum so curious a specimen of natural history. But as we have consented to admit the leading incident of the work, perhaps some of our readers may be of opinion, that to stickle upon lesser improbabilities, is to incur the censure bestowed by the Scottish proverb on those who start at straws after swallowing windlings.

Percy Bysshe Shelley, 'On "Frankenstein; or, the Modern Prometheus"' (1818), in E.B. Murray, ed., *The Prose Works of Percy Bysshe Shelley* (1993) Oxford: Clarendon Press, vol. 1: 282–4

Percy Shelley fiercely asserts the sociological reading of the novel: 'Treat a person ill, and he will become wicked . . . divide him, a social being, from

The novel of 'Frankenstein, or the Modern Prometheus', is undoubtedly, as a mere story, one of the most original and complete productions of the age. We debate with ourselves in wonder as we read it, what could have been the series of thoughts, what could have been the peculiar experiences that awakened them, which conducted in the author's mind, to the astonishing combination of motives and incidents and the startling catastrophe which compose this tale. There are perhaps some points of subordinate importance which prove that it is the Author's first attempt. But in this judgement, which requires a very nice discrimination, we may be mistaken. For it is conducted throughout with a firm and steady hand. The interest gradually accumulates, and advances towards the conclusion with the accelerated rapidity of a rock rolled down a mountain. We are held breathless with suspense and sympathy, and the heaping up of incident on incident, and the working of passion out of passion. We cry, 'hold, hold, enough'[1] – but there is yet something to come, and like the victim whose history it relates we think we can bear no more, and yet more is to be borne. Pelion is heaped on Ossa, and Ossa on Olympus. We climb Alp after Alp,[2] until the horizon is seen, blank, vacant, and limitless, and the head turns giddy, and the ground seems to fail under the feet.

This Novel thus rests its claim on being a source of powerful and profound emotion. The elementary feelings of the human mind are exposed to view, and those who are accustomed to reason deeply on their origin and tendency, will perhaps be the only persons who can sympathise to the full extent in the interest of the actions which are their result. But, founded on nature as they are, there is perhaps no reader who can endure any thing beside a new love-story, who will not feel a responsive string touched in his inmost soul. The sentiments are so affectionate and so innocent, the characters of the subordinate agents in this strange drama are clothed in the light of such a mild and gentle mind. – The pictures of domestic manners are every where of the most simple and attaching character. The pathos is irresistible and deep. Nor are the crimes and malevolence of the single Being, tho' indeed withering and tremendous, the offspring of any unaccountable propensity to evil, but flow inevitably from certain causes fully adequate to their production. They are the children, as it were, of Necessity and Human Nature. In this the direct moral of the book consists; and it perhaps the most important, and of the most universal application, of any moral that can be enforced by example. Treat a person ill, and he will become wicked. Requite affection with scorn; – let one being be selected, for whatever cause, as the refuse

---

1 An allusion to *Macbeth* 5.8.33–4: 'Lay on Macduff,/And damn'd be him that first cries, "Hold, enough!" '
2 A sophisticated out-troping of the zeugmas in *Hamlet* 5.1 in which Hamlet tries to outdo Laertes in grief (246–54, 274–83). Shelley's zeugmatic construction throughout this paragraph here reaches a peak (pun probably intended).

of his kind – divide him, a social being, from society, and you impose upon him the irresistible obligations – malevolence and selfishness. It is thus that, too often in society, those who are best qualified to be its benefactors and its ornaments, are branded by some accident with scorn, and changed, by neglect and solitude of heart, into a scourge and a curse.

The Being in 'Frankenstein' is, no doubt, a tremendous creature. It was impossible that he should not have received among men that treatment which led to the consequences of his being a social nature. He was an abortion and an anomaly, and tho' his mind was such as its first impressions formed it, affectionate and full of moral sensibility, yet the circumstances of his existence were so monstrous and uncommon, that when the consequences of them became developed into action, his original goodness was gradually turned into the fuel of an inexhaustible misanthropy and revenge. The scene between the Being and the blind de Lacey in the cottage is one of the most profound and extraordinary instances of pathos that we ever recollect. It is impossible to read this dialogue – and indeed many other situations of a somewhat similar character – without feeling the heart suspend its pulsations with wonder, and the tears stream down the cheeks! The encounter and argument between Frankenstein and the Being on the sea of ice almost approaches in effect to the expostulations of Caleb Williams with Falkland.[3] It reminds us indeed somewhat of the style and character of that admirable writer to whom the Author has dedicated his work, and whose productions he seems to have studied. There is only one instance however in which we detect the least approach to imitation, and that is, the conduct of the incident of Frankenstein's landing and trial in Ireland. – The general character of the tale indeed resembles nothing that ever preceded it. After the death of Elisabeth, the story, like a stream which grows at once more rapid and profound as it proceeds, assumes an irresistible solemnity, and the magnificent energy and swiftness of a tempest.

The church yard scene, in which Frankenstein visits the tombs of his family, his quitting Geneva and his journey thro' Tartary to the shores of the Frozen Ocean, resembles at once the terrible reanimation of a corpse, and the supernatural career of a spirit. The scene in the cabin of Walton's ship, the more than mortal enthusiasm and grandeur of the Being's speech over the dead body of his victim, is an exhibition of intellectual and imaginative power, which we think the reader will acknowledge has seldom been surpassed.

Further Reading

Anon. *The British Critic* 9 (April 1818): 432–8.
Anon. *Edinburgh Magazine* 2 (March 1818): 249–53.
Anon. *The Literary Panorama and National Register* 8 (1 June 1818): 411–14.
Croker, John. *Quarterly Review* 18 (January 1818): 379–85.

---

3   This and the following sentence refer to Mary Shelley's father William Godwin, author of *Caleb Williams*.

Why Did You Make Me Like This?! Performing *Frankenstein*

Introduction

Jeffrey Robinson, my colleague at the University of Colorado at Boulder, has for some years been telling stories to his young daughter Rachel at bedtime. Recently, instead of inventing them on the spot, he has been telling the stories of others. One night he approached Rachel with an offer to tell her the story of Frankenstein. 'I don't want to hear it now,' said Rachel. 'Tell me at Halloween.' Rachel was already well aware of the performative dimension of Shelley's novel. This is the extent to which it has permeated culture throughout the world.

In a sense it is easy to assess the performative impact of *Frankenstein*: the novel has taken on the status of a modern myth, and thus involves almost every layer of society. Notably, one could include politics, understood as a form of performance itself, under this rubric. Performance studies has recently been revealing the extent to which the social field is, in general, charged with performances of all kinds. For Marxist and cultural studies readers of the novel, this is evident in the ways in which *Frankenstein* has been used to depict the struggles of the nineteenth and twentieth centuries between owners and workers, and to cast an eye upon social structures based on commodity production.

This is the driving impulse of Chris Baldick's magnificent *In Frankenstein's Shadow*, a study of the ways in which class struggle has been encoded through Shelley's novel. The destiny traced by Baldick, in which the creature comes to stand in for the working class, is further extrapolated by the industrialisation of the Frankenstein story, and the detachment of the now-autonomous creature from that story, performed by the movie industry. Baldick also demonstrates how Shelley's story came to figure in the representation of the industrial age as an era of advancing technology and imperialism. Moreover, the myth of the creature has in recent times been taken as fruitful for the investigation of issues around nuclear technology (see the extract from Kathleen Sullivan, **pp. 55–8**). The type of the Frankenstein movie has now also split into its various themes, such as the risks of presumption (*Jurassic Park*) and the consequences of cloning (*The Sixth Element*).

Why has the novel's story taken on such mythic proportions? According to the structuralist anthropologist Claude Lévi-Strauss, a myth is rather like a computer program: it provides a way for people to think out certain basic social problems; problems that may not instantly be resolved but which require displacement into a narrative medium. Underlying these problems, claims Lévi-Strauss, is the basic question of *where we came from*. Was it from others – from the earth, from our mother's body, from our family, tribe or nation . . . – or was it 'from ourselves', as in the popular capitalist myth of the 'self-made man'? To put it in Lévi-Strauss's terminology, this is the opposition between *chthonic* and *autochthonous* origins. Does Frankenstein's creature, in the fullness of his personality, 'come from' his creator, or, as the second part of the novel indicates, is he self-making, self-taught, in some fashion? Throughout the nineteenth century, then, the question could be posed: who is responsible, if anyone, for the working class? Were they 'made' (by bosses, factory owners, and so forth) or did they just appear?

In the melancholy Ridley Scott film *Blade Runner* (1982), an adaptation of Philip K. Dick's *Do Androids Dream of Electric Sheep?* (1968), the struggle between bosses and workers is re-enacted through an extended allusion to *Frankenstein*. The replicants are workers whose very bodies have been manufactured. They work in dangerous jobs in the colony worlds, far from civilisation; they die (the euphemism being 'are retired') when they are four years old; the resulting emotional instability is corrected, thinks the Corporation who makes them, by implanted memories. Agents of the law, 'Blade Runners', are hired to 'retire' insurrectionary replicants such as the team confronted by agent Deckard in the movie.

Out of this material, what the film achieves derives from the ways in which it fully appreciates what really makes the novel *Frankenstein* disturbing. This is not the creature's difference from, but his *similarity to* human beings. In the language of the Enlightenment, familiar to Mary Shelley, he is *humane*, he displays humanity and pathos, principally through his speech, which never fails to strike the first reader as disturbing in its very dignity. His disgusting features are at odds with his noble eloquence. In other words, his body is one thing, but his mind another.

Surely this is the pathos of the character Roy Batty (played by Rutger Hauer), and also ultimately (at least in the director's cut) of Deckard (the character played by Harrison Ford). The uncanny truth is not that humans are different from the working-class 'replicants' whom they have made to carry out their dirty work in space colonisation, but that humans, in their very humanity, are replicants: beings whose core is artificial, just a sum of memories. What if artificial people could be made? When does a human being become a person? Shelley's novel, and Philip K. Dick's novel (and Ridley Scott's movie) dramatise this idea, through fantastic literalisation.

What makes the replicants sympathetic is their very short life span (four years), relative to the implanted memories of an entire life, with which they are equipped to function as pseudo-humans. It is not their concrete humanness but their obsession with the possibility of being human, encapsulated as a set of behaviours and responses (they cry at each other's deaths, they feel love, pain, misery . . .) – this is what makes them human. We could call this obsession with the possibility of being human *reflexive humanity*. It is a very Romantic notion and is thus, not surprisingly, found in *Frankenstein*. It is the creature's demand to be treated as a human being that makes him a human being: the contrast between the abstractness of that demand and the concreteness of his horrific body and his doomed situation is what makes this novel both tragic and utopian.

At the end of the movie, Deckard realises his love for a female replicant, and the possibility that he himself might be a replicant: the fragility and preciousness of human birth is made clear to him. And, as at the end of *Frankenstein*, the chief replicant, Roy, owns his own inevitable death in a moment that is at once highly ethical and supremely tragic: 'I've . . . *seen* things – some of you people wouldn't believe . . . Attack ships on fire off the shoulder of Orion . . . I watched C-beams glitter in the darkness at Tannhäuser Gate . . . All those – moments – will be lost in time, like . . . tears . . . in rain: time . . . to die' (my transcription). What Roy says has the same plangency as the creature's last words and actions: ' "But soon," he cried, with sad and solemn enthusiasm, "I shall die" . . . He was soon borne away by the waves, and lost in darkness and distance' (**p. 166**). Roy, like the creature, is intellectual (beating his maker at chess), literary (quoting lines from Blake's *America* about the fires of Orc),[1] and witty in a creaturely, heavy-handed way. The brilliance of *Blade Runner*, and of *Frankenstein*, is not so much to point out that artificial life and intelligence are possible, but that human life *already is this artificial intelligence*. René Descartes tellingly referred to the intelligence as the *res intellectus*, the 'thing which thinks'. *Frankenstein* and *Blade Runner*, then, are identical parodies of Enlightenment thought.[2]

What makes humans human, finally, is shown to be not some natural or essential component of their being, but a relationship that can never be fulfilled, between one's material conditions and one's mental or spiritual capacity. This asymmetrical relationship is perfectly captured in *Blade Runner* when Roy goads the manufacturer of replicants – in this story, as opposed to Shelley's, the roles subsumed by Frankenstein of entrepreneur and labourer are divided between the owner and the employees of the Corporation. Roy picks up a pair of eyes on which the scientist has been working and declares: 'If only you could see what I have seen . . . with your eyes.' On the one hand the eyes are physical and the property of the Corporation; on the other hand, mental or spiritual, reflecting the mind of the replicant. This is surely the reason for the pathos of the central section of *Frankenstein*, in which the creature narrates what *he* has seen with, as it were, Frankenstein's eyes.

Frankenphemes

In structural linguistics, words are seen as made of sonic elements (phonemes) and visual elements (graphemes). 'Frankenphemes' is the name I have chosen to

---

1 Orc is William Blake's revolutionary hero, depicted as a rebel against his own maker, the heavy-handed allegorical figure of dominant ideology, Urizen. See William Blake, *The Complete Poetry and Prose of William Blake*, ed. David V. Erdman (New York: Doubleday, 1965; revised 1998), 55 (*America* plate II).

2 For a masterful analysis of this theme in *Blade Runner*, see Slavoj Žižek, 'I or He or It (the Thing) which Thinks', in Slavoj Žižek, *Tarrying with the Negative: Kant, Hegel, and the Critique of Ideology* (Durham: Duke University Press, 1993), 10–44.

give to those elements of culture that are derived from *Frankenstein*, but that are less than a work of art in completion or scale. Some kernel of an idea derived from Shelley's novel has been repeated in another medium. These Frankenphemes are worth noting, although the list is necessarily not exhaustive, and keeps changing. They demonstrate the extent to which the novel has permeated the ways in which we see the world, the 'metaphors we live by'.[1] You will also find some graphic art in this section (see Figures 1 and 2, facing and overleaf). Race and class issues have consistently been coded through *Frankenstein*, from the speeches of Canning in the House of Commons (see Shelley's letters in Contemporary Documents), to the Mr Potato Head commercial in 1980s America. In the film *Better Off Dead*, John Cusack vivifies a hamburger, which then overpowers him with cool, does a rock guitar number and gets together with a live girl hamburger. In the 1990s there emerged 'Frankenfoods' and the 'Frankencell' project, on both sides of the Atlantic, to describe the new business and technology of genetic engineering. The frame of the current debate is still within the parameters set by *Frankenstein*: are the genetic engineers and biotech corporations at fault for imitating God, or are they to blame for objectifying the world and turning the very stuff of life into a commodity?

The first extract below is from the original dramatic adaptation of the novel (1823). In this play the creature begins to become an autonomous being in relation to the novel in which he first appears, as if he were rising from the table of the art that created him in the first place.

Richard Brinsley Peake, *Presumption: Or the Fate of Frankenstein.*
Copy text: Jeffrey Cox, ed., *Seven Gothic Dramas 1789–1825* (1992) Athens, OH: Ohio University Press

Adapted by Richard Brinsley Peake, produced by S.J. Arnold, with music by Mr Bennett; James Wallack as Dr Frankenstein, Thomas Potter Cooke ('a well-known villain of the stage, stole the show') playing the creature (see Figure 3, **p.52**).[1] Mary was in Turin when it opened, and while she travelled back to London, she heard inflated reports from her friend Horace Smith of its London staging (that the creature made women faint) as well as of its Paris reception. She reached London on Monday 25 August and went to the Lyceum on Friday 29 with her father, Jane and William (165). (See the extracts from Shelley's letters on **pp. 29–30** of this volume to find out what she thought of Cooke's part, and

1   See George Lakoff and Mark Johnson, *Metaphors We Live By* (Chicago and London: University of Chicago Press), 1980.

1   Radu Florescu, *In Search of Frankenstein* (Boston: New York Graphic Society, 1975), 165.

THE RUSSIAN FRANKENSTEIN AND HIS MONSTER.

Figure 1 **Anon., 'The Russian Frankenstein and His Monster',** *Punch,*
15 July 1854: 15. This image indicates the politicisation of
Frankenstein's creature. 'A Militarist Frankenstein: [this cartoon] . . .
celebrates the sending of an Allied force to the Crimea to punish the
presumptuous Tsar Nicholas I, whose militarism would surely
backfire on him' (Baldick, *In Frankenstein's Shadow,* 95).

Courtesy of the Bodleian Library, University of Oxford

THE BRUMMAGEM FRANKENSTEIN.

John Bright. "I HAVE NO FE—FE—FEAR OF MA—MANHOOD SUFFRAGE!"—*Mr. Bright's Speech at Birmingham.*

Figure 2 **John Tenniel, 'The Brummagem [Birmingham] Frankenstein', *Punch*, 8 September 1866: 103.** The liberal middle class tiptoes past the giant figure of the working class in this image: 'an enormous proletarian waits for the vote to be given to him by the Birmingham Liberal MP John Bright, a leader of the Reform agitation of the 1860s' (Baldick, *In Frankenstein's Shadow*, 85). The monster appears to have a healthy suspicion of the MP's motives, and not to be as stupid as portrayed in Tenniel's 'The Irish Frankenstein', *Punch*, 20 May 1882: 235, a negative comment on the Irish nationalism of Charles Stewart Parnell.

Courtesy of the Bodleian Library, University of Oxford

more.) The play ran from late July through October, when it was displaced by *Der Freischütz*. The playbill for Covent Garden shows that *Presumption* shared its date with *The West Indian* and *Yard Arm* and *Yard Arm; or, Two Ways of Telling a Story* (both preceding it). The bill states:

> 'The Evening's Entertainments to conclude with, for the first and only time at this Theatre, (by the kind permission of S.J. Arnold, Esq.) the highly popular Romance, of peculiar and terrific interest, called PRESUMPTION. The striking moral exhibited in this story, is the fatal consequence of that presumption which attempts to penetrate, beyond prescribed depths, into mysteries of nature … *Among the many striking effects of this Piece, the following will be displayed: Mysterious and terrific appearance of the Demon from the Laboratory of Frankenstein.* DESTRUCTION *of a* COTTAGE *by* FIRE. *And the* FALL *of an* AVALANCHE'.
>
> (164)

See the section 'Theatrical Adapations' **pp. 59–61** for further details of performances of *Presumption*.

Variant readings have been placed in square brackets. Stage directions have been placed in italics. Note how the text of *Frankenstein* has been incorporated into the play: 'We see the movement here away from Mary Shelley's being towards the bolt-neck monster of the movie tradition.'[2]

DRAMATIS PERSONAE

English Opera House, 28 July, 1823

Frankenstein	Mr. Wallack
Clerval (his friend, in love with Elizabeth)	Mr. Bland
William (brother of Frankenstein)	Master Boden
Fritz (servant of Frankenstein)	Mr. Keeley
De Lacey (a banished gentleman – blind)	Mr. Rowbotham
Felix De Lacey (his son)	Mr. Pearman
Tanskin (a gipsy)	Mr. Shield
Hammerpan (a tinker)	Mr. Salter
First Gipsy	
A Guide (an old man)	Mr. R. Phillips
——	Mr. T.P. Cooke[3]
Elizabeth (sister of Frankenstein)	Mrs. Austin
Agatha (daughter of De Lacey)	Miss L. Dance
Safie (an Arabian girl, betrothed to Felix)	Miss Povey
Madame Ninon (wife to Fritz)	Mrs. T. Weippert
Gipsies, Peasants, Choristers, and Dancers (Male and Female)	

---

2   Jeffrey Cox, *Seven Gothic Dramas*, 397.
3   Playing the part of the creature. See Contemporary Documents (**pp. 29–30**) and Modern Criticism (**p. 109**) for Shelley's thoughts on his anonymity.

MR. T. P. COOKE,
Of the Theatre Royal Covent Garden.
In the Character of the Monster, in the Dramatic Romance of Frankenstien.

Figure 3 Anon., T.P. Cooke as the creature in *Presumption*, Richard Brinsley Peake's adaptation of *Frankenstein* (London, 1823).

Courtesy of the Harvard Theatre Collection, The Houghton Library

*The sleeping Apartment of Frankenstein. Dark. The Bed is within a recess
between the wings, enclosed by dark green curtains. A Sword (to break) hanging.
A Large French Window; between the wings a staircase leading to a Gallery
across the stage, on which is the Door of the Laboratory above. A small high
Lattice in centre of scene, next the Laboratory Door. A Gothic Table on stage,
screwed. A Gothic Chair in centre, and Footstool. Music expressive of the rising
of a storm. Enter Frankenstein, with a Lighted Lamp, which he places on the
table. Distant thunder heard.*

FRANK. This evening – this lowering evening, will, in all probability, complete my
task. Years have I laboured, and at length discovered that to which so many men
of genius have in vain directed their inquiries. After days and nights of incredible
labour and fatigue, I have become master of the secret of bestowing animation
upon lifeless matter. With so astonishing a power in my hands, long, long did I
hesitate how to employ it. The object of my experiments lies there (*Pointing up to
the laboratory.*) – A huge automaton in human form. Should I succeed in animating it, Life and Death would appear to me as ideal bounds, which I shall break
through and pour a torrent of light into our dark world. I have lost all soul or
sensation but for this one pursuit. (*Storm.*) A storm has hastily arisen! – 'Tis a
dreary night – the rain patters dismally against the panes – 'tis a night for such a
task – I'll in and attempt to infuse the spark of life. –

*Music. – Frankenstein takes up lamp, cautiously looks around him, ascends the
stairs, crosses the gallery above, and exits into door of laboratory. Enter Fritz,
trembling, with a candle.*

FRITZ. Master isn't here – dare I peep. Only think of the reward Mr. Clerval
promised me, a cow and a cottage, milk and a mansion. Master is certainly not
come up yet. My candle burns all manner of colours, and spits like a roasted
apple. (*Runs against the chair and drops his light, which goes out.*) There, now,
I'm in the dark. Oh my nerves.

A blue flame appears at the small lattice window above, as from the laboratory.

What's that? O lauk; there he is, kicking up the devil's own flame! Oh my Cow!
I'll venture up – oh my cottage! I'll climb to the window – it will be only one peep
to make my fortune.

*Music. – Fritz takes up footstool, he ascends the stairs, when on the gallery
landing place, he stands on the footstool tiptoe to look through the small high
lattice window of the laboratory, a sudden combustion is heard within. The blue
flame changes to one of a reddish hue.*

FRANK. (*Within.*) It lives! it lives!

FRITZ. (*Speaks through music.*) Oh, dear! oh, dear! oh, dear!

*Fritz, greatly alarmed, jumps down hastily, totters tremblingly down the stairs in
vast hurry; when in front of stage, having fallen flat in fright, with difficulty speaks.*

FRITZ. There's a hob – [a] hob-goblin, [and] 20 feet high! [wrapp'd in [a mantle – mercy – mercy –

[*Falls down.*]

Music. – Frankenstein rushes from the laboratory, without lamp, fastens the door in apparent dread, and hastens down the stairs, watching the entrance of the laboratory.

FRANK. It lives! [It lives.] I saw the dull yellow eye of the creature open, it breathed hard, and a convulsive motion agitated its limbs. What a wretch have I formed, [his legs are in proportion and] I had selected his features as beautiful – beautiful! Ah, horror! his cadaverous skin scarcely covers the work of muscles and arteries beneath, his hair lustrous, black, and flowing – his teeth of pearly whiteness – but these luxuriances only form more horrible contrasts with the deformities of the Demon.

Music. – He listens at the foot of the staircase.

[It is yet quiet –] What have I accomplished? the beauty of my dream has vanished! and breathless horror and disgust fill my heart. For this I have deprived myself of rest and health, have worked my brain to madness; and when I looked to reap my great reward, a flash breaks in upon my darkened soul, and tells me my attempt was impious, and that its fruition will be fatal to my peace for ever. (*He listens again.*) All is still! The dreadful spectre of a human form – no mortal could withstand the horror of that countenance [– a mummy endued with animation could be so hideous as the wretch I have endowed with life!] – miserable and impious being that I am! [– lost – lost] Elizabeth! brother! Agatha! – faithful Agatha! never more dare I look upon your virtuous faces. 'Lost! lost! lost!'

Music – Frankenstein sinks on a chair.

[FRITZ. (*Looks up once or twice before he speaks.*) Oh my nerves; I feel as if [I had just come out of strong fits, and nobody to throw water in my [face – Master sleeps, so I'll, if my legs won't lap up under me – just – [make my escape.]

Sudden combustion heard, and smoke issues, the door of the laboratory breaks to pieces with a loud crash – red fire within.

[FRITZ. Oh – Oh. (*Runs out hastily*)

Music. The Demon discovered at door entrance in smoke, which evaporates – the red flame continues visible. The Demon advances forward, breaks through the balustrade or railing of gallery immediately facing the door of laboratory, jumps on the table beneath, and from thence leaps on the stage, stands in attitude before Frankenstein, who had started up in terror; they gaze for a moment at each other.

FRANK. The demon corpse to which I have given life!

Music. – The Demon looks at Frankenstein most intently, approaches him with gestures of conciliation. Frankenstein retreats, the Demon pursuing him.

[Its unearthly ugliness renders it too horrible for human eyes! [*The Demon approaches him.*]

Fiend! do not dare approach me – avaunt, or dread the fierce vengeance of my arm [wrecked on your miserable head –]

Music. – Frankenstein takes the sword from the nail, points with it at the Demon, who snatches the sword, snaps it in two and throws it on stage. The Demon then seizes Frankenstein – loud thunder heard – throws him violently on the floor, ascends the staircase, opens the large window, and disappears through the casement. Frankenstein remains motionless on the ground. – Thunder and lightning until the drop falls.

END OF ACT I

Kathleen Sullivan, 'This New Promethean Fire: Radioactive Monsters and Sustainable Nuclear Futures' (1999) PhD Thesis, University of Lancaster

This extract concerns one of the Frankenphemes: the ways in which nuclear radiation falls under the sign of *Frankenstein*.

Sublime aspects of the monster's monstrosity, or the monster's terrible and amazing 'otherness', affects *how he is seen*. This *act of seeing* further illustrates a human prejudice which persists wherein people translate the 'other' as the 'not normal'. It is the monster's abnormality that denies him access to the human community. Shelley revealed a prejudice in the early nineteenth century which still prevails. Sexism, racism, classism and homophobia result from a 'fear of others' and as such, these 'monsters' by birth or by choice are not accepted in those parts of the human community which are defined by fear and prejudice. But what about radioactive monsters? Part of the project of nuclear responsibility is developing the ability to look at 'monsters', to sustain 'the gaze'. But not all radioactive monsters are visible, undeniable representations like Frankenstein's creation. How is it possible to sustain a gaze upon the invisible? Making the invisible visible is the aim of this chapter, and to this end, I illustrate different visual representations of the monstrous nuclear.

Seeing the monstrous nuclear is paramount to the complexities and ambivalence implicit to the nuclear age, because *language alone cannot compensate for the enormous undertaking involved in nuclear responsibility*. As my research shows, the nuclear age problematizes concepts of modernity signified by its sociological/technological products, gender constructions in pre-modern and nuclear societies, the unique temporality of radioactive materials and the contradicting messages of nuclear stories. However, *seeing the nuclear* augments an understanding of nuclear processes and nuclear culture that exist in a written form. In previous chapters, my focus has remained with theoretical assumptions of the nuclear. In this chapter, I highlight that part of nuclear complexity that lies outside of written language, and that may be more readily accessed through a variety of visual representations.

Visual representations of the nuclear take on various and (at times) disparate forms in this chapter. I begin by revealing monstrous bodies as visual representations of the nuclear, because these 'monsters' are the result of radioactive contamination. Here, I draw parallels again to Shelley's monster. When invisible poisons interact with biological systems, subsequent disease, ill-health or mutagenic effects become potent 'signs' of nuclear contamination. By this trajectory, the invisible poison makes itself visible through its maligning effects. Drawing on the experience of Chernobyl, I point to the appearance of monstrous bodies in plant 'bodies' and in the bodies of children, born with gross genetic mutation due to excessive exposure to radiation. . . .

Embracing monstrosity: the angels of the nuclear age

Unlike the creature found in Hollywood archetypes of *Frankenstein*, the monster is not an inarticulate, stupefied hulk. He is an eloquent, sensitive and discerning creature [. . .]

The contradiction in Shelley's novel comes to life in the nuclear age. Radioactive monsters, as nuclear materials, *are spoken for* in contradictory ways, by opponents of the industry and representatives of the industry. The industry's view represents the 'sanctioned' voice of the nuclear through its sole assertion of 'expertise'. As such, the nuclear industry can itself be read as a 'persuasive participant in Western culture'. Here, the 'language' of radioactive monsters is akin to ventriloquism. A voice is 'thrown' from the industry. This voice symbolizes the persuasive, reasoned verbiage of the nuclear (industry), located in 'eloquent' discourses on 'safety' and 'sustainability'. However, the ventriloquist's voice represents a stark contrast to the monstrous bodies which result from nuclear contamination. The visual, embodied in the life forms or 'monsters', that contradict the verbal reasoning of the nuclear industry, points to something entirely different. The plants, animals and humans beings reproduced as deformed or maligned through radioactive poisoning are not the stuff of fiction. These products are not only defined by social and political phenomena, or by the contradiction between the verbal and visual, but are defined by *a physical embodiment*; that is, *they are complex, living beings*. [. . .] The monsters of the nuclear age, typified by Shelley's monster, have become a part of 'nature'. Due to radioactive contamination, the genetic code is being altered, new beings are taking form and reproducing which problematize definitions of the 'natural'. As Donna Haraway argues, in the late twentieth century 'the certainty of what counts as nature – a source of insight and a promise of innocence – is undermined, probably fatally'.[1]

1   Donna J. Haraway, *Simians, Cyborgs, and Women: the Reinvention of Nature* (London: Verso, 1991), 194.

Chernobyl Monsters

Edward Tenner [. . .] claims that 'one of industrial and post-industrial humanity's perennial nightmare is the machine that passes from stubbornness to rebellion'.[2] Using Shelley's novel which 'first connected Promethean technology with unintended havoc' (14) he argues that

> Frankenstein's fateful error was to consider everything but the sum of the parts he had assembled. . . . A machine can't appear to have a will of its own unless it is a system, not just a device. It needs parts that interact in unexpected and sometimes unstable ways. (15)

If, as Langdon Winner [. . .] argues, nuclear technology is autonomous, it can be asserted that this technology is not only creating and dispensing nuclear 'devices', but also 'nuclear systems'.

Recognizing visible aspects of nuclear systems is part of the project of seeing the invisible. The Chernobyl disaster is one such invisible/visible nuclear system that has been unleashed onto the world. The unintended consequences from that accident will continue to occur into a vast, indeterminable future. Chernobyl represented as the return of the modern Prometheus, who has stolen a new fire from the gods. But the gods are laughing because the fire that Promethean Chernobyl has stolen is a poisonous mutagen and carcinogen that lasts beyond any conventional notion of time.

My first encounter with radioactive monsters from Chernobyl occurred in 1989 when I met Ryuichi Hirokawa, a Japanese photographer, who had traveled to Colorado to take photographs of Rocky Flats. He was writing and photographing for a book about the most dangerous nuclear places on earth. At that time, I was working for the local nuclear freeze campaign, and he interviewed me about my concerns regarding plutonium and my nuclear neighbor, Rocky Flats. He had been to Chernobyl the previous year, and had taken photographs of genetic muta- tions that had been occurring in plants and animals, two years after the disaster. He showed me a photograph of a dandelion leaf which has had a lasting effect on me. In his photograph, the leaf appears to be ten times its normal size and not only green in colour, but also a burnt brown – a grotesque, monstrous body. [. . .]

The Chernobyl dandelions will spread their seeds in this way. But the genetic code of that seed has been forever altered. When the seeds from the dandelion that I saw in the photograph are taken up by the wind, and dispersed, what will grow there is not my childhood memory of yellow flowers and salad greens. What will grow there, and continue to reproduce itself year after year is the monstrous green and brown leaf. As a further aspect of the 'nuclear sublime', it is a leaf that dwarfs its former self. When I saw the Chernobyl dandelion, a memory of childhood innocence was destroyed for me. I no longer look at the yellow flower as a sign of

---

2   Edward Tenner, *Why Things Bite Back: Technology and the Revenge of Unintended Consequences* (New York: Knopf, 1996), 3.

spring, or as a miracle of 'nature's design' in seed distribution. From 1989 and onwards, when I see a dandelion, I think of Chernobyl.

Adaptations and Hybrids

Many and varied are the versions of *Frankenstein*, and uses of its themes and figurative language. I have included a selection of texts in this section, in media from print and film to internet sites and video games. Many of these are to be found in Donald Glut's extraordinary *The Frankenstein Catalog* (which also lists many other forms of media, including music), and sources such as the Internet Movie Database and Romantic Circles were also used. I have placed the films in chronological order in eight subsections, which seek roughly to divide up the films into categories. These reflect some of the themes that feature in Frankenstein films: the generation of life (for example in genetic engineering), sexuality, comedy. The categories also show the extent to which the content of the movies is in part conditioned by their form and status as commodities: the industrialisation that gives rise to endless Frankensteinian sequels featuring other monsters created in Hollywood, such as the Wolfman and the Mummy.

On the whole I have preferred to cite earlier rather than more recent works, although I have made note of the more unusual recent ones. And I have preferred to cite plays and novels over movies, simply because of the sheer weight of numbers in the latter section. Nevertheless, all the most notable movie adaptations have been mentioned. I have placed titles first, rather than authors' names.

Translations

Frankenstein. Trans. Jules Saladin. Paris: Coréard, 1821. This, in French, was the first edition to appear in another language.[1]

Frankenstein, or The Modern Prometheus. Trans. Masaki Yamamoto, illus. Ichiro Fukuzawa. New York: Harrison Smith and Robert Haas, 1934. The first edition in Japanese.

Frankenstein. Trans. Mazhar-ur-Haw 'Alvi. Lucknow: Nasim Book Dept, 1959. A translation into Hindi.

Frankenstein. Trans. M.R. Naryana Pilla. Kozhikode Brothers, 1959. A rare, perhaps unique, translation into Sanskrit.

---

1   For further information, please consult Donald F. Glut, *The Frankenstein Catalog* (Jefferson and London: McFarland and Company, 1984), 11–13.

Frankensteinian fictions

Heart of a Dog. Mikhail Bulgakov. (Written 1925.) Trans. Mirra Ginsburg. New York: Grove, 1968. Sharik the dog is turned into an oafish brute in charge of the purging of Moscow's cats, ironically by the transplantation of a petty human criminal's pituitary gland and testes. The novel employs the inset-narrative techniques used in *Frankenstein*, including a scientific journal.

Sirius: A Fantasy of Love and Discord. Olaf Stapledon. London: Secker & Warburg, 1944. A dog named Sirius is surgically retrofitted with vocal cords and a larger brain, and becomes tortured by his part-human condition.

'Human Monsters of the Future: Dr Frankenstein's Personal Diary'. Eugene Aiello. *Gruesome Creatures*, no. 1 (n.d. [1961?]), 9–12.

Do Androids Dream of Electric Sheep? Philip K. Dick. London: Orion, 2000 (first edition published 1968). See the discussion of *Blade Runner* (**pp. 46–7, 75**).

'Getting Along'. James Blish and Judith Lawrence. In *Again, Dangerous Visions*, ed. Harlan Ellison. Garden City: Doubleday, 1972, 614–18. The story features a reclusive professor called Turnkistan.

Frankenstein Unbound. Brian Aldiss. London: Jonathan Cape, 1973.

Forests of the Night. Andrew S. Swann. New York: Daw Books, 1993. This is a cyberpunk detective story that features the genetic manipulation of animals.

Frankenstein. Mary Shelley. Adapted by Malvina G. Vogel. New York: Baronet Books, 1993. An example of the very many illustrated versions of the novel for children.

Patchwork Girl. Hypertext by Shelley Jackson (available at www.eastgate.com), 1995. The female creature *is* completed, by Shelley herself, and the two become lovers; each of the creature's body parts has a biography.

The Memoirs of Elizabeth Frankenstein. Theodore Roszak. New York: Random House, 1995. A pro-ecofeminist novel with Frankenstein's bride as its heroine: she foresees the consequences of the doctor's experiments.

Lives of the Monster Dogs. Kirsten Bakis, 1997. Dogs turn on and kill their masters when they understand that a twisted German scientist plans to enslave them as military weapons by modifying them with voice boxes and prosthetic limbs. The dogs escape to New York where they are celebrated. Farcically, one of the dogs writes an opera about the canine revolution.

Frankensteinian erotica

The Adult Version of Frankenstein. Hal Kantor. Los Angeles: Calga Publishers, 1970.

Theatrical adaptations

Presumption, or, The Fate of Frankenstein (alternatively *Frankenstein; or, The Danger of Presumption, Presumption; or, The Fate of Episcopals* and *Franken- stein; a Romantic Drama*; manuscript title: *Frankenstein, a Melo-Dramatic*

Opera). Richard Brinsley Peake. English Opera House (Lyceum), London, from Monday 28 July to October 1823. Theatre Royal, Covent Garden, London, England, Friday 9 July 1824. English Opera House and Covent Garden, London, England, 1824. 'Revival of the play.'[2] Brasenose College, Oxford, 1824. ('Comedy version . . . with the Demon portrayed as a spring-operated mechanical man', 153.) New York City, USA, 1825. Grand Guignol, Paris, France, 1826. English Opera House, 1826. Second Witchcraft and Sorcery Convention at Baltimore Hotel, Los Angeles, USA, 20 October 1972. ('The creation scene only' – this was produced by Glut (153).)

Frankenstein. Coburg Theatre, London, England, 1823. 'Adapted from Mary Shelley's *Frankenstein.* Climaxes with the Monster perishing in a burning church.'[3]

Frankenstein. Royalty Theatre, London, England, 1823.

Frankenstitch. Surrey Theatre, London, England, 1823. A burlesque version; title character 'created his monster from the corpses of nine men using needle and thread'.[4] Frankenstitch the tailor is 'the "Needle Prometheus"'; the nine victims are journeymen; the Creature or 'Blue Demon' perishes in 'an explosion of household materials'.[5]

Frank-n-Steam. Adelphi Theatre, London, England, 1823. A burlesque version; 'a story of an ambitious student who steals a still-living though seemingly dead body'.[6] 'Burlesque of the play *Presumption* . . . Reviving a bailiff who had been buried in a state of catalepsy, a poor medical student believes he has given life to a corpse.'[7]

Frankenstein. Davis's Royal Amphitheatre, London, England, 1823. A burlesque version.

Frankenstein! or, The Demon of Switzerland. H.M. Milner. Royal Coburg Theatre, London, England, 18 August 1823.

Another Piece of Presumption. Richard Brinsley Peake. Adelphi Theatre, London, England, from 20 October 1823.

Frank-n-stein, or the Modern Promise to Play. Olympic Theatre, London, England, 13 December 1824. Burlesque version; 'may have been the logical precursor to Mel Brooks's *Young Frankenstein*'.[8]

Le Monstre et le magicien. Merle and Anthony. La Porte of St Martin, Paris, France, 1826. Gâité Theatre, Paris, France, 1826. West-London Theatre, London, England, 1826. Thomas Potter Cooke also acted in this version on eighty successive nights.

Frankenstein; or, the Man and the Monster! (alternatively *The Fate of Frankenstein, The Man and the Monster; or, The Fate of Frankenstein*). H.M. Milner. London: Thomas Hailes Lacy, 1826. London: J. Duncombe, 1826. (Includes illustration of O. Smith as the creature.) Repr. in *The Hour of One.* Ed. Stephen

2 Ibid., 153.
3 Ibid., 145.
4 Florescu, *In Search of Frankenstein*, 166.
5 Glut, *The Frankenstein Catalog*, 145.
6 Florescu, *In Search of Frankenstein*, 166.
7 Glut, *The Frankenstein Catalog*, 145.
8 Florescu, *In Search of Frankenstein*, 166.

Wischhusen. London: Gordon Fraser, 1975, 103–38. Royal Coburg Theatre, London, England, 3 July 1826.

The Devil Among the Players. Opera Glass, London, England, 9 October 1826. This 'featured a trio of monsters: Frankenstein, Faust, and the Vampire'.[9] It was the precedent for later film productions that conflate the stories of various monsters.

Presumption; or, The Fate of Episcopals. Richard Brinsley Peake. England, 1832. 'Performance requested by John Bull', the mythical figure of a stout English patriot.[10]

The Man in the Moon. England, 1847. This is *Hamlet* to which 'a new act has been added, wherein the Frankenstein Monster rises from Hell through a trapdoor and sings and drinks with the Ghost'.[11]

Frankenstein; or, the Vampire's Victim. The Brough Brothers. Adelphi Theatre, London, England, 26 December (Boxing Day) 1849. This burlesque was the last production to run in Mary's lifetime.[12] Florescu quotes the atrocious rhymes of the actor Otto von Rosenberg:

> You must excuse a trifling deviation
> From Mrs. Shelley's marvellous narration.
> You know a piece could never hope to go on
> Without Love – Rivals – tyrant pa's and so on.
> Therefore to let you know our altered plan
> I'm here to represent the 'nice young man'
> And in the hero's person you'll discover
> On this occasion the obnoxious lover.[13]

The Model Man. (Alternatively *Frankenstein*.) Richard Butler and H. Chane Newton. Gaiety Theatre, London, England, 24 December 1887 to 23 April 1888. A burlesque in which a woman, Miss Nellie Farren, 'the Gaiety's top star', played Dr Frankenstein; Fred Leslie played the creature.[14]

The Last Laugh. New York City, USA, 1915. 'A short-lived farce' based on *Frankenstein*.[15]

Frankenstein. Peggy Webling. Preston Theatre, London, England, 1927. Little Theatre, London, England, from 10 February 1930. USA tour, 1930. This stage adaptation written by Peggy Webling was the basis for James Whale's film (Universal, 1931). Henry Hallet played Dr Frankenstein; Hamilton Deane played the creature.

Goon with the Wind. Fairmont Public School, Manion, USA, 1940. A 'comic version'; James (Byron) Dean played the creature 'made up with a high forehead – soon to be seen on Karloff'.[16]

9 Ibid., 166.
10 Ibid., 153.
11 Ibid., 148.
12 Florescu, *In Search of Frankenstein*, 168.
13 Ibid., 168.
14 Ibid., 169.
15 Glut, *The Frankenstein Catalog*, 148.
16 Florescu, *In Search of Frankenstein*, 169.

Arsenic and Old Lace. Joseph Kesselring. Broadway, New York City, USA, 1944. A 'Broadway digression' featuring B. Karloff which 'was immensely popular, and ran . . . for some 1444 performances'.[17]

Frankenstein and His Bride. Strip City, Los Angeles, USA, late 1950s? A burlesque featuring these songs: 'Oh, What a Beautiful Mourning', 'Ghoul of My Dreams' and 'Rock 'n' Roll Dirge' with a five-member cast.[18]

Get the Picture. LeShow, Chicago, USA, mid 1960s? 'Satire mixing the theme of Mary Shelley's Frankenstein with local politics.'[19]

Frankenstein. Julian Beck and Judith Malina. *City Lights Journal.* Ed. Lawrence Ferlinghetti. San Francisco: City Lights Books, 1966, 51–70.

Frankenstein. 'Les quatre étapes de la genese du Frankenstein'. *Entretiens avec le living theatre.* Paris: Editions Pierre Belford, 1969, 272–91. Mandel Hall, Chicago, USA. Berlin, Germany, October 1965. Teatro La Perla, Venice (Biennale), Italy 26 September 1965. Bovard Auditorium (USC), Los Angeles, USA, 27 February 1969. Performed by *The Living Theatre* (Julian Beck and Judith Malina, his wife).[20]

My Fair Zombie. Carroll Borland. Staged for the Count Dracula Society, Los Angeles, USA, 31 October 1965. A '[s]poof of the show *My Fair Lady* with monsters', including Luna, Count Dracula, and Frankenstein's 'Monster'.[21]

Frankenstein. San Francisco Mime Troupe (part of the Radical Theatre Repertory). San Francisco, USA, 1967.

Frankenstein's Wife. Tom Eyen. Café La Mama, New York City, USA, 6 February 1969.

I'm Sorry, the Bridge is Out, You'll Have to Spend the Night. Coronet Theatre, Hollywood, USA, 28 April 1970. This is a musical by Sheldon Allman and Bob Pickett featuring 'the contemporary cast of horror's creatures: Dracula, the Mummy, Wolf Man, Igor, and, of course, [Frankenstein's] Monster'.[22] The plot is reminiscent of *The Rocky Horror Show* (1975).

H.R. Puffnstuff. United States Tour, 1972. A children's production: Witchiepoo the witch 'creates a Frankenstein Monster, brings it to life with her spells, lets it stalk into the audience, then dance on stage'.[23]

The World Festival of Magic & Occult. Black Magic, Inc. Madison Square Garden, New York City, USA, Spring 1973. Called itself 'The Weirdest Show on Earth'; apparently a mix of *Frankenstein* with a magic trick, featuring Al Carthy, 'the master builder of human robots'. The creature is assembled on stage, comes to life and attacks Carthy; finally Carthy emerges from behind the creature's 'mask'. Carthy staged this for other gatherings and for British TV in the 1970s.[24]

The Rocky Horror Show. Richard O'Brien. Royal Court Theatre Upstairs,

17 Ibid., 169.
18 Glut, *The Frankenstein Catalog*, 145.
19 Ibid., 146.
20 Florescu, *In Search of Frankenstein*, 169.
21 Glut, *The Frankenstein Catalog*, 138.
22 Florescu, *In Search of Frankenstein*, 171.
23 Glut, *The Frankenstein Catalog*, 147.
24 Ibid., 155.

London, England, 19 June 1973 (five weeks, with previews on 16 and 18 June). Kings Road Theatre, London, England, 3 November 1973. Roxy Theatre, Los Angeles, USA, from 21 March 1974. Belasco Theatre, New York, USA, from 9 March 1975. Glad Saxe Theater, Tokyo, Japan, from 13 August 1975. Pigelle Café Concert, Argentina, August 1975. Regent Palace, Fitzroy, Australia, from 24 October 1975. Wellington, New Zealand, 1975. Norway, 1975. (Songs translated.) Montgomery Playhouse, San Francisco, USA, from 3 February 1976. North American Tour, 1980–1: Queen Elizabeth Theatre, Toronto, Canada. Harvard Square Theatre, Boston, USA. The Granada Theatre, Chicago, USA. Aquarius Theatre, Hollywood, USA, etc.

Brad Majors and Janet Weiss, prudes who have pledged their love after attending their friends' wedding, are stranded in front of an old house. They are greeted by Frank-n-Furter, a transvestite from the planet Transexual in the galaxy Transylvania, and his odd associates. Frank-n-Furter shows them his creation Rocky Horror, a physically perfect male lover to replace the leather-clad rocker Eddie. Frank seduces both Brad and Janet; Janet offers herself to Rocky. Eddie, protesting his rejection by Frank, gets melted in a freezer. Wheelchair-bound Dr Everett Scott arrives to the save the young couple but is defeated by Frank. Brad and Janet are saved when the servants revolt and the hunchbacked alien Riff Raff kills Frank-n-furter for his transgressions.[25]

Frankenstein. Tim Kelly. New York: Samuel French, 1974. Sagebrush Theatre, Scottsdale, USA, 1975. Hollywood Actor's Theatre, Los Angeles, USA, 15 June– 14 July 1979. This is a reconfiguration of *Frankenstein* incidents with these notable changes: the story is told by Victor as he waits to be attacked by the creature on his wedding night (the creature is furious that Victor destroyed his mate).[26]

Frankenstein. Megan Terry. Scorpio Rising Theatre, Los Angeles, USA, from 26 July 1974, two acts. A futuristic and adaptation with political overtones: '[s]et in Amerika . . . a little bit in the future' in which a 'handsome' Frankenstein (the common misnomer) is a clone made from the highest quality biological materials 'of all time'; his destiny is to 'save the world from oppression', although he falls because he is 'corrupted by revolutionaries'; the 'maker' kills his Mate and is himself killed by Frankenstein's clone, who then plans to 'launch himself into the sun, reducing himself to primal matter to be reborn in the future'.[27]

The Crime of Dr Frankenstein, a Pop Myth and Monster Show. Theodore Roszak. Vancouver, from 9 April 1975. The production's literature identifies it as a 'multimedia rhapsody on Frankensteinian themes [tracing the] antecedents of Mary Shelley's myth'; Glut adds that it touched upon the Jewish legend of the Golem, the medieval myth of the homunculus and eighteenth-century automata, Paracelsus, Rousseau, Gershom Scholem, Thomas Hobbes, Julien LaMettrie, William Harvey and the soundtrack from *Frankenstein* (Universal, 1931).[28]

---

25 Ibid., 150.
26 Ibid., 147–8.
27 Ibid., 154.
28 Ibid., 153.

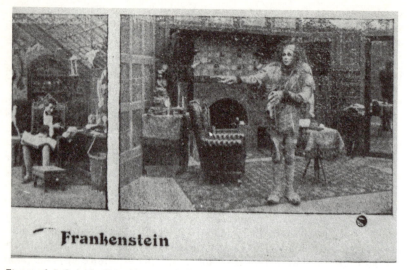

Figure 4 J. Searle Dawley, prod. Thomas Edison, *Frankenstein* (1910). Charles Ogle playing the creature, standing in the living room.

Source: Universal, Courtesy of the Kobal Collection, London

Film adaptations

Early films: genesis of a genre

Frankenstein. USA, dir. J. Searle Dawley. Prod. Thomas Edison, 1910, 1 tinted reel, silent (see Figure 4). This is a film-school classic. Its portrayal of Victor is Faustian. 'Leaving his sweetheart and his father, Frankenstein goes away to college where he becomes obsessed with creating a perfect human being. The Monster comes to life in a cauldron of blazing chemicals. On his wedding day, Frankenstein sees the Monster reflected in a mirror. Later, with Frankenstein's love for his bride at full strength, the Monster returns for acceptance by his maker. Standing before the mirror, the Monster vanishes, leaving behind only his reflection. Frankenstein enters the room and stands before the mirror, seeing the Monster's image vanish, having been conquered by love and his creator's better nature'. Long thought to be lost, this 'first filmed version of the story is extant, scenes having been incorporated into a late 1970s documentary on motion pictures shown on European television'.[29]

Life Without Soul. USA, dir. Joseph W. Smiley. Ocean Film Corporation, 1915, 5 reels, silent. 'The film was later reissued by the Raver Film Corporation including new scientific documentary footage (conjugations of cells, the workings of the circulatory system, the reproduction of fishes, etc.).'[30] The title curiously echoes

---

29 Ibid., 172–3. See Philip J. Riley, ed., *Frankenstein* (Absecon, NJ: MagicImage Filmbooks, 1989), 17–21.
30 Ibid., 187.

one of Defoe's pamphlets of 1726, 'Mere Nature Delineated: Or, a Body without a Soul', a discussion of Peter the Wild Boy, a young man allegedly brought up by wolves in the forests near Hanover, who had become something of a media celebrity of the day, and who was an object of fascination for radical language theorists such as **Lord Monboddo**, and thus eventually worked into *Frankenstein*.

Il Mostro di Frankenstein. Italy, dir. Eugenio Testa, Albertini Film. UCI, 1920, black and white, silent. ' Includes a confrontation in a dark cave between Frankenstein and the Monster. This is the same film as *Le Monstre*, which was advertised in *Revue Belge du Cinema* (August 5, 1921 issue). *Le Monstre*, released in France and Belgium by Etablissements Georges Petit, is described as "Vision Mystérieuse en 4 parties, d'après le célèbre roman de Miss SHELLY [*sic*]". The Monster is depicted in the advertisement as attacking the laboratory with an axe while a man, presumably Frankenstein, sneaks down the stairs'.[31]

Frankenstein. (Spain: *El Dr Frankenstein, autor del monstruo* ('Dr Frankenstein, perpetrator of the monster').) USA, dir. James Whale. Universal, 1931. The credits of this film claim that a play by Peggy Webling, adapted by John Balderston, was its inspiration. Webling's play was based on the earliest theatrical adaptations of Shelley's novel by Peake and Milner. Whale's *Frankenstein* with Boris Karloff's performance has proved itself a strong influence on the contemporary reception of the story, having established lasting popular images. See Figure 5. In the credits, 'The Monster' is played by '?', similar to the first theatrical adaptation, *Presumption*. The creature has been dumbed down since his appearance in Shelley's novel.

Florescu notes a 'revised screenplay credited to Garrett Ford and Francis Edwards Faragoh'; that the Doctor part is called 'Henry Frankenstein'; that the Fritz part procures a defective brain for the creature; and that this film is shot like a 'photographed stage play (as was even more true in the screen version of Dracula)'.[32] It 'end[s] on a happy note with Henry's father toasting the recovery of his son after having been thrown from the fiery windmill'.[33]

Glut explains that 'Henry Frankenstein and his hunchbacked assistant Fritz rob a corpse from a graveyard, after which they steal another corpse from a gallows. When the latter corpse's brain proves useless, Henry sends Fritz to the local medical school to steal a good brain. Frightened by a gong, Fritz inadvertently drops the good brain and absconds with the inferior brain of a criminal. Concern for Henry's welfare brings his fiancée Elizabeth, friend Victor Moritz and Dr Waldman, from whose laboratory the brain was stolen, to Frankenstein's watchtower, where he has assembled a giant being. The group watch as Henry uses his electrical equipment to bring the creature to life during a lightning storm. Days later Waldman and Henry observe the Monster's fascination with light. When the sadistic Fritz attacks the Monster with a torch, the creature becomes violent and is subdued by a hypodermic injection. Later the Monster kills Fritz to end his

31 Ibid., 188.
32 Florescu, *In Search of Frankenstein*, 192.
33 Ibid., 194.

Figure 5 James Whale, *Frankenstein* (1931). Boris Karloff as the creature. The creature has suffered a haemorrhage of intelligence since his first appearance, thus stunting social and political readings of the novel in favour of caveats against technology and the imitation of God. Has the creature been reduced to an object?

Source: Universal, Courtesy of the Kobal Collection, London

torments, after which Henry realizes that his creation must be destroyed. Returning to Elizabeth and his estate, Henry entrusts the Monster to Waldman for dissection. The Monster slays Waldman and escapes to the woods where he encounters a young girl Maria. Through his own innocence the Monster accidentally kills Maria . . . the villagers . . . pursue the Monster with torches on the day of Henry's intended wedding to Elizabeth. In the hills Henry is subdued by his creation, who drags him into a windmill which is set ablaze by the townspeople. After hurling his creator down from the windmill, the Monster apparently dies in flames. . . . During the early 1930s, some prints of Frankenstein were issued in green tint.'[34]

Revisions and multiple-monster films

Bride of Frankenstein. (Production title: *The Return of Frankenstein*; initial title: *Frankenstein Lives Again!*; France: *La fiancée de Frankenstein*). USA, dir.

---

34 Glut, *The Frankenstein Catalog*, 200–1.

James Whale. Universal, 1935. The historical opening of this film features a representation of Mary Shelley with her circle (Percy and Byron) discussing her novel; the actress who plays Mary (Elsa Lanchester) also plays the bride of the creature; a classic Universal horror that delights in parody and satire. Most commentators agree that this one is not a 'horror film' and tends towards comedy and even criticism of 'sacred institutions' and a possible gay subtext. The bride herself is an extraordinary combination of the hair of Queen Nefertiti and the appearance of the woman robot in *Metropolis*. Dr Praetorious works with Frankenstein on the bride and can grow miniature humans like seedlings. Florescu attributes the screenplay to William Hurlbut and John L. Balderston.[35] The film features progressive music compositions by Franz Waxman and 'huge panning and traveling shots'.[36] See Figures 6–8.

Son of Frankenstein. (Spain: *La sombra de Frankenstein* ('The shadow of Frankenstein').) USA, dir. Rowland V. Lee. Universal, 1939.

Third Dimensional Murder. (Advertisement title: *Murder in 3-D*.) USA, dir. George Sidney. Metro-Goldwyn-Mayer (A Pete Smith Metroscopix Special), 1941 (filmed in 1940), red and green anaglyph technique, 7 minutes. 'At midnight, a man goes to the old Smith Mansion looking for his Aunt Tillie. He finds the house haunted by the Frankenstein Monster (here called "Frankenstein"), a witch, skeleton, zombie, masked archer, walking suit of armor and other apparitions, all of whom try to kill him. "Frankenstein" traps him outside, emptying a cauldron of molten metal from the roof, then throwing down the kettle.'[37]

Frankenstein's Cat. Dir. Mannie Davis, 1942. Short animated film in English.

Frankenstein Meets the Wolf Man. USA, dir. Roy William Neill. Universal, 1943. Features the older Bela Lugosi (depicted in Tim Burton's *Ed Wood*) and Lon Chaney Jr; less about Frankenstein than a sequel for a previous Wolf Man movie.

House of Frankenstein. (Filming title: *The Devil's Brood*; initial title: *Chamber of Horror*; Spain: *La zingara y los monstruos*.) USA, dir. Erle C. Kenton. Universal, 1944. This film includes the Wolfman, Dracula and a cameo by Frankenstein's creature.[38]

Torticola contre Frankensberg ('Twisted Neck vs. Frankensberg'). France, dir. Paul Paviot. Les Films Marceau, 1952.–'Lorelei, forced by poverty to live at Todenvald, castle of Dr Franken[s]berg, her uncle and guardian, meets a talking cat, a man with a cat's brain, and a monster called Torticola whom the doctor has made from corpses.'[39]

Frankenstein's Daughter. (France: *La fille de Frankenstein*; Italy: *La figlia di Frankenstein*.) Dir. Richard E. Cunha. Astor, 1958. 'Oliver Frank, actually Frankenstein, uses a drug to transform young Trudy Morton into a female monster.

---

35 Florescu, *In Search of Frankenstein*, 193.
36 Ibid., 193.
37 Glut, *The Frankenstein Catalog*, 194.
38 Ibid., 207–8.
39 Ibid., 194–5.

Figure 6 James Whale, *Bride of Frankenstein* (1935). Elsa Lanchester
playing Mary Shelley.

Source: Universal, Courtesy of the Kobal Collection, London

Then, in a wine cellar-turned laboratory, he hopes to emulate his father and
grandfather and create a living woman, which he believes will obey his com-
mands. Using the head of a woman he killed when she refused his romantic
advances, Oliver brings to life his female creation, which later escapes into the
streets and kills a garage mechanic. Returning to the laboratory for more
electrical power, the Monster is ordered by Oliver to kill Trudy and her boyfriend Johnny. The boy throws acid at the Monster, hitting Oliver's face instead.

Figure 7 **James Whale, *Bride of Frankenstein* (1935), O.P. Heggie (De Lacey) and Karloff.** The pathos in the movie comes from the way in which the creature, reduced to a grunting but fast-learning sort, interacts with the old De Lacey: their sharing a cigar is a notable addition to Shelley's story.

Source: Universal, Courtesy of the Kobal Collection, London

Watching her screaming creator fall, the monster brushes against a Bunsen burner and is fatally set ablaze.'[40]

Orlak, el infierno de Frankenstein ('Orlak, the hell of Frankenstein'). Mexico, dir. Rafael Baledón. Filmadora Independiente (Columbia), 1960, black and white. 'Dr Frankenstein creates Orlak, a monster with a robot head. He gives it a fleshlike face which melts when getting too near a fire.'[41]

Frankenstein, el Vampiro y Cia ('Frankenstein, the Vampire and Company'). (Alternatively *Frankenstein, el Vampiro y Compañía*). Mexico, dir. Benito Alazraki. Calderón (Azteca), 1963 (shot in 1961), black and white, Spanish. Based on the film *Abbott and Costello Meet Frankenstein*.[42]

Furankenshutain tai chitei kaijû Baragon. (Initial title: *Frankenstein vs. the Giant Devil Fish*; USA: *Frankenstein Conquers the World* (1966); Italy: *Frankenstein alla conquista della Terra*; Germany: *Frankenstein: Der Schrecken mit*

---

40 Ibid., 176–7.
41 Ibid., 189.
42 Ibid., 177.

Figure 8 James Whale, *Bride of Frankenstein* (1935). **Lanchester as the bride.** By using Lanchester for the roles of both Mary Shelley and the bride, the implied inclusion of the author as the female creature whose creation concludes the story is a pleasant Romantic conceit.

Source: Universal, Courtesy of the Kobal Collection, London

dem Affengesicht ('Frankenstein: The Terror with the Monkey Face', 177, 180).) Japan, dir. Ishirô Honda. Toho International (American International Pictures), 1964 (US release in 1966), colour. 'Toward the end of World War II, the undying heart of Frankenstein's Monster, capable of regenerating itself, is forcibly removed from a laboratory in Germany and taken to Japan, to be lost in the Hiroshima atomic holocaust. Twenty years later a youth resembling the Monster is found in Hiroshima. Examined by Dr James Bowen, the boy begins to grow in size and ugliness, proving to be either the regenerated heart of the Monster or a mutated boy who had eaten the heart. Now giant size, "Frankenstein," leaving behind a living severed hand, flees into the hills where he terrifies people and devours live-stock. During an earthquake Baragon (as he is called in the Japanese version), a prehistoric reptile, appears and causes destruction for which Frankenstein is blamed, though Bowen believes him to be innocent and a gentle creature. Frankenstein saves the doctor and his party. Standing over the vanquished saurian, Frankenstein is swallowed by another earthquake.'[43]

---

43 Ibid., 179–80.

The Hammer films

Note: These films warrant their own subsection, as they represent the results of one company's industrial production of the narrative: the English Hammer House of Horror.

The Curse of Frankenstein. (France: *Frankensteins' est échappé* ('Frankenstein has escaped'); Italy: *La machera di Frankenstein* ('The mask of Frankenstein'). England, dir. Terence Fisher. Hammer Films (Warner Bros.), 1957, colour. Christopher Lee joins Peter Cushing. The film, in which both creature and creator are ruthless, got the equivalent of an X-rating at that time for its gore; the film also touches upon sexuality. See Glut, *The Frankenstein Catalog*, 211–12.

The Revenge of Frankenstein. (Germany: *Ich bin Frankenstein*.) England, dir. Terence Fisher. Hammer Films (Columbia), 1958, colour. Sequel to *The Curse of Frankenstein*; considered one of the best from this studio and of the entire genre.

Frankenstein Created Woman. (Title publicised in 1958: *And Frankenstein Created Woman*. (Italy: *La meledizione dei Frankenstein* ('The curse of Frankenstein').) England, dir. Terence Fisher. Hammer Films (20th Century–Fox/Seven Arts), 1967, colour. The fourth Frankenstein film from Hammer deals with the issue of souls and the effects of past psychological trauma on future action. Victor uses a dead woman's body and the captured soul of an executed young man whose memories compel the female creature, Christina, to murder those who falsely accused the young man, her lover. See Glut, *The Frankenstein Catalog*, 216–17.

Frankenstein Must Be Destroyed! (Italy: *Distruggete Frankenstein* ('Destroy Frankenstein').) England, dir. Terence Fisher. Hammer Films (Warner Bros./Seven Arts), 1969, colour. The focus is more on Victor than on the creature in this film, considered to be some of Fisher's and Cushing's best work.

Comedy

The Inventors. USA, William Watson and Sig Herzig. Educational Pictures, 1934, 20 minutes. 'Based on the *Stoopnagle and Budd* radio program. At a girls' school, Stoopnagle and Budd [decide] to build a "Stoopenstein" ("a second cousin to a Frankenstein"), sending the students out for such materials as an automobile motor and a set of false teeth.'[44]

One in a Million. USA, dir. Sidney Lanfield. 20th Century–Fox, 1936. 'Al Ritz impersonates the Frankenstein Monster in an ice skating number and joins his brothers in a song about movie villains Boris Karloff, Charles Laughton and Peter Lorre.'[45]

Sing, Baby, Sing. USA, dir. Sidney Lanfield. 20th Century–Fox, 1936. 'The Ritz Brothers perform a Frankenstein Monster comedy skit.'[46]

Hellzapoppin. (Spain: *Loquilandia*). USA, dir. H.C. Potter, Universal, 1941. 'Based on the Olsen and Johnson stage show (which did not feature the

---

44 Ibid., 186.
45 Ibid., 189.
46 Ibid., 193.

Frankenstein Monster). After being thrown into the orchestra pit, Martha Raye is helped up by the Frankenstein Monster (or an actor made-up as the Monster) and tossed back onto the stage.'[47]

Arsenic and Old Lace. USA, dir. Frank Capra. Warner Bros., 1944. Based upon the Broadway play with the same name, containing a role created for Boris Karloff (later played by Bela Lugosi and Charles Laughton).[48]

Abbott and Costello Meet Frankenstein. USA, dir. Charles Barton. Universal–International, 1948 (filmed in 1947).[49]

Haram Alek ('Shame on You'). Egypt, dir. Issa Karama. Studio Guizan, 1953. 'Comedy featuring the Frankenstein Monster, a mummy and a werewolf.'[50]

El castillo de los monstruos. Mexico, dir. Julian Soler. Producciones Sotomayor, 1957. 'Comedy in which a castle handyman encounters various horrors created by a mad scientist, including a Frankenstein Monster called "Frentenstein" ("Forehead-stein"), a vampire, lagoon creature, mummy and gorilla.'[51]

I Was a Teenage Frankenstein. (Belgium: *Des filles pour Frankenstein* ('The godson of Frankenstein'); England: *Teenage Frankenstein*; France: *La légende du nouveau Frankenstein* ('The legend of the new Frankenstein'); Italy: *La strange di Frankenstein* ('The massacre of Frankenstein').) USA, dir. Herbert L. Strock. American International Pictures, 1957, colour (ending). A British Doctor, descended from Frankenstein, comes to America as a University lecturer, and lives in a house with crackling labs and an alligator-pit for the disposal of organs; he believes that dead youths are the best components for his creature and he finds a recently deceased boy; his mistress discovers the creature and is killed by it, as well as others on campus; a respected B-movie.

Carry on Screaming. England, dir. Gerald Thomas. Anglo-Amalgamated (Audio Film Center), 1966, colour. In this, one of the celebrated 'Carry On' films, the creature is 'actually a prehistoric hominid' whose fingers can regenerate as a form of procreation. The creature is represented 'like Universal's Monster' as animated by electric energy given by 'electrodes hooked to the neck'. The Frankenstein part is called Dr Watts, who 'admits' that he was schooled with Frankenstein and Dr Jekyll. The plot centres around the creature 'captur[ing] a young woman' and losing one of his lively fingers, which makes offspring, until a Jekyllian concoction is used to kill the lot of them.[52]

Munster, Go Home! (France: *La famille Frankenstein, Frankenstein et les faux monayeurs* ('Frankenstein and the false money'); Italy: *La dolce vita non piace ai mostri* ('The sweet life not pleasant to a monster'); Spain: *La herencia de los Munsters* ('The inheritance of the Munsters').) USA, dir. Earl Bellamy. Universal, 1966, colour.[53] See the entry on *The Addams Family* ('Television adaptations', **p. 78**).

---

47 Ibid., 203.
48 Ibid., 159.
49 Ibid., 209–10.
50 Ibid., 181.
51 Ibid., 163.
52 Ibid., 162.
53 Ibid., 210–11.

Young Frankenstein. (Germany: *Springtime for Frankenstein*; Italy: *Franken-stein Junior*.) USA, dir. Mel Brooks. 20th Century–Fox, 1974. 'Inspired by Mary Shelley's *Frankenstein* and the Universal *Frankenstein* film series.'[54] Brooks plays with the motifs of repetition and spontaneous motion that characterise Shelley's novel. The Frankensteinian opposition between voluntary and involuntary reactions is transferred onto the Freudian one between the conscious and the unconscious, such that young Froedrick (who insists that his name is pronounced 'Fronkensteen') stabs himself in the act of insisting, with a gesture involving a knife, that he only wishes to preserve life. The very difference that he insists upon between himself and his ancestor is ironically transformed into its opposite, kinship – thus revealing the truth of the original Victor's overbearing will. Brooks's use of Gothic allows him to fuse horror and comedy, both marked by their fixation upon the involuntary spasms of terror or laughter.

Films exploring sexuality

Note: Obviously, sexuality (like technology and class) permeates many if not all adaptations of *Frankenstein*. The following films are simply those that make a generic or thematic virtue of it.

Kiss Me Quick. (Alternatively *Dr Breedlove*, *Dr Breedlove's Lab*.) USA, dir. Russ Meyer. Fantasy Films, 1963, colour. 'The alien Sterilox comes to Earth because his own world has no women. He meets Dr Breedlove, who not only creates living women, but has also made his own Frankenstein Monster (called "Frankie Stein"), Dracula and living mummy [*sic*]. Sterilox falls in love with a vending machine, then returns home with one of the women.'[55]

Angelic Frankenstein. USA, dir. Bob Mizer. Athletic Models Guild, 1964, 6.5 minutes. Gay film. 'Frankenstein creates a perfect male from a small doll he has fashioned. When Frankenstein tries teaching him how to use a gun, the creature rebels, attacking his maker and then leaving.'[56]

Fanny Hill Meets Dr Erotico. USA, dir. Barry Mahon. Chancellor Films, 1968, colour. 'Sequel to *Fanny Hill Meets Lady Chatterley*. Hoping to find Lady Chatterley, Fanny Hill meets Dr Erotico at the castle where he has created a Frankensteinian monster. Working as his chairwoman, Fanny accidentally throws the life-giving switch. The monster falls in love with Fanny and sees the doctor's lesbian maid trying to make love to her. Thinking Fanny is being harmed, the monster kills the maid. The monster dies in a shack set ablaze by the villagers. Sequel: *Fanny Hill Meets the Red Baron*.'[57]

Hollow-My-Weenie, Dr Frankenstein. (Alternatively *Frankenstein De Sade*.) USA. Anon, 1969, colour, short film. 'Gay sex film in which Dr Frankenstein and his hunchbacked assistant create a monster in a basement laboratory.'[58]

54 Ibid., 196–7.
55 Ibid., 187.
56 Ibid., 227.
57 Ibid., 168.
58 Ibid., 181.

Flesh for Frankenstein. (Initial titles: *The Devil and Dr Frankenstein, Up Frankenstein,* Warhol's Frankenstein.) (Alternatively known as *Andy Warhol's Frankenstein, The Frankenstein Experiment.* Italy: *Il mostro è in tavola, Barone Frankenstein* ('The monster and the table, Baron Frankenstein'); France: *De la chair pour Frankenstein* ('Some flesh for Frankenstein').) USA/Italy, dir. Antonio Margheriti/Paul Morrissey.[59] Carol Ponti-Braunsberg-Rassam (Bryanston Pictures), 1974, 3D colour. The movie was presented by Andy Warhol, and features well-done 3D production. 'Baron Frankenstein, who believes sex is dirty and gets thrills from disemboweling female corpses,' contrives to engender 'two "zombies", one male and the other female, and mating them to produce a super-race. Needing the head of a lustful male for one zombie, he waits with Otto outside a brothel, then inadvertently beheads a farm boy planning to be a monk, with no interest in women. After bringing his two zombies to the dinner table as "guests", he sends the male to learn sex from his sister/wife whom the creature kills. Sex-starved Otto, imitating his master, disembowels the female zombie. The male returns to the Baron's laboratory with his dead wife, then cuts off his maker's hand and impales him through the back. Finally the male zombie disembowels himself. Frankenstein's two children then enter the laboratory to begin work on their own creation.'[60]

The Rocky Horror Picture Show. (Alternatively known as *Rock Horroar, They Came from Denton High.*) USA, dir. Jim Sharman (screenplay by Jim Sharman and Richard O' Brien). 20th Century–Fox, 1975, colour. This unforgettably bold musical comedy casts the Frankenstein part and his creature as bisexuals in a sci-fi pop-cult. See the entry for *The Rocky Horror Show* (**pp. 162–3**) for a summary. Glut notes 'major changes from the show: An opening wedding scene and a dining room scene are added. The usherette singing "Science Fiction" has been deleted. Some songs have been changed. Eddie is now an earlier creation of Frank. In the end the Transylvanians come to Earth to punish Frank.'[61]

Cybernetics, doppelgängers, genetic engineering and replicants

Fearless Frank. (Production title: *Frank's Greatest Adventure*). USA, dir. Philip Kaufman. American International Pictures, 1969 (filmed in 1967), colour. Jon Voigt plays 'Frank/False' in this film whose story appears similar to the later Verhoeven film *Robocop.* Frank is 'shot to death while trying to save the beautiful Plethora from the Boss's gangsters'; Frank is 'rebuilt and given a radio-controlled mind by the Good Doctor, who sends him out to fight crime. Frank becomes a bullet-proof superhero with superhuman strength and the ability to fly, lashing out against the Boss's gang. Claude, the Good Doctor's evil brother, creates a Frankenstein Monster type double of Frank with unsightly stitches and the name False Frank. The two Franks fight with the original using unfair tactics. After the

59 Ibid., 172.
60 Ibid., 169, 172.
61 Ibid., 190.

Good Doctor dies, Frank, affected by society, becomes evil and egotistical, while False Frank gradually becomes more like the original. Finally no longer able to fly, Frank drops to the pavement and disintegrates, leaving his double to capture the criminals, save Plethora and take his place.'[62]

Blade Runner. USA, dir. Ridley Scott. Ladd Company, 1982. The basic concepts of *Frankenstein* placed in the year 2019, in this classic cyberpunk film, are filtered through noir detective narrative, cyborgs and genetic engineering in the late techno-capitalism of Los Angeles. The movie featured an innovative soundtrack by Vangelis, eventually released in its proper form (Warner Music, 1994).[63] See the introduction to this chapter, the frontispiece to the book and Figure 9.

Slapstick. USA, dir. Steven Paul. Steven Paul Productions, 1982, colour. Glut lists Kurt Vonnegut as screenwriter, and acting by Jerry Lewis, Madeleine Kahn, John Abbott (in Dr Frankenstein role). 'Based on the novel *Slapstick* by Kurt Vonnegut, Jr. Dr Frankenstein delivers two monstrous babies. The children seem to be morons but, when in the company of each other, are actually geniuses. The children are entrusted to Dr Frankenstein's care.'[64]

Figure 9 **Ridley Scott, *Blade Runner* (1982). Harrison Ford and Rutger Hauer in the rooftop scene.** One could read this scene as a moment of homosexual panic similar to the pursuit of the creature by Frankenstein.

Source: Universal, Courtesy of the Kobal Collection, London

62 Ibid., 168–9.
63 For further discussion, please see Jay Clayton, 'Concealed Circuits: Frankenstein's Monster, the Medusa, and the Cyborg', *Raritan* 15 (1996): 53–69.
64 Glut, *The Frankenstein Catalog*, 193.

The Terminator. USA, dir. James Cameron. Pacific Western, 1984. The *Terminator* story is similar to *Frankenstein* not only as a story about technology and biology, but also as a meditation upon whether one 'comes from' others or from oneself (chthonic or autochthonous origin, as discussed by the anthropologist Lévi-Strauss; see **p. 46**). How can one be one's own parent? This is the plot of *Terminator*, enabled by the fiction of the time loop. The *Frankenstein* story is rewritten as human versus machine, as in the more recent film *The Matrix*.

Re-Animator. USA, dir. Stuart Gordon. Empire Pictures, 1985. A witty version of the *Frankenstein* story in which rebellious, squirming limbs, notably the disembodied head of a psychiatrist, wreak havoc upon the student inventor of a revivifying liquid.

Politics, race and class

Flick. (UK: *Frankenstein on Campus*; USA: *Dr Frankenstein on Campus*.) Canada, dir. Gilbert Taylor. Astral Films, 1970, colour. An R-rated B-movie set in contemporary Canada. A young Victor is expelled twice for acting strange while developing a mind-control serum. He is set up by campus radicals who take an incriminating picture of him holding a joint, and ultimately he injects a martial arts expert with his creation, setting him on a murderous rampage.[65]

Blackenstein. USA, dir. William Al Levey. Eddie C. Stewart and Exclusive International Pix, 1973, colour. In this blaxploitation version, Victor is 'Nobel prize winner Dr Stein', solicited by Winnifred Walker with regards to her fiancé Eddie Walker, a Vietnam veteran who lost his limbs. Stein treats Eddie in his castle and succeeds in prompting the growth of new limbs. Trouble arises when Stein's assistant Malcolm (in love with Winnifred) switches Eddie's DNA therapy with RNA, which animalises him into Blackenstein, a murderous creature who disembowels people on romps outside the castle; the police pursue him back to the castle and he kills Malcolm (who tries to rape Winnifred) along with other DNA patients Eleanor and Bruno Stragour. Glut notes that a 1976 sequel called *Black Frankenstein Meets the White Werewolf* did not get made.[66]

Biographical and historical films

Gothic. UK, dir. Ken Russell. Virgin Vision, 1986. This film is about the night of the ghost-story contest (see **pp. 2, 13, 27** in this sourcebook). Opium is consumed by all in its liquid tincture form as laudanum, and the sexual fantasies and nightmares of Byron, Mary and Percy Shelley and Polidori are explored; without terribly much good taste or surprise, Mary Shelley's is represented as being concerned with miscarriage.

Mary Shelley's 'Frankenstein'. USA, dir. Kenneth Branagh. American Zoetrope/

---

65 Ibid., 172.
66 Ibid., 159, 162.

Tristar, 1994. Robert De Niro (the creature), Kenneth Branagh, Helena Bonham Carter. Billed as an attempt to be more faithful than other films to the original novel, the plot does nevertheless diverge in places. De Niro's pathos as the creature, however, is strong. See Eberle-Sinatra.

Gods and Monsters. USA, dir. Bill Condon. BBC et al., 1998. Ian McKellen plays James Whale at the end of his life. The film makes a strong connection between his representation of Frankenstein (1931) and his experience of the First World War.

Other films

Lisztomania. UK, dir. Ken Russell. Goodtimes Enterprises Production (Columbia–Warner), 1975, colour. '[A] combination Frankenstein Monster/Hitler/Wagner rises from a grave to shoot Jews with a machinegun-guitar, showing how Hitler uses Strauss' music as a "monster." Then Liszt comes out of the sky in a love-powered spaceship and kills the creature.'[67] (Incidentally, the music director on this project was my father, Garth Morton.) 'A junior version of the Frankenstein Monster appears at a wedding ceremony'; see also the Ken Russell film of the Who's *Tommy* (1975).[68]

Frankenstein's Island. USA, dir. Jerry Warren. Chriswar Pictures, 1982 (Internet Movie Database has it in 1981) (initiated in 1980), colour. An endearingly laughable movie that features a dog caught urinating on seaweed during the credits. 'Balloonists are stranded on an island where mad scientists perform weird experiments.'[69]

The True Adventures of Bernadette Soubirou. USA, dir. David McNeill. Timber Films (McMillan Films), 1982, colour. 'Among her adventures, Bernadette is captured by Dr Frankenstein, who wants to transfer her youth into Adolph Hitler's ailing body. Simon Wiesnethal interrupts the experiment and kidnaps Hitler. Superman, Dr Frankenstein's boyfriend, enters the laboratory, but it is Tarzan who saves Bernadette. (Other characters include Dracula, Quasimodo, Eva Peron, Charles de Gaulle, Omar Sharif and St Nicholas.)'[70]

Videodrome. USA, dir. David Cronenberg. Guardian Trust Company, 1982. A disturbing science-fiction horror movie about the power of the media in capitalist corporate society. A pornographic television programme contains a signal which creates a brain tumour that alters the viewer's perception of reality. The theme of 'uncontrollable flesh' is in line with other contemporary horror movies in which the autonomy and determinacy of flesh is a theme. Determinacy in this respect is clearly also a theme in *Frankenstein*. The movie also literalises a metaphor about figurative language and authorship, as does Mary Shelley's novel.

Frankenweenie. USA, dir. Tim Burton. Walt Disney Pictures, 1984.

Frankenstein's Great Aunt Tillie. USA, dir. Myron J. Gold, 1984. Tagline:

---

67 Ibid., 188.
68 Ibid., 194.
69 Ibid., 177.
70 Ibid., 195.

'You've seen Frankenstein . . . wait until you meet his Great Aunt Tillie . . . more fun than a barrel of monkeys.' Donald Pleasence plays both Victor and 'Old Baron Frankenstein' and Zsa Zsa Gabor plays 'Clara'.

Robocop. USA, dir. Paul Verhoeven, Orion, 1987. A critique of automated society and capitalist corporate culture. A shattered police officer is cybernetically rebuilt and is compelled to re-encounter his human past, while outsmarting a fully automated (and ruthlessly Kantian) police-officer machine.

Tetsuo: The Ironman. Japan, dir. Shinya Tsukamoto. Kaijyu Theater, 1988. The protagonist finds himself growing nails and other sharp metal objects from his body. He and his friend/lover mutate into a hybrid metal phallus on the rampage. Hardcore cyberpunk. See also Tsukamoto's *Tetsuo II: Body Hammer* (1992).

Rock 'n' Roll Frankenstein. USA, Brian O'Hara II. R & R Productions, 1999. A record producer who makes a creature to be a rock-and-roll star using Elvis's head, Jimi Hendrix's hands and Liberace's penis, resulting in a sexually confused creature. The film was advertised in part by paying the homeless to put the poster on their shopping carts.

Television adaptations

The Addams Family. USA, dir. Stanley C. Cherry and Arthur Hiller, 1964–6. Written by Charles Addams. Lurch (played by Ted Cassidy) is a butler whose physique resembles the Whale Frankenstein's creatures, while his alter ego (played by the same actor) is surely the ultimate in working-class alienation, the disembodied hand, Thing. There was also a 1973–5 TV series, and a cartoon series in 1992–5 (Jim Cummings played Lurch). The concept also spawned the movies *The Addams Family* (1991), *Addams Family Values* (1993) and *Addams Family Reunion* (1998).

Frankenstein Jr and the Impossibles. USA, dir. Joseph Barbera, William Hanna, 1966–8, animated; Creature Jr (erroneously named 'Frankenstein Jr') is teamed up with Coil Man, Fluid Man, etc.

Frankenstein: The True Story. USA, dir. Jack Smight. Universal TV and NBC, 1972. Features writing by Christopher Isherwood, and acting by James Mason, Jane Seymour, Michael Sarrazin, David McCallum, John Gielgud, Ralph Richardson, Agnes Moorehead and Tom Baker (of *Doctor Who* fame).

Frankenstein. USA, dir. Glenn Jordan. Dan Curtis Productions and ABC, 1973. Features a purportedly excellent creature performance by Bo Svenson.

Frankenstein. UK, dir. James Ormerod. Lightning Video and Live Video, 1984. Carrie Fisher as Elizabeth (limited to short cameos) and Shakespearean actors such as John Gielgud as Blind Man.

Frankenstein's Baby. UK, dir. Robert Bierman. BBC, 1990, 75 minutes. Yvonne Bryceland as Victor.

Frankenstein. UK, dir. David Wickles. Turner Pictures, 1993. British made-for-cable production with Patrick Bergin (Victor) and Randy Quaid (creature); introduces the twist of a creature cloned from Victor himself.

'Ship in a Bottle', *Star Trek: The Next Generation*, episode 138. USA, created by Gene Rodenberry. Paramount Television, 1993. Frankensteinian themes appear in other episodes, notably those involving the Borg, beings who are grafted to a hive-like collective in a process of 'assimilation' that renders them part humanoid and part cyborg.

Frankenstein in music

'Monster Mash'. Bobby Pickett and Leonard Capizzi. Garpax, 1963.

'Stoned Innocent Frankenstein'. Daevid Allen. Daevid Allen, *Banana Moon*. Charly Records, 1970.

'Frankenstein Goes to the Disco'. Billy Cobham. Billy Cobham and George Duke, *Live on Tour in Europe*. Atlantic Records, 1993.

The Clones of Dr Funkenstein. Parliament. Polygram, 1976.

'Iron Man', on Black Sabbath, *We Sold Our Soul For Rock and Roll*. WEA, 1976. Later covered by the Cardigans (*First Band on the Moon*. Stockholm Records, 1996).

Iron Maiden's mascot (appearing on all of their album covers and in their stage shows) resembles Frankenstein's creature.

Multimedia and interactive

The Interactive History of Frankenstein. Video game, 1995. Rick Baker, Jack P. Pierce, Kevin Pollak and the voice of Boris Karloff. (See Shelley Jackson's *Patchwork Girl*, **p. 59**.)

Frankenstein: Through the Eyes of the Monster. Video game. Interplay Productions and Amazing Media Inc., 1996. Tim Curry as Victor.

Rocky Interactive Horror Show. Video game, Enteractive, Inc., 1999. Narrated by Christopher Lee, with Richard O'Brien (who wrote the original play) as 'The Game Devil' (Internet Movie Database).

Other media

The Frankenstein Monster. USA. Marvel Comics, 1973–5. The early 1970s' Marvel comics tended to divert from superheroes towards horror and fantasy (Werewolf, Silver Surfer, Dr Strange). Many of the story's elements were retained at the beginning of the series, to disappear as it continued.

Hard Boiled. Frank Miller and Geof Darrow. Milwaukie, OR: Dark Horse Comics, 1992). An android cop thinks that he is human.

Modern Criticism

Introduction

The point of this section is not to duplicate the work of others, but to guide you around some of the salient issues in *Frankenstein* criticism, an industry that has been burgeoning since the 1980s. This period witnessed a real explosion of interest after the trickle of academic work earlier in the twentieth century; of course, the (traditionally) less academic spheres of science-fiction studies kept the torch burning. I have not intended to reproduce material here that is easy to find elsewhere, nor to commission special essays. Instead, I would like to point out some interesting, significant, curious and hard-to-find material on *Frankenstein*. The purpose here has not been to present an entirely exhaustive selection of readings, but, first, to present material from such sources that have proved indispensable, such as the work of Mary Jacobus, **pp. 99–102**, or Eve Sedgwick, **pp. 103–4**, and, second, to gather material from sources that are less easy to find. Further reading materials are discussed in each section.

This chapter has been organised alphabetically by category, then alphabetically within each category. Where I was unable to include an entry, for reasons of space, I have substituted a short summary, rather than supply long and relatively unmediated lists of further reading. Each work has been chosen for its significance for *Frankenstein* studies in general and/or for its specific interest. I have chosen not to include any work from other collections of essays and anthologies, which are listed at the end of this section.

Here are the six categories into which extracts are subdivided, with brief explanations. The distinctions I have made are necessarily arbitrary. The work of such a writer as Gayatri Spivak, for example (**pp. 121–3**), defies the categories I have invented.

(i) *The body, medicine and science.* Some of the readings here are inspired by the work of the post-structuralist historian and philosopher of history, Michel Foucault. But not all of them; I have decided simply to group together all those readings that deal with issues of materiality and the physical universe.

(ii) *Commodity culture and social structure.* These readings show the influence of the many varieties of Marxist thought, and also of cultural studies and the rise of historicist literary criticism (see Richardson, **pp. 92–5**). As the novel is concerned with the manufacture of an artificial being, the story seems ripe for an interpretation that takes into account the rise of industrial capitalism in Shelley's time (such an interpretation may also be applied to the film *Blade Runner*: see **p. 46** of the chapter on Performance).

(iii) *Gender and queer theories.* Such an enormous variety of different kinds of reading that could be included in this section makes such a category necessarily inadequate to the task. But I have endeavoured to take note of some of the recent developments, including those inspired by Jacobus and Sedgwick. These readings stress that gender is apparent in and through language, or focus on historical and cultural contexts for images of gender (feminine *and* masculine). Less recent late-twentieth-century feminist readings tend to emphasise the role of Shelley as a woman writer: for example, see Gilbert and Gubar (a significant reading of Shelley's parody of Milton); Ellen Moers's exploration of what she dubbed 'female Gothic'; or even a more recent biographical approach such as Mellor's. Mary Poovey's work provides a significant bridge to questions of commodity culture again, via notions of *propriety*.

(iv) *Genre, literary form and literary history.* These extracts consider the novel with regard to its literary form, both internally, and as it relates to other literary forms. Much significant work has been done, for example, on the fact that the novel is structured as a set of narratives arranged as Chinese boxes, each framed by the other. Also in this section is the work of such writers as Zachary Leader, **p. 104**, who have considered Shelley's role as a writer of literary texts.

(v) *Language and psyche.* This cluster of readings is grouped around the work of the psychoanalyst Jacques Lacan and Jacques Derrida (who was a student in Lacan's seminars in the 1950s). Those readings that emphasise either psychoanalysis or deconstruction appear under this heading. Since the creature grapples with language and since we as readers experience this as part of his coming to awareness (the growth of his psyche, if you like), it seemed appropriate to group these readings together. If you are unfamiliar with deconstruction and the psychoanalytic literary criticism, it will be helpful to have an explanatory text nearby, such as Rivkin and Ryan's literary theory anthology, or one of the Routledge New Accents studies such as Christopher Norris (on deconstruction) or Elizabeth Wright (on psychoanalysis).

(vi) *Race, colonialism and orientalism.* This section examines the novel in the light of the developments in colonialism and imperialism in Shelley's time. One could generalise that during Shelley's life Europe moved from its colonialist into its imperialist phase. For further discussion of the Romantic period, orientalism and imperialism, please see Saree Makdisi's *Romantic Imperialism*. Two significant collections of essays on these issues have recently appeared, one edited by Sonia Hofkosh and Alan Richardson, the other by Timothy Fulford and Peter Kitson.

As elsewhere, I have silently corrected some tiny solecisms in the original sources. Numbers in bold indicate page numbers from the novel printed in this sourcebook (Key Passages). I have also included cross references to the preface material and to anything else that happens to be reprinted here.

The Body, Medicine and Science

Marilyn Butler, 'The Shelleys and Radical Science', in Marilyn Butler, ed., *Frankenstein* (1994) Oxford and New York: Oxford University Press, xv–xxi

While Mary Shelley had points to teach her husband about novel-writing, [Percy Shelley] had a start over her with science. His interest dates back, as is well known, from preparatory-school days at Syon House, and the inspiration of an unorthodox scientist and brilliant itinerant teacher, **Adam Walker** (1731–1821). Shelley became fascinated by major scientific topics of the day, the solar system, microscopy, magnetism, and electricity. First at Eton, afterwards at University College, Oxford, he was noted for his interest in chemical and electrical experiments. He told his cousin Thomas Medwin that when his career as an Oxford undergraduate, 1810–11, was brought abruptly to an end because of his share in the pamphlet *The Necessity of Atheism*, he began a professional training as a surgeon; that, together with his cousin Charles Grove, he 'walked the wards' of Bart's (St Bartholomew's) Hospital, and attended the London anatomy lectures of a senior surgeon whose notions and writings afterwards figure in *Frankenstein*: John Abernethy (1764–1831). Shelley's visit or visits to Bart's may however have dated from 1813–14, when he was getting to know Abernethy's demonstrator and former pupil, William Lawrence (1783–1867), who was soon to become Abernethy's professional antagonist, and one of the most publicised scientists of the day. It is in fact hard to date Shelley's early meetings with Lawrence, because of Lawrence's membership of the Godwin circle – to which another avant-garde scientist important to Percy Shelley at this time, John Frank Newton, also belonged.

  Whether or not Percy Shelley contemplated the professional training, his industry in reading science is well documented.[1] A long reading list for the years 1813–17 can be culled from Percy's letters, the footnotes to annotated works like *Queen Mab*, and Mary Shelley's *Journal*; it organises itself into the pursuit of Enlightenment scepticism (Hume, Voltaire, Volney), anthropology (Buffon, [Jean-Jacques] **Rousseau**, Monboddo), and the so-called French materialists, Holbach as author of *The System of Nature*, and from the French-revolutionary period [Marquis de] **Condorcet**, [Pierre-Jean-Georges] **Cabanis** and [Marquis de] **Laplace**. This litany has appeared over time in a number of studies of the science in *Frankenstein*, notably for instance by Samuel Holmes Vasbinder and Anne Mellor. But, though a useful outline sketch to the modern reader otherwise ignorant of late-Enlightenment science, the litany alone will not necessarily serve as a

---

1 Shelley, *Letters* 1.429.

guide to what Mary Shelley was able or willing to incorporate in her novels. In pre-professional times readers' knowledge of so specialised a discourse could not be assumed. The academic reading-list needs qualifying or replacing with a form of newspaper and journal-talk which *could* be thought of as current language, to which Lawrence, who was known to both Shelleys, conspicuously contributed.

What is more, there is good and bad evidence when we come to explore the growth of a particular idea in an author's imagination. Lawrence was a high-flying professional who could have guided the couple's reading in the physical sciences from the time they became partners in 1814 to the moment of the novel's emergence, some four years later. But we have arrived at a new, much more particularised insight when we find in the Shelley circle's letters of August–September 1815, when Lawrence was playing a particularly important role as Percy Shelley's physician, a cluster of words, ideas, events which surely recur in *Frankenstein*. Facts Mary Shelley learnt of during the trip up the Thames have been cited – Shelley's use of his rooms when an undergraduate for a noncurricular and potentially threatening form of science, and at the same time, his challenge to religion. But there seems to be another bridge which may connect Lawrence to *Frankenstein*: Percy Shelley's train of thought on returning to Bishopsgate reinvigorated in September 1815, when he shows a new interest in keeping records of the processes of his own mind, notably his early thinking and his dreams. Later that autumn he began work on a stylised poetic biography, which is also autobiography, 'Alastor'.

The fragment which records and reflects on some of his dreams or fantasies is datable from 1815. Mary Shelley afterwards claimed to have been present when this was written, and grouped it with other fragments on 'Metaphysics', 'Mind', and the germ of the 'little treatise' on 'morals'. While they still draw on Shelley's reading in Berkeley and Hume, these writings sound a distinctive note [. . .] When Percy Shelley talked with Lawrence, different traditions of thinking about mind plainly converged. The consultations must also have focused on Shelley's nervous condition, his suggestibility and his dreams, those presentations of the non-rational. Like *Alastor* (1816), *Frankenstein* can be read as the testimonies of three deliberately differentiated autobiographers, who together bear witness to a story of universal significance. Thanks to the dialogue set up with Lawrence, such 'records' not only mimic, but imaginatively contribute to current 'science of mind'. Meanwhile almost all Lawrence's own publications in the vitalist and evolutionary field fall into the years of the conceiving and writing of *Franken-stein*. The dialogue continues, embraces the novel, becomes its essential context and at times its text.

It was in 1814 that a schism in the life-sciences between strict materialists and those willing to share a vocabulary with the religious came out into the open in Britain. [. . .] Edinburgh, long Britain's leading university for medicine, was situ-ated in a powerfully theological culture. As President of London's Royal College of Surgeons, the Scottish-trained John Abernethy chose the College and the public occasion of the Hunterian lectures, named after his own old teacher John Hunter, to make a conciliatory move in an issue which threatened to bring believers into collision with outright materialists: the origin and ultimate nature of what afterwards became known as the life-principle.[2] Abernethy attributed his 'Theory of Life' broadly to Hunter, Humphry Davy, and other notables, a modest and diplomatic move. As a moderate willing to conform to religious scruples, he conceded that the modern catchwords 'organization', 'function', 'matter' could not *explain* what was distinctively life-giving. Life, that which vitalised, had to be thought of as something independent. Attributing the view to Hunter, Abernethy declared that a 'superadded' element was needed, some 'subtile, mobile, invisible substance', perhaps a superfine fluid 'analogous to electricity', which would appear as a correlative to or confirmation of the idea of an (immortal) Soul. Scientists would be free to pursue their enquiries, so long as these did not necessarily entail a major victory over religion.

The secular-minded *Edinburgh Review* wittily contested Abernethy's conclusions. But the issue became a notable professional quarrel, waged in public, only after Abernethy's former pupil William Lawrence was appointed in 1815 as a second Professor at the Royal College of Surgeons. In March 1816 Lawrence gave two public inaugural lectures on Abernethy's topic. The first, an introduction to comparative anatomy (21 March), described work currently being done in France, with a comprehensiveness no doubt aimed to convey to his student audience that he was a more fully qualified professional than Abernethy. Lawrence's second lecture, 'On Life', by contrast focuses as rigorously on the issue as physiology and anatomy (but no other specialism) can explicate it, in the spirit and avant-garde medical terminology of **M.F.X. Bichat** (1771–1802), who had brought new standards of precision to French physiology. For biologists (a word Lawrence allegedly introduced to Britain), life is the 'assemblage of all the functions' a living body can perform. We have done what we can, Lawrence says, to find origins and 'to observe living bodies in the moment of their formation . . . when matter may be supposed to receive the stamp of life. . . . Hitherto, however, we have not been able to catch nature in the fact'. On the contrary, what we can observe of animals is that 'all have participated in the existence of other living beings . . . the motion proper to living bodies, or in one word, life, has its origin in that of their parents'.[3] The power that animates animals resists abstraction from matter; for the materialist thinker, an abstracted approach to Life yields nothing.

Lawrence made an outright attack on Abernethy a year later, in 1817, when, for the first time, he named his colleague and President as his adversary. There he unmistakably ridiculed the argument that electricity, or 'something analogous' to it, could do duty for the soul – 'For subtle matter is still matter; and if this fine stuff can possess vital properties, surely they may reside in a fabric which differs only in being a little coarser.'[4] But even in the more guarded 1816 lectures there was an offensive tone of superiority in (for instance) the demand that the Life question should be left to the real professionals; that would mean, on this issue, excluding chemists: 'Organised bodies must be treated differently from those which have inorganic matter for their object . . . the reference to gravity, to

2   Abernethy, *Inquiry*, 48, 52; see Contemporary Documents for a complete citation.
3   Lawrence, *Introduction* 140–2; see Contemporary Documents for a complete citation.
4   Ibid., 84.

attraction, to chemical affinity, to electricity and galvanism, can only serve to perpetuate false notes in philosophy.' Lawrence then gravely suggests that the great John Hunter, after whom his and Abernethy's lectures are named, would have taken the Lawrence side on the question of method:

> He did not attempt to explain life by . . . *a priori* speculations, or by the illusory analogies of other sciences . . . he sought to discover its nature in the only way, which can possibly lead to any useful and satis-factory result; that is, by a patient examination of the fabric, and close observation of the actions of living creatures.[5]

Mary and Percy Shelley, Lawrence's friends, were living near London in that March of 1816, when Lawrence's materialist case against spiritualised vitalism was first sketched out. It would not be surprising, then, if Mary's contribution to the ghost-story competition to some degree acts out the debate between Aber-nethy and Lawrence, in a form close enough for those who knew the debate to recognise. Frankenstein the blundering experimenter, still working with super-seded notions, shadows the intellectual position of Abernethy, who proposes that the superadded life-element is analogous to electricity. Lawrence's sceptical commentary on that position finds its echo in Mary Shelley's equally detached, serio-comic representation – though the connection between her satire and Lawrence's is masked by her use of a comic analogy out of the folk tradition, concerning the over-reacher who gets more than he bargains for.

Tim Marshall, *Murdering to Dissect: Graverobbing, Frankenstein, and the Anatomy Literature* (1995) Manchester: Manchester University Press; and New York: St Martin's Press, 19–23

> Tim Marshall investigates the 'auto-icon' of Jeremy Bentham, the philosopher, somewhere between a mummy and a waxwork. Bentham's utilitarianism had rendered him not squeamish to the use of the human body in medical research. Marshall studies the legitimation of such research in the Romantic period. A cultural 'association between dissection and murder' was transformed into the theatrical display of the dissected poor. Marshall employs the work of the post-structuralist historian Michel Foucault to support this argument.

[. . .] **Jeremy Bentham**, the utilitarian philosopher [. . .] died in 1832, aged eighty-five. Bentham left instructions that after his death his body was to go to the surgeons for the purpose of a public dissection in a London anatomy school. His wishes in this respect went back to a will made as early as 1769, which he revised two months before his death to confirm his special request. It was his desire that

5   Ibid., 161–3.

his body should be used to illustrate the structure and the functions of the human body, and to promote a recognition within society of the usefulness of this kind of knowledge. It was a gesture of solidarity with the medical profession of the day and a recognition of the legitimacy of the then relatively new science of morbid anatomy.

The auto-icon, as it is called, was made as Bentham ordered it. It is a waxwork likeness of himself, dressed in his own clothes and with his walking stick in his hand; it is mounted on the skeleton which the surgeon articulated in a sitting posture. The dried head beside him is his actual preserved head, but it was felt by his close associates to be so unlike the live Bentham that a commissioned wax-head was substituted shortly after his death. The auto-icon is kept in a cabinet in the cloisters of University College, London, and is exhibited on ceremonial occasions. It is but a step from this rather strange artefact to the famous novel *Frankenstein*. The connection concerns the study of human anatomy by dissection; more precisely, it concerns the legitimation of dissection as indispensable to the advance and improvement of medical knowledge and education. Bentham's subtitle for his representation of himself was 'further uses of the dead to the living'. The figure in the glass showcase understood science in an eighteenth-century sense, that is to say, as a practical art based on empirical knowledge. In this conviction the great philosopher of utility sits in his own self-representation – disembodied, and offering his body to medical science.

The gesture is ambiguous, and the story of its ambiguity is told in *Frankenstein*. The auto-icon denies, or negates, the full reality of what has been done to the body. It is a remarkably intact-looking Jeremy Bentham who countenances the clinical dismantlement of the human body to a point beyond all ordinary recognition.

Bentham's gesture needs to be understood in its contemporary context. It is not an isolated gesture. On the contrary, it is part of a concerted but only partially successful programme of propaganda within officialdom in the 1820s which aimed to secure the legitimacy of dissection, and with it the legitimation of the medical profession. [T]he low public standing of the medical profession in the early nineteenth century was due to a large extent to its reluctant but necessary trade complicity with the graverobbers. The dead body business connection brought with it an unwelcome association with the unclean and the profane which inevitably made it next to impossible for the profession to present itself as properly scientific and in alliance with polite society.

Since the 1790s, particularly in the context of the armed forces, an urgent requirement for trained surgeons had arisen. In a sixteen-month course in surgery and anatomy every student required a minimum of three corpses to dissect. The traditional source of supply, sanctioned by royal grant, were the bodies of convicted murderers supplied by the hangman to the surgeons. This supply-line, however, as I have noted, bound the profession into an unwelcome association with the gallows. The result, as Ruth Richardson observes, was that 'the surgeon-anatomist became an executioner of the law'.[1] This was an identity

---

1   Ruth Richardson, *Death, Dissection and the Destitute* (Harmondsworth: Penguin, 1989), 34.

which regularly earned the surgeons a hostile reception from the large crowds that attended public executions in the eighteenth century.

The 1752 Act of Parliament for 'better Preventing the horrid Crime of Murder' is an illustration of some of these difficulties. In respect of sentences for murder, it gave the Bench the discretion to order a public dissection of the criminal's body in place of a gibbeting.[2] The move added a further punitive dimension to the punishment for murder. However, over the course of time the intention and the effect of the law placed complications in the way of the medical profession's long bid for legitimacy. By design, the law associated dissection with the punishment meted out to the worst offenders; henceforth, dissection was invested with a stigma which was difficult if not impossible to remove in the long term. The ruling elite made dissection an object of dread or superstitious fear – as the Act explicitly stated, an object of 'further Terror'.[3] The popular perception had long had reason to link dissection with punishment; and it is in this context that Bentham's opportunist donation of his own body gains its significance.

Furthermore, the gallows theatre confronted the beleaguered surgeons with their chief practical problem, for the number of corpses from this source was not equal to their requirements. It was an awkward point, but from their professional point of view there was not enough murder in society. By the 1820s several thousand bodies were required per annum, but no legal provision existed to supply them on this scale. The need to obtain corpses by some other legal source, and to end the compromising association with the hangman, is the crux of the medical profession's legitimacy problem in the early nineteenth century. Bentham's auto-icon stands as testimony to his lifelong commitment to break the popular association between dissection and murder, and with it to dissolve the stigma. It happens, indeed, that in the decade before his death Bentham devised the enduring solution to the surgeons' difficulties.

Bentham's solution was the Anatomy Act of 1832. In the national context, the legislation is a milestone in the transition to modernity that Michel Foucault describes in *Discipline and Punish*, the story of the development of the techniques and practices of 'disciplinary' society. One reader of Foucault has characterised the transition in a way that has an apt application to Bentham's proposal. Michel de Certeau comments that:

> what Foucault analyses is a chiasmus: how the place occupied by humanitarian and reformist projects at the end of the eighteenth century is then 'colonised' or 'vampirised' by those disciplinary procedures that have since increasingly organised the social realm itself. This mystery story narrates a plot of substituted corpses, the sort of game of substitution that would have pleased Freud.[4]

2 Gibbeting is an aspect of capital punishment: the corpse is placed on display in a gibbet, a metal frame suspended from a gallows.
3 Richardson, *Death*, 37.
4 Michel de Certeau, *Heterologies* (Manchester: Manchester University Press, 1986), 185.

The historical context suggests that it is not Freud but the caste of surgeons, in fiction as well as reality, who had best reason to appreciate *a plot of substituted corpses*. A plot of this kind was in hand when the third edition of *Frankenstein* appeared in 1831. The Anatomy Act became law just months afterwards, in August 1832. It was long in design and the early stages of its inception were surrounded by secrecy. As its architect and patron intended, it achieved the utilitarian objective of obligating the dead to be useful to society. It has been commented that the auto-icon is 'the sacred relic of a secular creed' which gained in stridency after 1832.[5] The creed, utilitarianism, is one face of the middle-class hegemony which begins with the new political arrangements of the Great Reform Bill.

The class issue is central to the reading that I shall give of *Frankenstein* as an allegory of 1832. In the period preceding the legislation, grave robbery and dissection crossed class boundaries and this fact is the key to the labyrinth of the social implications of the new law. In a remarkable synchronicity of parliamentary discourse, the Anatomy Act leads a low profile, peek-a-boo existence, overshadowed by the monumental public moment of the Reform Bill. The legislation – after a number of bureaucratic teething problems – delivered a reliable supply of corpses to the slab. The surgeons were granted automatic access to unclaimed bodies from the workhouse. As the chronology shows at 1832, the Reform Bill receives Royal Assent in the days between Bentham's death and his dissection, and on 1 August 1832 the Anatomy Act becomes law. The complex history of the new anatomy law is described by Ruth Richardson in *Death, Dissection and the Destitute*. The backcover summary of her book spells out the plot of substituted corpses:

> Before 1832 dissection was a feared and hated punishment for murder. The 1832 Anatomy Act requisitioned instead the corpses of the poor, transferring the penalty from murder to poverty. The Act contributed to the terrible fear of the Victorian workhouse and influences attitudes to death even today.

Before 1832 the surgeons' dependency on the resurrectionist connection was usually accompanied by a barely disguised disdain for the men who provided the developing science with its materials. **Sir Astley Cooper**, the President of the Royal College of Surgeons, told a Parliamentary Select Committee in 1828 that the graverobbers were 'the lowest dregs of degradation', and that he traded with them out of necessity. He observed that 'there is no crime they would not commit'.[6] This emphasis plainly anticipates murder as a logical development, as the Burke and Hare scandal later in the same year was to prove. The events in Edinburgh in 1828 were to clarify the fact that the dead body business had always been – in all but name – the medicine of murder.

---

5   R. Harrison, *Bentham* (London: Routledge & Kegan Paul, 1983), 22.
6   Richardson, *Death*, 117. Also quoted in D. Low, *Thieves' Kitchen* (Guernsey: Alan Sutton, 1987), 91.

Alan Rauch, 'The Monstrous Body of Knowledge in Mary Shelley's *Frankenstein*', *Studies in Romanticism* 34.2 (1995): 227–53

Rauch's discussion of the 'nature of knowledge' in *Frankenstein* (228) starts by examining Victor's scientific knowledge. Shelley 'erodes Frankenstein's credibility' (233) by having him dismember the female creature, an irrational response to the idea of 'a *female* embodiment of knowledge' (232). Frankenstein reads alchemical texts, an esoteric and anachronistic discipline. His secrecy cuts against what **John F. W. Herschel** argued was the necessary openness of scientific inquiry (234–5). Luigi Galvani and **Giovanni Aldini** proposed that electricity could resuscitate the 'fatally ill', not instil life in lifeless matter (238; please consult the Directory). John Birch's *Essay on the Medical Applications of Electricity* (1802) recounts experiments in this vein. Why does Frankenstein not know how to restore life to the creature's victims (239)? In contrast, saving a young girl from drowning, 'The monster, equipped only with the rudiments of scientific knowledge (gleaned perhaps from the notes on his own creation), makes the best use of it when it is needed' (240–1). Shelley and Percy were fascinated by galvanism; Polidori may have learnt about it while studying medicine in Edinburgh (242). Rauch supplies more context for the childbirth theme: **Princess Charlotte**, the popular Royal, died in childbirth while *Frankenstein* was being written.

Paul Youngquist, '*Frankenstein*: The Mother, the Daughter, and the Monster', *Philological Quarterly* 70: 3 (1991): 339–59

Youngquist remarks that Shelley wanted her feminism to be more concrete, more rooted in contingency, than Wollstonecraft's (339). Wollstonecraft reaches beyond sex to a universalist Enlightenment view of 'humanity'. But Shelley deviated from this 'humane standard' (341), unconfident that 'the imperatives of the body' can or should be overcome. In 'reconstructing female beauty as male ugliness' in the creature, Shelley revises her mother's insistence that female beauty is mere enculturation. Frankenstein's workshop is sexualised as a womb, displaced to the very top of the house (347). Shelley keeps insisting that birth and sex are inherently polluted and irreducible, only capable of being kept at bay (348–9). Sexually innocent women in *Frankenstein* are depicted according to a figurative register of virginity (349–50). Mothers, on the other hand, sustain the paradox that life breeds death (351–2). The increased presence of Frankenstein's mother, Caroline Beaufort, in the 1831 edition, reinforces both 'proto-Victorian [. . .] domesticity' and an underlying 'tragic paradox of impure birth' (352). Youngquist writes: 'To the extent that Shelley looks to art to set her free from the ruins of motherhood she becomes the purveyor of a Romantic idealism' (355). But her swerving 'from the fate of motherhood' ironically reinforces the undeniable determinacy of the body (356).

Commodity Culture and Social Structure

Elsie B. Michie, 'Production Replaces Creation: Market Forces and *Frankenstein* as Critique of Romanticism', *Nineteenth-Century Contexts* 12:1 (1988): 27–33

In *Frankenstein*, as in Marx, not only the end product of capitalist processes (the commodity), but also its very manufacture, is shot through with alienation. Michie shows that in order to make the creature, Frankenstein is compelled to alienate himself from the ecosystem in general (he handles corpses and tortures animals) and from other human beings in particular (isolating himself in his laboratory). In the 1831 edition, Victor feels even more alienated from the creature he has made (28–9). For Marx, Hegel's theory of absolute spirit – that becomes disalienated by fully knowing itself – is an inadequate, Romantic solution to the desire for liberation, as it is only free in an abstract way. We may have come to know who we are, but has this really changed the social conditions in which we take our place and suffer? Likewise, Frankenstein's Romantic, imaginative attitude towards creation is not adequate to the concrete status of the artwork as *product*. (In general, this was a commonly perceived asymmetry, and genuine artistic problem, in the Romantic period. Authors were grappling with the fact that they had to produce work in an alienated marketplace rather than to a familiar reading public.) Thus Michie declares that *Frankenstein* dramatises the nature of the novel itself as a commodity form.

Franco Moretti, *Signs Taken for Wonders: Essays in the Sociology of Literary Forms*, trans. Susan Fischer, David Forgacs and David Miller (1983) London: Verso, 83–90

Moretti's Marxist reading of *Frankenstein* is based on the notion that in a capitalist society there is a necessary split between property owners and workers. The creature is a displaced version of the working class, brought to life from the 'limbs' of the feudal poor. As in the nineteenth-century cartoons from *Punch* in this sourcebook, the creature is the image of what most disturbs the property-owning bourgeoisie: the class it has created, as 'a race apart' (87), that is inherently monstrous to its gaze. Walton frames the story in order to suggest that '*capitalism has no future*' (89), that the narrative of *Frankenstein* is just a freak case study. Here are no factories, unions and class struggles. The novel's terrifying elements are reduced to mere domestic 'fable': Mary Shelley 'erases history' (90).

The fear of bourgeois civilisation is summed up in two names: Frankenstein and Dracula. The monster and the vampire are born together, one night in 1816, in the drawing room of the Villa Chapuis near Geneva, out of a society game among friends to while away a rainy summer. Born in the full spate of the industrial revolution, they rise again together in the critical years at the end of the nineteenth century, under the names of Hyde and Dracula. In the twentieth century they conquer the cinema: after the First World War, in German Expressionism; after the 1929 crisis, with the big RKO productions in America; then in 1956–57, Peter Cushing and Christopher Lee, directed by Terence Fisher, again, triumphantly, incarnate this twin-faced nightmare.[1]

Frankenstein['s creature] and Dracula lead parallel lives. They are two indivisible, because complementary, figures; the two horrible faces of a single society, its *extremes*: the disfigured wretch and the ruthless proprietor. The worker and capital: 'the whole of society must split into the two classes of *property owners* and propertyless *workers*'.[2] That 'must', which for Marx is a scientific prediction of the future (and the guarantee of a future reordering of society) is a forewarning of the end for nineteenth-century bourgeois culture. The literature of terror is born precisely *out of the terror of a split society*, and out of that desire to heal it. It is for just this reason that Dracula and Frankenstein, with rare exceptions, do not appear together. The threat would be too great: and this literature, having produced terror, must also erase it and restore peace. It must restore the broken equilibrium, giving the illusion of being able to stop history: because the monster expresses the anxiety that the future will be monstrous. His antagonist – the enemy of the monster – will always be, by contrast, a representative of the present, a distillation of complacent nineteenth-century mediocrity: nationalistic, stupid, superstitious, philistine, impotent, self-satisfied. But this does not show through. Fascinated by the horror of the monster, the public accepts the vices of its destroyer without a murmur, just as it accepts his literary depiction, the jaded and repetitive typology which regains its strength and its virginity on contact with the unknown. The monster, then, serves to displace the antagonisms and horrors evidenced *within* society *outside* society itself. In *Frankenstein* the struggle will be between a 'race of devils' and the 'species of man'. Whoever dares to fight the monster automatically becomes the representative of the species, of the whole of society. The monster, the utterly unknown, serves to reconstruct a universality, a social cohesion which – in itself – would no longer carry conviction. [. . .]

Like the proletariat, the monster is denied a name and an individuality. He is the Frankenstein monster; he belongs wholly to his creator (just as one can speak of a 'Ford worker'). Like the proletariat, he is a *collective* and *artificial* creature. He is not found in nature, but built. Frankenstein is a productive *inventor*-scientist, in open conflict with Walton, the contemplative *discoverer*-scientist (the pattern is repeated with Jekyll and Lanyon). Reunited and brought back to life in the monster are the limbs of those – the 'poor' – whom the breakdown of feudal relations has forced into brigandage, poverty and death. Only modern science – this metaphor for the 'dark satanic mills' – can offer them a future. It sews them

---

1   See the section on performance, pp. 65–7, 71.
2   Karl Marx, 'Economic and Philosophical Manuscripts' (1844), in *Early Writings* (Harmondsworth: Penguin, 1975), 322.

together again, moulds them according to its will and finally gives them life. *But at the moment the monster opens its eyes*, its creator draws back in horror: 'by the glimmer of the half-extinguished light, I saw the dull yellow eye of the creature open ... How can I describe my emotions at this catastrophe ...?' (**p. 137**). Between Frankenstein and the monster there is an ambivalent, dialectical relationship, the same as that which, according to Marx, connects capital with wage-labour. [. . .]

The monster's explicit 'demands' cannot in fact produce fear. They are not a gesture of challenge; they are 'reformist'/'Chartist' demands. The monster wishes only to have rights of citizenship among men: 'I will not be tempted to set myself in opposition to thee. I am thy creature, and I will be ever mild and docile to my natural lord and king, ... I was benevolent and good; misery made me a fiend. Make me happy, and I shall again be virtuous' (**p. 143**). Furthermore, when all friendly relations with humans have failed, the monster humbly accepts his marginalisation, begging only to have another creature who is 'as deformed and horrible as myself' (**p. 155**). But even this is denied him. The monster's sheer *existence* is frightening enough for Frankenstein, let alone the prospect of his producing children and multiplying. Frankenstein – who never manages to consummate his marriage – is the victim of the same impotence that Benjamin describes: 'Social reasons for impotence: the imagination of the bourgeois class stopped caring about the future of the productive forces it had unleashed ... Male impotence – key figure of solitude, in which the arrest of the productive forces is effected.'[3] The possibility of the monster having descendants presents itself to the scientist as a real nightmare: 'a race of devils would be propagated upon the earth who might make the very existence of the species of man a condition precarious and full of terror.'

Alan Richardson, *Literature, Education, and Romanticism: Reading as Social Practice, 1780–1832* (1994) Cambridge and New York: Cambridge University Press, 203–12

The Gothic novel, a form which developed alongside the domestic novel and which was also particularly associated with women writers, invites rather than silences the representation of erotic or aggressive wishes. Within the 'spectral arena of the Gothic castle', as Poovey writes, women novelists of the Romantic era could 'dramatise the eruption of psychic material ordinarily controlled by the inhibitions of bourgeois society'.[1] What must always remain tacit in the post-Jacobin domestic novel becomes overt in the lurid domain of the Gothic, much to the chagrin of conservatives like More. If its more salient treatment of the

3   Walter Benjamin, 'Zentralpark', in *Gesammelte Schriften*, ed. Rolf Tiedemann, Hermann Schweppenhäuser, Theodor W. Adorno and Gershom Scholem, 7 vols (Frankfurt a/M: Suhrkamp, 1972–89), 1.655–90.

1   Mary Poovey, *The Proper Lady and the Woman Writer: Ideology as Style in the Works of Mary Wollstonecraft, Mary Shelley, and Jane Austen* (Chicago and London: University of Chicago Press, 1984), 321.

problematic nature and expression of female desire differentiates the 'female Gothic' from the contemporary domestic novel, however, its concern with questions of women's education and moral development, which has largely gone unnoted, provides an unexpected bridge between the two genres. In Radcliffe's *Romance of the Forest* (1791), for example, the heroine finds herself in the midst of a Rousseauvian educational idyll, nursed through a mental and physical breakdown in Savoy by a benevolent pastor who applies the 'philosophy of nature' to the 'gradual unfolding of [his children's] infant minds'; the object lesson by which this Savoyard vicar teaches his daughter the value of moderation reads like an excerpt from *Emile* or *Sandford and Merton*.[2] In *The Mysteries of Udolpho* (1794), Radcliffe carefully describes the 'unfolding' of the heroine's character under the tutelage of her father, St Aubert; Emily's education, including a 'general view of the sciences', 'every part of elegant literature' and the inculcation of 'modesty, simplicity, and correct manners', represents (despite the novel's Renaissance setting) the most advanced eighteenth-century liberal thinking, anticipating the educational programs of [Erasmus] **Darwin** and the Edgeworths.[3]

Such unexpected appearances of the rational pedagogue in the haunted castle might seem merely to reflect the insistent presence of education within Romantic culture, an accidental rather than integral feature of the female Gothic. And yet, as Judith Wilt has pointed out, the implicitly tyrannical relation of (male) teacher and (female) student, the 'exercise of power by the knowing over the ignorant', is a 'pure Gothic' convention and recognisable as such even in the domestic novels of Austen, troubling such 'charming young man/naive young woman relationships' as those of Willoughby and Marianne in *Sense and Sensibility* and Henry and Catherine in *Northanger Abbey*.[4] The power/knowledge dynamic underlying the relation of Emily St Aubert and her father is structurally cognate with that which facilitates Emily's exploitation by the villain Montoni, who cruelly plays on this very resemblance, taking on the voice of the father-instructor, when she balks at his designs [. . .] The same inequality informs the pedagogical-romantic relations we have seen in the domestic novel, marking not only doomed couplings like that of Clarence Hervey and Virginia St Pierre in *Belinda*, but successful ones like that of Edmund and Fanny in *Mansfield Park* as well. [. . .]

Mary Shelley's *Frankenstein* (1818) presents an especially complex and elaborate version of the critique of female education which Radcliffe brought into the Gothic, and which Austen comically varies in *Northanger Abbey*. Shelley's concern with education – which her father (Godwin) had described as inherently connected with 'despotism' and which her mother (Wollstonecraft) had shown as central in establishing and maintaining male hegemony – emerges in the opening pages of the novel's epistolary frame, in which Walton laments his 'neglected' studies and the limitations of a 'self-educated' intellect [. . .] Walton's reliance on

2   Ann Radcliffe, *The Romance of the Forest*, ed. Chloe Chard (Oxford University Press, 1986), 245–53.
3   Ann Radcliffe, *The Mysteries of Udolpho: A Romance* (London: Oxford University Press, 1970), 5–6, 24.
4   Judith Wilt, *Ghosts of the Gothic: Austen, Eliot, and Lawrence* (Princeton, NJ: Princeton University Press, 1980), 138–9.

a self-directed program of reading in place of a more regular and directed course of studies allies him with most women of the period, who could hope at best for a few years in a finishing school which might (as Austen puts it in *Emma*) allow them to 'scramble themselves into a little education'. His sense of inferiority to a schoolboy also reflects a common female dilemma, what Swift, in his 'Letter to a Young Lady', had insisted that even the most 'learned Women' must endure, and the unflattering comparison had become commonplace in the discourse on female education of the period.[5] Anne Mellor has shown how Shelley's critique of a 'sexual education' troubles the 'cult of domesticity' informing such later novels as *Mathilda* (1819), *Lodore* (1835) and *Falkner* (1837), all of which feature 'father-guardians' who mold the heroines along lines set out in Rousseau's *Emile*.[6] This critique is already present, however, in *Frankenstein*, which exposes the programmatic silences of domestic fiction by inflecting its discourse and conventions with a Gothic exposure of pedagogical tyranny and demonised female desire. Shelley's novel may be read as a 'birth myth', but it does not stop there, taking up such 'domestic' (and pedagogical) themes as the development and education of children as well.[7] More particularly, *Frankenstein* addresses the dilemma of the middle-class adolescent girl, caught between the equally unhappy alternatives of a haphazard self-education and a 'sexual education' in passivity and self-containment.

Rousseau has been invoked in a number of recent critical discussions of *Frankenstein*. The monster is often compared to the 'natural man' of Rousseau's *Second Discourse*, although such comparisons elide a crucial distinction between the two: man in Rousseau's imagined state of nature is essentially solitary, and barely recognises other individuals as such, whereas Shelley's creature is instinctively social, and longing to join the De Lacey family almost from the moment he observes them (110/**p. 146**). More plausible (and more far-reaching in their implications) are the associations made between Victor Frankenstein and the autobiographical Rousseau of *The Confessions* and the *Reveries* who similarly abandons his children (earning Shelley's scorn in her essay on Rousseau for the *Cabinet Cyclopedia*); between the creature and Rousseau as self-styled victims who dwell upon their persecution by an unjust society; and between the often remarked relation of Victor and his creature as two halves of a divided self and the literal self-division of Rousseau in the *Dialogues* or *Rousseau Juge de Jean-Jacques*.[8] What has gone unnoticed, however, is that the narrative at the heart of

5   Jane Austen, *Emma*, ed. Ronald Blythe (Harmondsworth: Penguin, 1966), 52; Jonathan Swift, 'A Letter to a Young Lady, On Her Marriage', in *Irish Tracts 1720–1723 and Sermons*, ed. Louis Landa (Oxford: Basil Blackwell, 1948), 92; Hannah More, *Strictures on the Modern System of Female Education*, 6th edn, 2 vols (London, 1799), 1.188.

6   Anne Mellor, *Mary Shelley: Her Life, Her Fiction, Her Monsters* (New York: Methuen, 1988), 184, 212.

7   Ellen Moers, 'Female Gothic', in George Levine and U.C. Knoepflmacher, eds, *The Endurance of Frankenstein: Essays on Mary Shelley's Novel* (Berkeley: University of California Press, 1979), 77–87 (82).

8   David Marshall, *The Surprising Effects of Sympathy: Marivaux, Diderot, Rousseau, and Mary Shelley* (Chicago: University of Chicago Press, 1988), 178–227, esp. 187–93; James O'Rourke, ' "Nothing More Unnatural": Mary Shelley's Revision of Rousseau', *ELH* 56 (1989), 543–69, esp. 545–6, 559.

Frankenstein – the creature's long speech describing his first sensations, his developing ideas of the natural and social worlds around him, and the 'progress of [his] intellect' (127) – may well have been suggested by a passage in *Emile*, which Shelley had read in 1815 (a year before beginning *Frankenstein*):

> Let us suppose that a child had at his birth the stature and the strength of a grown man, that he emerged, so to speak, fully armed from his mother's womb as did Pallas from the brain of Jupiter ... Not only would he perceive no object outside of himself, he would not even relate any object to the sense organ which made him perceive it ... all his sensations would come together in a single point ... he would have only a single idea, that is, of the *I* to which he would relate all his sensations; and this idea or, rather, this sentiment would be the only thing which he would have beyond what an ordinary baby has.[9]

Given life by a 'creator' or god-figure without the mediation of woman, the monster is indeed a kind of Pallas Athena, and his 'confused and indistinct' memories of his first moments are much as Rousseau describes them: 'A strange multiplicity of sensations seized me, and I saw, felt, heard, and smelt, at the same time; and it was, indeed, a long time before I learned to distinguish between the operations of my various senses'.[10] If the scenario which Shelley develops in *Frankenstein* owes something to Rousseau's book on education, however, it is developed in a manner which suggests a critical engagement with *Emile* in the spirit of her mother's more overt attack.

In describing the education of a monster, Shelley challenges, through a program of critical hyperbole, the tradition of writing on female education and conduct associated especially (after Wollstonecraft) with *Emile*, in which women are at once sentimentalised and viewed, anxiously, as deformed or monstrous in comparison with an explicitly male norm. For Rousseau, woman's subordinate position in society is rooted both in her physical difference from man – her weakness, her capacity to bear children – and in certain moral differences which characterise her as well: her tendency to 'unlimited desires' and to be 'extreme in everything', which together make her life a 'perpetual combat against herself' that can only be won with the aid of modesty and 'habitual constraint'.[11] The notion that women are morally, as well as physically, deformed in comparison to men surfaces throughout British writing on female conduct and education as well, despite the growing emphasis on women's beneficial moral influence on their children, husbands and the larger society around them informing these same works.

9 Jean-Jacques Rousseau, *Emile or Education*, trans. Allan Bloom (New York: Basic Books, 1979), 61.
10 [Richardson's note.] Ibid., 102. There are also some important differences between Rousseau's sketch and the creature's narrative: Rousseau imagines the man/child as an 'imbecile, an automaton, an immobile and almost insensible statue' who would learn to stand, if he attempted it at all, with the greatest difficulty and would not connect hunger with food (61–2), while Shelley's monster gains motor control almost at once and instinctively slakes his hunger with berries.
11 [Richardson's note.] Ibid., 359, 369–70.

Gender and Queer Theories

Rolf Eichler, 'In the Romantic Tradition: *Frankenstein* and *The Rocky Horror Picture Show*', in Michael Gassenheime and Norbert H. Platz, *Beyond the Suburbs of the Mind: Exploring English Romanticism* (1987) Essen: Blau Eule, 95–114

Eichler comments on the autonomy of movies of *Frankenstein* from the novel. *The Rocky Horror Picture Show* links sexuality and death in the tradition of American Gothic (and indeed of the Romantic tradition of the *Schauerroman* or 'shudder novel', a point not discussed here). But the real point of comparison is the creation of Rocky by Frank N. Furter, an act whose homosexual connotations are exploited with reference to *Frankenstein*, through the theme of the *doppelgänger* or double. Eichler does not observe that Rocky's expression of sorrow at not belonging, '"Oh, woe is me – my life is a misery"', alludes to William Wordsworth's 'The Thorn' (which Mary Shelley would have known), where it is the cry of a grief-stricken mother over her dead child. This would have strengthened his contrast between the pathos of the creature and the presumption of the creator. See **p. 74** in the section on performance for more on *The Rocky Horror Picture Show*.

The premier of the musical *The Rocky Horror Show* took place in London in 1973. Text and music were by Richard O'Brien, who also directed the show. It was nominated best musical of the year, and there followed a film version (directed by Jim Sharman) under the title *The Rocky Horror Picture Show*, which was first screened in New York in 1976. To an even greater extent than the stage version, the film refers to and parodies past horror and science fiction films. The basic theme of the musical is society's old fear of sexual deviation. The film paints this attitude with broad strokes, but with its substantial element of science fiction it takes on a highly imaginative character, as well as being provided with a narrative framework which always highlights the moral message. [. . .]

The pivotal incident of *RHPS* is Frank N. Furter's creation of Rocky. With elaborate technology, a parody in itself, Frank brings his creature to life in the laboratory. The pink triangle that Frank wears on his green apron symbolises his homosexual desires, explains why here a man is giving birth to a man, and demonstrates that in Rocky Frank is creating his own pleasure object: 'good for relieving my tension'.[1] At first Rocky's body, wrapped round like a mummy, floats in a giant aquarium; for a few moments he is shown up in X-Ray as a skeleton, and then for the first time he moves and emerges from the 'waters'. Rocky's entry into the world is marked by fear: 'The sword of Damocles is hanging over my head' (13) – and he feels that he does not belong in the society

---

1   Richard O'Brien, *The Rocky Horror Picture Show* (London, 1983), 9.

into which he was born: 'Oh, woe is me – my life is a misery.' Frank, however, celebrates his feat by alluding to Genesis: 'in just seven days, I can make you a man' (15). The presumptuousness of his deed is highlighted by the arrival of the punk Eddie. This leather-jacketed Rocker rides into the laboratory on his motor bike from a deep-freeze (in which Frank had put him), and he brings into Frank's scientifically cloaked world of pleasure a new, anarchic mode of satisfaction.

Eddie has a Boris Karloff scar on his forehead (an allusion to Whale's film) – the result of an operation in which Frank removed half his brain to be transplanted into Rocky.[2] Eddie is the wild and ugly source that was sacrificed in order to produce his double, the gentle, handsome Rocky. Eddie was merely the store from which Frank took his materials to make his artificial man. Mary Shelley had used just a few terse sentences to enable the reader to imagine, or rather not to imagine, the manner in which Victor Frankenstein had robbed corpses, but in the film this perversion is given a macabre twist: at Rocky's birthday party the cloth is removed from the table, and under a sheet of glass lies Eddie, his body slit open, his guts spilling out. The guests realise with horror what they have been eating. In this age of organ transplants, Victor's 'romantic' violation of a taboo (his 'brico-lage' of corpses) loses its vigour, and the addition of the cannibalism taboo enhances the horror.

The recreation of paradise that Victor strives for with his 'new Adam', and which Walton also hopes to achieve through his discovery of the North Pole, takes on a real form in 'Frankenstein Place', the space ship disguised as a medi-eval castle. Here people dance the 'Time Warp' in order to enter another age. The resultant paradise is staged, as it were, on two levels: for the spectator it is set in motion through a commentator leafing through a photo album; within the film itself, the action is experienced by those attending the Transylvanian con-gress. Paradise is conceived here as the greatest possible sexual liberty. In the trend-setting musical *Hair*, there was a quasi-religious song that raised the ques-tion: 'Sodomy, Fellatio, Cunnilingus, Pederasty, Father why do these words sound so nasty?' With such cries the generation of Flower Power demanded a 'resurrection of the body'. In *RHPS* the demand is given a more subtle, though never pornographic optical expression. The focal scenes are the 'wedding' between Frank and Rocky, i.e. the union of creator and creature, and the two sequences when Janet and Brad are in separate bedrooms, and are visited in turn by Frank, who tricks them by imitating their respective voices. The double nature of all the participants, in respect of their sexual activities, is mirrored and parodied filmically by the doubling of one and the same scene: the silhouettes's movements, and the Frank–Janet, Frank–Brad dialogues are (apart from one clause) absolutely identical. The fact that the first scene is shot in pink, and the second in blue, makes the distinction between them highly artificial. In these scenes Frank converts his creature and his guests to his message of sexual liberty, and to a removal of all restrictions that reaches its climax in the swimming-pool

2 See **pp. 62–3** in the chapter on performance.

orgy, in which all the participants appear as Frank's double. Frank's invitation to them runs as follows:

Give yourself over to absolute pleasure,
Swim the warm waters of sins of the flesh,
Erotic nightmares beyond any measure.
And sensual day dreams to treasure forever.
Don't dream it. Be it! (29)

[. . .]

Inseparably linked to the theme of the new Eden is that of its creator, the *overreacher* – as he is called in Frankenstein criticism – or the *superhero*, as science fiction critics dub him. Frank N. Furter has one foot in either camp. He has come to earth from another galaxy with a message whose contents remain open. But his actions on earth, where he creates a being to serve his own desire, are condemned by his rebelling servants Riff-Raff and Magenta: 'your mission was a failure' (29). His excessive lifestyle is then punished by death. Like other themes in the film, that of the superhero is echoed elsewhere, maintaining its presence by thematic *Doppelgängerei*: the castle, 'Frankenstein Place', was General De Gaulle's refuge during the Second World War; the speech that Brad and Janet hear on the car radio when they have got lost at night is Nixon's speech of resignation; the film that Frank wants to show them is about Super-man: the recognisable earthly art and sculpture in the midst of Frank's world of wonders stem from Michelangelo and Leonardo, the giants of the Renaissance. But every illusion to the superhero devalues him. This is even to be seen from the examples of 'David' and the 'Mona Lisa', for each of them is duplicated; and as one looks left and one looks right, we are made thoroughly aware of the fact that they are reproducible. Against this background of movable pieces from an age that designated man as the pinnacle of creation we have Frank N. Furter, the superhero, stripping his superhuman creative powers of all that is socially acceptable, and using them only to further his own lustful ends. The fall of this decadent hero occurs only indirectly through his creature, for Rocky is the narcissistic and not the demonic double. It is others who bring him down, notably Dr Scott, a guardian of morality from the real, everyday world, who significantly is paralysed from the waist downwards. Scott: 'We've got to get out of this trap, before this decadence saps our will . . . society must be protected' (29, 30). Riff-Raff and Magenta are the instruments of Frank's destruction. In the closing scene they both resume the 'American Gothic' position they had taken up at the beginning of the film. But this time the reference is to the future – the pitchfork, for example, having now turned into a triangular laser gun. This is used to dispose of Frank N. Furter. The silent accusation of the earlier image has become an explicit judgment: 'Your lifestyle's too extreme' (29). Here the two servants appear to represent a sexual concept that is composed of the double elements of repression and sublimation. As beings from a transexual planet they have gone beyond the various forms of human sexuality, and as 'American Gothic' figures, they do not even wish these forms to be allowed.

Mary Jacobus, 'Is There a Woman in This Text?', New Literary History 14 (1982): 117–41

In this extremely influential and powerful essay, Jacobus names 'theory' as the sudden impact in the US and UK academy of the 1980s of French post-structuralist thought and its affiliates (notably the work of Stanley Fish). She argues that theory poses its intellectual operations over the 'bodies of women', something she calls 'textual harassment'. Jacobus discusses Freud's reading of Jensen's novel *Gradiva* and Frankenstein, focusing on Victor's 'uncreation of a female monster, while drawing on a theoretical debate which similarly has as its focus the elimination of the woman' (119). Jacobus points out the ways in which male scientists bond over understanding women, or science figured as a woman, exploring the story of Watson's and Crick's discovery of the structure of DNA (128–30). Using René Girard's notion of how desire is always triangulated (the argument in *Violence and the Sacred* that desire is always mediated through an other), she indicates the parallel between the DNA story and the formation of Shelley's novel, supposedly in conversations between Byron and Percy Shelley (128).

[In certain forms of misogynistic figurative language t]he function of the object of desire is [. . .] to mediate relations between men; female desire is impossible except as a mimetic reflection of male desire. The same paradigm shapes Mary Shelley's *Frankenstein* – at once a drama of Promethean scientific enquiry and of oedipal rivalry, a myth of creation that encompasses both a quest for the origins of life and the bond of love and hate between creator and creation; 'Did I request thee, Maker, from my clay/To mould Me man?' (*Paradise Lost* 10.743–44) demands the novel's epigraph in Adam's words to God (**p. 129**). Significantly, what Mary Shelley recalls at the inception of her novel are conversations between Byron and Shelley in which she took almost no part. Perhaps we should see *Frankenstein* not simply as a reworking of Milton's creation myth in the light of Romantic ideology but as an implicit critique of that ideology for its exclusive emphasis on oedipal politics.[1] *Frankenstein* would thus become the novel that most accurately represents the condition of both men and women under the predominantly oedipal forms of Byronic and Shelleyan Romanticism. Read in this light, the monster's tragedy is his confinement to the destructive intensities of a one-to-one relationship with his maker, and his exclusion from other relations – whether familial or with a female counterpart. The most striking absence in

---

1 [Jacobus's note.] See also Mary Poovey, 'My Hideous Progeny: Mary Shelley and the Feminization of Romanticism', *PMLA*, 95 (May 1980), 332–47, for a reading of *Frankenstein* in the light of its relation to Romantic egotism.

Frankenstein, after all, is Eve's. Refusing to create a female monster, Frankenstein pays the price of losing his own bride. When the primary bond of paternity unites scientist and his creation so exclusively, women who get in the way must fall victim to the struggle. Indeed, if we look in this text for a female author, we find only a dismembered corpse whose successful animation would threaten the entire structure of the myth. It was more appropriate than he knew for James Whale to cast the same actress, Elsa Lanchester, as both the angelic Mary Shelley and the demonic female monster in his film sequel to the novel, *The Bride of Frankenstein* (1935).[2]

In Mary Shelley's own version, Frankenstein's creation of the monster is immediately followed by the vivid nightmare and yet more appalling awakening which had been her own waking dream and the starting point of her novel. Frankenstein's postpartum nightmare strikingly conflates the body of his long neglected fiancée and childhood sweetheart, Elizabeth, with that of his dead mother [. . .] (**p. 138**). The composite image, mingling eroticism and the horror of corruption, transforms Frankenstein's latently incestuous brother-sister relationship with Elizabeth into the forbidden relationship with the mother. The grave as well as the source of life, bringing birth, sex, and death together in one appalling place, the incestuously embraced mother figures Frankenstein's unnatural pursuit of nature's secrets in his charnel house labors. Like Irma's throat [in Freud's analysis 'The Dream of Irma's Injection'], the mother's shrouded form is unwrapped to reveal decay and deformity in the flesh itself.[3] It's not just that the exclusion of woman from creation symbolically 'kills' the mother, but that Frankenstein's forbidden researches give to the 'facts of life' the aspect of mortality. Elizabeth in turn comes to represent not the object of desire but its death. In a bizarre pun, the monster – 'the demonical corpse to which I had so miserably given life' – is compared to 'a mummy again endued with animation' (**p. 138**). Exchanging a woman for a monster, Frankenstein has perhaps preferred monstrosity to this vision of corrupt female flesh. From this moment on, the narrative must move inexorably towards the elimination of both female monster and Elizabeth herself on her wedding night. Only when the two females who double one another in the novel – the hideous travesty of a woman and her anodyne ideal – have cancelled each other out is the way clear for the scene of passionate mourning in which the monster hangs, loverlike, over Frankenstein's deathbed at the conclusion of Walton's narrative.

2   See **pp. 66–7** in the chapter on performance.
3   [Jacobus's note.] See Jacques Lacan, 'Le rêve de l'injection d'Irma', *Le séminaire de Jacques Lacan*, ed. Jacques-Alain Miller (Paris: Editions du Seuil, 1978), 2.193–204: 'Tout se mêle et s'associe dans cette image, de la bouche à l'organe sexuel féminin. . . . Il y a là une horrible découverte, celle de la chair qu'on ne voit jamais, le fond des choses, l'envers de la face, du visage, les secrétats par excellence, la chair dont tout sort, au plus profond même du mystère, la chair en tant qu'elle est souffrante, qu'elle est informe, que sa forme par soi-même est quelque chose qui provoque l'angoisse' (186). [Editor's translation: 'All is mingled and associated in this image, from the mouth to the female sex organ. . . . There is, there, a horrible discovery, that of the flesh which one may never see, the bottom of things, the other side of the front, the face, the 'secretories'/secretory glands [a pun] par excellence, the flesh from which all comes out, to the most mysterious depths, the flesh in so far as it is suffering, in so far as it is without form, that its form in itself is something which provokes anguish.']

In Mary Shelley's novel, intense identification with an oedipal conflict exists at the expense of identification with women. At best, women are the bearers of a traditional ideology of love, nurturance, and domesticity; at worst, passive victims. And yet, for the monster himself, women become a major problem (one that Frankenstein largely avoids by immersing himself in his scientific studies). A curious thread in the plot focuses not on the image of the hostile father (Frankenstein/ God) but on that of the dead mother who comes to symbolise to the monster his loveless state. Literally unmothered, he fantasises acceptance by a series of women but founders in imagined rebuffs and ends in violence. Though it is a little boy (Frankenstein's younger brother) who provokes the monster's first murder by his rejection, the child bears the fatal image of the mother – the same whose shroud had crawled with grave worms in Frankenstein's nightmare [. . .] (**p. 138**). Immediately after the monster has his vision of this lovely but inaccessible woman, shifting in imagination from looks of benignity to disgust, he finds the Frankensteins' servant girl Justine asleep in a nearby barn: 'She was young: not indeed so beautiful as her whose portrait I held; but of an agreeable aspect, and blooming in the loveliness of youth and health. Here, I thought, is one of those whose joy-imparting smiles are bestowed on all but me. And then I bent over her, and whispered, "Awake, fairest, thy lover is near – he who would give his life but to obtain one look of affection from thine eyes: my beloved, awake!"' (**p. 173**). But in this travesty of the lover's *aubade*, the beloved's awakening will shatter the dream, so she must sleep forever. On Justine's person the monster wreaks his revenge on all women, planting among her clothes the incriminating evidence of the mother's portrait as the supposed motive for her murder of the little boy. She is duly tried and executed, even confessing to the crime – for in the monstrous logic of the text, she is as guilty as the monster claims: 'The crime had its source in her: be hers the punishment!' (**p. 173**).

In this bizarre parody of the Fall, Eve is to blame for having been desired. By the same monstrous logic, if woman is the cause of the monster's crimes, then the only cure is a mate, 'one as deformed and horrible as myself' (**p. 155**). The monster's demand for a mate provides the basis for James Whale's sequel. In *The Bride of Frankenstein*, Frankenstein and his crazed collaborator Dr Praetorius undertake what neither Mary Shelley nor her hero could quite bring themselves to do – embody woman as fully monstrous. Shelley's Frankenstein gives several different reasons for dismembering the female corpse which he is on the point of animating: that she might prove even more malignant than her mate; that between them they might breed a race of monsters to prey on mankind; and that 'they might even hate each other' – he loathing her for a deformity worse than his because it 'came before his eyes in the female form', while 'she also might turn in disgust from him to the superior beauty of man' (**p. 158**). This last fear, taken up by James Whale's horror movie, is a demonic parody of the moment in Milton's creation myth when Eve prefers her own image to that of Adam – 'less fair,/Less winning soft, less amiably mild,/Than that smooth watery image' (*Paradise Lost* 5.478–80). As in Renaissance representations of the Fall, where the serpent's face is hers, Eve appeared in the guise of the narcissistic woman – that self-sufficient (the more desirable because self-sufficient) adorer of her own image. God tells her firmly that Adam is 'he/Whose image thou art' (*Paradise Lost* 4.471–72), but she knows better. If it is the function of *Paradise Lost* to cast out female self-love, it is the function of *The Bride of Frankenstein* to destroy its monstrous version of Eve's rejection of Adam. Behind this fantasy lies yet another, that of the female monster who might desire men instead of monsters. The threat to male sexuality lies not only in her hideous deformity, refusing to accommodate the image of his desire, but in the dangerous autonomy of her refusal to mate in the image in which she was made. It is as if Irma's throat had suddenly found its voice.

Bette London, 'Mary Shelley, *Frankenstein*, and the Spectacle of Masculinity', *PMLA* 108.2 (1993): 253–67

London discusses Henry Weekes's monument (in Christchurch Priory, Dorset), in which Percy Shelley is embraced by Mary, like Christ by his mother in Michelangelo's *Pietà* (253). London notes the 'unseemly' 'wranglings' for Percy's heart between Shelley and Leigh Hunt (254). The monument's emphasis on the male phallus echoes *Frankenstein*'s monumental, 'frieze'-like depictions of the lifeless male body (255). Explicit male sexuality, however, is repressed: masculinity is supposed to be invisible, as opposed to femininity, which is supposed to be marked, visible (255). James Rieger's edition of the novel, claims London, makes Shelley's biographical monstrosity visible: 'a figure marked . . . by unnatural bodily extension' (256). In Rieger, Shelley is 'always "Mary" to Percy's "Shelley"'. Percy's 'assistance' on the manuscript, by analogy, is seen as another invisible masculine support of a visible feminine and ambiguous 'excess and lack'. Shelley herself contributed to this analogy in her preface to the third edition (1831), which calls her original idea '"hideous"' for '"a young girl"' (257/p. 167). Against this London asserts that *Frankenstein* literalises the idea of writing as 'grafting', an explicitly monstrous production in which men and masculinity are implicated (258/p. 136). (This monstrosity might be understood via classical poetics, the indecorous splicing of one kind of rhetoric onto another is compared in Horace to the making of a monster out of different parts of different animals.)[1] Percy's biographer, Newman Ivey White, objected to Onslow Ford's monument to Percy (University College, Oxford), as feminising 'Shelleyana'. But, London asks, why should masculinity be the sole positive standard against which even Mellor judges *Frankenstein*, albeit in opposition to Rieger? London claims that the novel presents, and questions, the male body as fetishistic: simultaneously 'self-contained' and different. There is a trace of this in what she calls the novel's 'ornate' prose style, added by Percy and drawing attention to his hand; though one could also suggest that this is not technically ornate but certainly a 'high' classical rhetorical style. The representation of Frankenstein as

---

1   Horace, *On the Art of Poetry*, in *Aristotle Horace Longinus: Classical Literary Criticism*, tr. T.S. Dorsch (Harmondsworth: Penguin, 1965, 1984), 79.

a martyr makes him both 'spectator and spectacle': 'a body culturally coded as feminine . . . but subject to discursive appropriation in the masculine domain' (263). In conclusion, London asks whether this spectacle is posed for a female reader, thus inverting the normalised hierarchy of who gets to see and who gets to be seen (264–5).

Eve Kosofsky Sedgwick, *Between Men: English Literature and Homosocial Desire* (1985) New York: Columbia University Press, 91–2, 116–17

The impact of Sedgwick's work cannot be underestimated. In *Between Men* she establishes and explores the notion of homosociality: the ways in which social power structures are often hierarchically organised so as to cause men to bond (but homophobically, and at the expense of women). It is evident that *Frankenstein* is a classic example of such negative bonding, in that the pursuit of the creature by the creator is based on a kind of fatal attraction, a desire to destroy that which one wishes to love. See also Eve Kosofsky Sedgwick, *Epistemology of the Closet* (Berkeley and Los Angeles: University of California Press, 1990), 186–7.

[. . .] Particularly relevant for the Gothic novel is the perception Freud arrived at in the case of Dr Schreber: that paranoia is the psychosis that makes graphic the mechanisms of homophobia. In our argument about the Gothic in the following chapter, we will not take Freud's analysis on faith, but examine its grounds and workings closely in a single novel. To begin with, however, it is true that the limited group of fictions that represent the 'classic' early Gothic contains a large subgroup – *Caleb Williams, Frankenstein, Confessions of a Justified Sinner*, probably *Melmoth*, possibly *The Italian* – whose plots might be mapped almost point for point onto the case of Dr Schreber: most saliently, each is about one or more males who not only is persecuted by, but considers himself transparent to and often under the compulsion of, another male. If we follow Freud in hypothesising that such a sense of persecution represents the fearful, phantasmic rejection by the recasting of an original homosexual (or even merely homosocial) desire, then it would make sense to think of this group of novels as embodying strongly homophobic mechanisms. (This is not to say that either the authors [as distinct from the characters], or the overall cultural effects of the novels, were necessarily homophobic, but merely that through these novels a tradition of homophobic thematics was a force in the development of the Gothic.) [. . .]

The writing on the paranoid Gothic that is most closely relevant to this discussion has come [. . .] not from a gay male but from a feminist perspective. For instance, the history of feminist readings of *Frankenstein*, including particularly Mary Jacobus's sketch of a feminist Girardian reading (Jacobus 130–5), makes amply clear several ways in which the kind of analysis I am proposing would find resonances in that text [. . .]

Besides (but, as we have discussed, in relation to) their thematisation of homophobia, the paranoid Gothic novels [. . .] have in common a relation to the family like the one I have sketched in Hogg: in *Frankenstein* and in *Caleb Williams* as in the *Confessions*, the hero intrusively and in effect violently carves a *small, male, intimate* family for himself out of what had in each case originally been an untidy, nonnuclear group of cohabitants.

Genre, Literary Form and Literary History

Zachary Leader, 'Parenting Frankenstein', in *Revision and Romantic Authorship* (1996) Oxford and New York: Oxford University Press, 167–205

Shelley allowed Percy Shelley to revise *Frankenstein* while she was composing it. Leader points out that recent feminist scholarship that condemns this distorts contemporary pictures of Shelley as a powerful intellect in her own right (169). (Leader does not indicate that Percy also allowed Mary to do likewise to *his* writing; evidence that would have helped his argument.) The collaboration between Shelley and Percy reflects the ways in which *Frankenstein* undermines the Romantic image of the lone genius, creating art directly out of their head like Zeus giving birth to Athena (a common and sexist image of literary production). (Incidentally, the image of the lone genius may not itself have been as strong a part of Romantic culture as previously thought.)[1] Leader sees *Frankenstein* as a critique of Percy's idealism, his beliefs that the world could be improved, and in particular his notions about the power of the mind. According to Leader, Shelley's anxiety about authorship (she declared '"an immediate objection to the seeing of my name in print"', 186), was connected to her fraught relationship with Percy and her feelings about parenting. The collaboration of Shelley and Percy on *Frankenstein* anticipated her work with Byron (188–90). Leader carefully traces the ways in which Shelley authorised Percy's changes to the novel. He argues that what Anne Mellor calls Percy's '"Ciceronian"' (Latinate) alterations are in keeping with the fact that Frankenstein, Walton *and* the creature are 'at least in part figures of Percy Shelley himself' (197–9). For Leader, as for George Levine, the creature becomes *more* frightening when he speaks in dignified polysyllables (189). Likewise, Frankenstein's character gains in subtlety from Percy's revisions. Sorting out who wrote what – for instance how much Shelley would have agreed with Percy's support of republicanism – cannot be reduced to the simple promotion of one solidified view over another.

---

1   See Jeffrey Cox, *Poetry and Politics in the Cockney School* (Cambridge and New York: Cambridge University Press, 1998).

David Marshall, *The Surprising Effects of Sympathy: Marivaux, Diderot, Rousseau, and Mary Shelley* (1988) Chicago and London: University of Chicago Press, 178–227

> Marshall traces the influence of Rousseau on Mary Shelley. Specifically, her depiction of the creature is related to Rousseau's representation of myths of the origins of human culture (language and fire). Frankenstein's remorse recalls Rousseau's guilt in the *Confessions* and elsewhere. The creature's early life also resembles Rousseau's autobiographical writings. And in general the *idea* that the creature has an autobiography *at all* is a major connection. From this Marshall demonstrates that *Frankenstein* is 'a parable about the failure of sympathy' (synonymous here with pity, empathy and compassion), the feeling named by Rousseau as fundamental to ethics and politics, but also awkwardly straddling the divide between nature and culture.[1]

Michael Scrivener, '*Frankenstein*'s Ghost Story: The Last Jacobin Novel', *Genre* 19:3 (Fall, 1986): 299–318

> Scrivener sees in *Frankenstein* a response to the trauma of the 1790s, as perceived by Mary Shelley's immediate radical family circle. The novel thematises what Scrivener calls 'errant utilitarianism', since utilitarianism was the dominant social theory of the 1790s Enlightenment radicals. The creature's radical reading list, for example, emphasises both empiricism and 'spontaneous benevolence' (315), making the creature stand for the progressive 'intelligentsia'.

[...] Victor's father, Alphonse Frankenstein, marries the daughter of his best friend Beaufort, who dies in poverty and despair. Beaufort had 'a proud and unbending disposition, and could not bear to live in poverty and oblivion in the same country where he had formerly been distinguished for his rank and magnificence'. **John Thelwall** published a novel in 1801 entitled *The Daughter of Adoption*, using a pseudonym, John Beaufort. Thelwall, like Godwin, was one of the principal English Jacobins who enjoyed a brief moment of fame in the '90s until the political repression and cultural reaction forced him to retreat from active political life. Godwin too employed a pseudonym, Edward Baldwin, to publish his juvenile library for the same reason Thelwall did: he had to make his living by writing and his 'name' was too notorious for the book-buying public. I draw out the Beaufort allusion to make several points. For Godwin, Thelwall, and their circle the 1790s was *traumatic*. As intellectuals who lived by their writing, the actual political repression was not perhaps as profoundly disturbing

---

1 For further discussion, see Jacques Derrida, *Of Grammatology*, tr. Gayatri Chakravorty Spivak (Baltimore and London: Johns Hopkins University Press, 1987), 171–92.

as the cultural reaction which buried them in abuse by at least 1802, if not earlier. That this terrible sense of trauma was communicated to the author of *Frankenstein* as she was growing up can be taken for granted without resorting to deeply psychological speculation. By the time her novel was published, the phrase 'novels of the Godwin school' signified not the Jacobin novel of the '90s but a Romantic novel which probed the psychological complexities of a deeply disturbed protagonist, such as Godwin created in *Fleetwood* (1805) and *Mandeville* (1817). [. . .]

Although 'utilitarianism' primarily signifies to us the philosophy of Bentham and Mill, 'utility' was of course a key concept for the Enlightenment intellectuals and radicals of the '90s and still possessed powerful associations for Shelley's generation. Utility signified what was best for humanity's interests. Quite deservingly the word has been subjected to all kinds of skeptical analysis, but if one situates it in the context where it was most meaningful, as the antithesis to 'custom', 'prejudice', 'egoism', 'privilege', 'luxury', 'superstition', 'corruption', and so on, one sees that it was the inevitable concept by which aristocratic, monarchical and church-dominated culture would be opposed. Although the second generation of English intellectuals was critical of the '90s' concept of utility as defined by Godwin, Paine, Thelwall and their circle, the second generation ([William] Hazlitt, Hunt, the Shelleys, Byron, [John] Keats, [Thomas Love] Peacock, et alia) accepted the philosophical authority of utility in this sense: an intellectual's duty was to write and speak as someone opposing established power and promoting the interests of humanity and not of a sect, party or even nation. Defining what those interests were was more problematic for the second generation than for the earlier, but the younger group accepted utilitarian criteria.

The narrative of the errant utilitarian was perhaps first composed by Godwin himself in the most famous Jacobin novel, *Caleb Williams*, when he revised the original ending. The first ending had Caleb in prison slowly going mad, thus maintaining to the end his status as a victim of aristocratic prejudice. The new ending has the long suffering victim become consumed by guilt for having wreaked his revenge on his oppressor Falkland. Although the new ending does not soften the relentless critique of injustice, it signals a new direction for reformist narratives. [. . .] The defensive tone of the errant utilitarian narrative is obvious, and the reasons for the defensiveness are equally obvious (the political repression, the cultural reaction, the failure of the French Revolution to live up to its advocates' highest ideals, and so on). Nevertheless, to mistake the narrative of the errant utilitarian with apostate testaments or anti-Jacobin propaganda is to do extraordinary violence to the political culture in its historical context. In short, 'utility' survived the '90s but only in the form of the utility whose demonic deviations from the true interests of humanity were exorcised. [. . .]

Since [*Frankenstein*] seems to fit so neatly into the category of Jacobin novel, why then has it so rarely been interpreted as such? As I mentioned earlier, the novel disguises its generic identity in many ways. First, there is the Preface, which except for one paragraph (the third) would be unexceptional in a Jacobin novel. The author, according to the Preface, is 'by no means indifferent' to the novel's 'moral tendencies' (the double negative here is peculiarly understated for a didactic novel). The moral concern is 'limited' to avoiding popular novels' 'enervating effects' and exhibiting 'the amiableness of domestic affection, and the excellence of universal virtue'. A Jacobin novelist would not 'limit' the novel's moral province, even if the domain were as large as Shelley has created it. Then there is the key sentence, the first part of which merely points out that the protagonist's 'opinions' cannot be equated always with the author's, but the second part would never appear in a Jacobin novel: 'nor is any inference justly to be drawn from the following pages as prejudicing any philosophical doctrine of whatever kind' (**p. 131**). Although one can read this disclaimer as ironic (that is, orthodox and established ideas are mere prejudice and cannot qualify as philosophical), such casuistry is hardly the most obvious way to interpret this statement, which on the surface seems to signal the novel as something other than a didactic narrative. [. . .]

The monster [. . .] is not simply a rebellious social victim or a Gothic villain spawned by a reforming intelligentsia; he is also a representation of that intelligentsia, particularly the innovating intellectual who is not permitted to employ his educated powers to reform society. After he understands Volney's radical social critique, he realises that without aristocratic blood or wealth, even if he were not ' "hideously deformed and loathesome" ', his *best* prospects would have been ' "as a vagabond and a slave, doomed to waste [my] powers for the profit of the chosen few" ' (**p. 149**). The monster himself challenges established social views more fundamentally than either Walton or Frankenstein, and he initially at least employs the methods most esteemed by reformist fiction to become a useful reformer of society: benevolent deeds and 'reason'. In the monster's failure to remove the prejudice against himself, he reproduces the failure of the English Jacobins. To the reading public, the Jacobin intellectuals were monsters permitted back into the culture only if they disguised themselves as something else: Thelwall became an expert in 'elocution' and speech therapy (an interesting career change for a radical orator), while Godwin produced Romantic novels and educational books, but withheld from publication his most heretical writings on religion. By the novel's end the monster uses his 'powers' to forgive his tormentors, to understand the Necessitarian process by which he became a criminal, and condemn himself ultimately on utilitarian grounds, so that he affirms the doctrine which gave him birth, which betrayed him, which he tried to actualise, and by whose logic he must destroy himself. Although Percy Shelley, relying on the generic logic of Jacobin fiction, read the monster's monstrosity as a creation by social prejudice, another possibility suggests itself, not as a better interpretation, but as a supplement: the monster was so monstrous, so deserving of extinction, precisely because he was such a pure embodiment of utilitarian doctrine. Whether the reader judges established opinion (the reviewers) or the New Philosophy (Percy Shelley) as the most morally desirable hardly matters in this instance because in either case the gap between the values affirmed by the monster and those governing society is so huge, so monstrous, so disproportionate, that no happy compromise is possible. Violence is inevitable, one way or another.

Language and Psyche

Peter Brooks, 'Godlike Science/Unhallowed Arts: Language and Monstrosity in *Frankenstein*', New Literary History 9.3 (Spring, 1978): 591–605

Brooks begins by noting the eloquence of the creature. In language, the creature can be recognised and can achieve a sort of beauty, in contrast to the 'specular relationship' between him and Victor (593), which only renders him visibly ugly. Brooks here draws on Lacan's theory of the Imaginary and the Symbolic to illustrate this. In brief, the Symbolic Order is the linguistic network in which we, as subjects, find our sense of identity; the Imaginary is that fantasy of identity itself. In noticing that there are some words that do not correspond to visual objects, the creature discovers the radical arbitrariness, the 'immotivation', of language, and consequently 'intuitively grasps that it will be of importance to him because by its very nature it implies the "chain of existence and events" within which he seeks a place, defines the interdependency of senders and receivers of messages in that chain, and provides the possibility of emotional effect independent of any designation' (594). For Brooks, 'Creation of the monsteress . . . would be a *substitute* for inclusion of the Monster within the human chain'; Frankenstein cannot do this as it would blow his cover, reveal his own monstrous rejecting desire for what it is (597). In a perverse symmetry, as Victor refuses to help the creature to such a substitution, the creature attacks substitutes for Victor (Clerval and Elizabeth), mimicking Frankenstein's own cruelty (598). Brooks moves to a study of the ambiguity of nature in *Frankenstein* (benign and malignant). The novel is 'a counterexample to such pedagogical utopias as Rousseau's *Emile*', presenting a naturally good creature corrupted by social maltreatment (600–1). Brooks remarks: 'It is a nature that eludes any optimistic Romanticism, finally most to resemble Freud's "uncanny": the Monster perfectly illustrates the *Unheimliche*, a monstrous potentiality so close to us – so close to home – that we have repressed its possibility and assigned an *un* as the mark of censorship on what is indeed to *heimisch* for comfort' (602). This monsterism is finally associated with *Frankenstein*'s textuality, addressed to Walton's sister Mrs Saville, a 'faceless addressee' who has 'no more existence, in the novel, than a postal address . . . a kind of lack of being, which means that what we are left with is a text, a narrative tissue that never wholly conceals its lack of ultimate reference' (604).

Bernard Duyfhuizen, 'Periphrastic Naming in Mary Shelley's *Frankenstein*', Studies in the Novel 27.4 (1995): 477–92.

Duyfhuizen investigates the obvious confusion, in common speech, between Frankenstein and his creature. When Shelley attended the first stage adaptation of *Frankenstein*, she was impressed that the creature was referred to as '——', a habit repeated later in plays and movies (not naming either the creature or the actor, 479; see **p. 51** in the chapter on performance). The creature's lack of a proper name is a feature of his lack of a place in the social symbolic order. This is an idea derived from the psychoanalyst Jacques Lacan. Duyfhuizen goes on to discuss the many and varied uses of the word 'wretch' in the novel, a periphrasis (or nickname) often applied to the creature, but also to the ways in which Frankenstein responds to his creation. 'Wretch' serves to identify the creature with Frankenstein, despite the latter's conscious wishes, as Frankenstein finds *himself* experiencing wretchedness. So also does 'wretch' reach out to Wollstonecraft's *A Vindication of the Rights of Woman*, which Shelley reread while composing *Frankenstein*. In Wollstonecraft, women are described as being made 'wretched' by their education. In Renaissance English, 'wretch' could also be a term of endearment applied to a lover. How might this play on words complicate the creature's relationship with his creator?

Barbara Johnson, 'My Monster/My Self', in *A World of Difference* (1987) Baltimore and London: Johns Hopkins University Press, 144–54

In a feminist deconstructive essay, Johnson examines the tendency of readings of *Frankenstein* to account for 'the monstrosity of autobiography'. In what does this monstrosity consist? *Frankenstein*, she argues, stages the ambiguous idea of creating 'a being like oneself', whose exemplar is the autobiographical text. Johnson indicates the uncanny parallel between biological life and textuality.

[. . .] The notion that *Frankenstein* can somehow be read as the autobiography of a woman would certainly appear at first sight to be ludicrous. The novel, indeed, presents not one but three autobiographies of men. Robert Walton, an arctic explorer on his way to the North Pole, writes home to his sister of his encounter with Victor Frankenstein, who tells Walton the story of his painstaking creation and unexplained abandonment of a nameless monster who suffers excruciating and fiendish loneliness, and who tells Frankenstein *his* life story in the middle pages of the book. The three male autobiographies motivate themselves as follows:

> [Walton, to his sister:] 'You will rejoice to hear that no disaster has accompanied the commencement of an enterprise which you have regarded with such evil forebodings. I arrived here yesterday, and my first task is to assure my dear sister of my welfare.'[1]

1   Mary Shelley, *Frankenstein; or, The Modern Prometheus* (New York: Signet, 1965), 15.

[Frankenstein, with his hands covering his face, to Walton, who has been speaking of his scientific ambition:] 'Unhappy man! Do you share my madness? Have you drunk also of the intoxicating draught? Hear me; let me reveal my tale, and you will dash the cup from your lips!' (26)

[Monster, to Frankenstein:] 'I entreat you to hear me before you give vent to your hatred on my devoted head.' [Frankenstein:] 'Begone! I will not hear you. There can be no community between you and me.' [Monster places his hands before Frankenstein's eyes:] 'Thus I take from thee a sight which you abhor. Still thou canst listen to me and grant me thy compassion. . . . God, in pity, made man beautiful and alluring, after his own image; but my form is a filthy type of yours, more horrid even from the very resemblance.' (95, 96, 97, 125)

All three autobiographies here are clearly attempts at persuasion rather than simple accounts of facts. They all depend on a presupposition of resemblance between teller and addressee: Walton assures his sister that he has not really left the path she would wish for him, that he still resembles *her*. Frankenstein recognises in Walton an image of himself and rejects in the monster a resemblance he does not wish to acknowledge. The teller is in each case speaking into a mirror of his own transgression. The tale is designed to reinforce the resemblance between teller and listener so that somehow transgression can be eliminated. Yet the desire for resemblance, the desire to create a being like oneself – which is the auto-biographical desire par excellence – is also the central transgression in Mary Shelley's novel. What is at stake in Frankenstein's workshop of filthy creation is precisely the possibility of shaping a life in one's own image: Frankenstein's monster can thus be seen as a figure for autobiography as such. Victor Frankenstein, then, has twice obeyed the impulse to construct an image of himself: on the first occasion he creates a monster, and on the second he tries to explain to Walton the causes and consequences of the first. *Frankenstein* can be read as the story of autobiography as the attempt to neutralise the monstrosity of autobiography. Simultaneously a revelation and a cover-up, autobiography would appear to constitute itself as in some way a repression of autobiography. [. . .]

[I]t is not merely in its depiction of the ambivalence of motherhood that Mary Shelley's novel can be read as autobiographical. In the introductory note added in 1831, she writes:

The publishers of the standard novels, in selecting *Frankenstein* for one of their series, expressed a wish that I should furnish them with some account of the origin of the story. I am the more willing to comply because I shall thus give a general answer to the question so very frequently asked me – how I, then a young girl, came to think of and to *dilate* upon so very hideous an idea. (vii/**p. 167**; emphasis mine)[2]

---

2   For a detailed study of the idea of 'dilation' as it pertains to Shelley's figuring of obstetrics in the novel, see the discussion of the essay by Alan Bewell in Further Reading.

As this passage makes clear, readers of Mary Shelley's novel had frequently expressed the feeling that a young girl's fascination with the idea of monstrousness was somehow monstrous in itself. When Mary ends her introduction to the reedition of her novel with the words, 'And now, once again, I bid my hideous progeny go forth and prosper', the reader begins to suspect that there may perhaps be meaningful parallels between Victor's creation of his monster and Mary's creation of her book.

Such parallels are indeed unexpectedly pervasive. The impulse to write the book and the desire to search for the secret of animation both arise under the same seemingly trivial circumstances: the necessity of finding something to read on a rainy day. During inclement weather on a family vacation, Victor Frankenstein happens upon the writings of Cornelius Agrippa and is immediately fired with the longing to penetrate the secrets of life and death. Similarly, it was during a wet, ungenial summer in Switzerland that Mary, Shelley, Byron, and several others picked up a volume of ghost stories and decided to write a collection of spine-tingling tales of their own. Moreover, Mary's discovery of the subject she would write about is described in almost exactly the same words as Frankenstein's discovery of the principle of life: 'Swift as light and as cheering was the idea that broke in upon me' (xi/**p. 171**), writes Mary in her introduction, while Frankenstein says: 'From the midst of this darkness a sudden light broke in upon me' (51). In both cases the sudden flash of inspiration must be supported by the meticulous gathering of heterogeneous, ready-made materials: Frankenstein collects bones and organs; Mary records overheard discussions of scientific questions that lead her to the sudden vision of monstrous creation. 'Invention', she writes of the process of writing, but her words apply equally well to Frankenstein's labors, 'Invention . . . does not consist in creating out of the void, but out of chaos; the materials must, in the first place, be afforded: it can give form to dark, shapeless substances but cannot bring into being the substance itself' (x/**p. 169**). Perhaps the most revealing indication of Mary's identification of Frankenstein's activity with her own is to be found in her use of the word 'artist' on two different occasions to qualify the 'pale student of unhallowed arts': 'His success would terrify the artist' (xi/**p. 170**), she writes of the catastrophic moment of creation, while Frankenstein confesses to Walton: 'I appeared rather like one doomed by slavery to toil in the mines, or any other unwholesome trade than an artist occupied by his favorite employment' (55). [. . .]

But what can Victor Frankenstein's workshop of filthy creation teach us about the specificity of *female* authorship? At first sight, it would seem that *Frankenstein* is much more striking for its avoidance of the question of femininity than for its insight into it. All the interesting, complex characters in the book are male, and their deepest attachments are to other males. The females, on the other hand, are beautiful, gentle, selfless, boring nurturers and victims who never experience inner conflict or true desire. Monstrousness is so incompatible with femininity that Frankenstein cannot even complete the female companion that his creature so eagerly awaits.

Steven Vine, 'Filthy Types: *Frankenstein*, Figuration, Femininity',
Critical Survey 8.3 (1996): 246–58

Vine analyses the ways in which characters in *Frankenstein* find themselves via some other figure (246–7). The act of reading (a tale told by Frankenstein to Walton or the creature looking at books) is itself an example of this, and thus the reader is implicated in this theme (247–8). What is feared in these encounters is the possibility of misrepresentation or 'disfiguration' (248), a word that conveniently stands both for bodily and linguistic referents. Vine observes that 'the monster . . . wishes to "forget" his disfiguration by acquiring a continuous history' (250). He cites Brooks's argument about the creature's desire to be given a place from which to speak. For Vine, the 'monster' (Latin: *monstrare*, to display, de-monstrate) is putting on display the rhetorical trope of prosopopoeia, 'that gives a face to facelessness' (252). Victor's narcissism is expressed as a desire to attract greater and greater approval for his creation; this is reflected in the creature's desire to be approved of, if not by humans then by a mate (253). Vine declares that 'the monster's longing for a metaphor of himself, his longing for a likeness, is coterminous with a desire for woman'; thus, 'In an uncanny doubling, Frankenstein and the monster share the same wish: a wish *for the same*, for self-reflection and self-mirroring – and for woman to ground that mirroring. In this sense, the monster's demand for figuration repeats Frankenstein's assimilation of femininity to patriarchal narcissism' (254).

Race, Colonialism and Orientalism

Elizabeth A. Bohls, 'Standards of Taste, Discourses of "Race", and the Aesthetic Education of a Monster: Critique of Empire in *Frankenstein*', *Eighteenth-Century Life* 18.3 (1994): 23–36.

Bohls examines the extent to which *Frankenstein*, as a text of English literature, is caught up in imperialism, part of a cultural 'portfolio' (23) – her entrepreneurial metaphor is apt, as English literature, as a subject of study at universities, was originally developed to serve the interests of the new entrepreneurial class in the eighteenth century. Shelley read widely in literature pertaining to colonialism while writing *Frankenstein*: *Gulliver's Travels*, Thomas Pennant's *View of Hindoostan* and Bryan Edwards's *History of the West Indies* among others (25).[1] But it is in the intersection of colonialism and aesthetics (for example in Burke), that Bohls discovers the most fruitful way of rereading *Frankenstein*. The ugliest

---

1   See Shelley, *Journals*, 2.631–84.

bodies, according to Burke, are the most suitable for colonial domination (30–1). For Burke, ugliness is empirically encoded in the bodies of non-white races (not simply in the eye of the beholder). When Gulliver falls for the Houyhnhnms, he finds himself just as ugly as a Yahoo when he beholds himself in a lake, just as Frankenstein's creature sees himself as intrinsically ugly, though no one has taught him a white European aesthetic standard of physical beauty (32–3).[2] But the creature's 'riveting speech', so strong and eloquent, casts doubt on this standard (34).

H.L. Malchow, 'Frankenstein's Monster and Images of Race in Nineteenth-Century Britain', *Past and Present* 139 (1993): 90–130

Malchow writes: 'Shelley's portrayal of her monster drew upon contemporary attitudes towards non-whites, in particular on fears and hopes of the abolition of slavery in the West Indies, as well as on middle-class apprehension of a Luddite proletariat or Mary Shelley's "birthing trauma"' (91–2). In the Napoleonic era, as 'fantastic' literature about other parts of the world 'was exchanged for a natural science of plants, animals and foreign peoples, there was an inevitable compulsion to rank not only creatures but also types of people' (93). Malchow charts the growth in the Romantic period of 'pseudo-scientific racism' towards its wider acceptance in the Victorian period. Even Godwin, champion of universal reason, affirmed 'common theories about Negro "differences" which one can find in the pro-slavery literature, as well as among the armchair theorists generally' (95). Malchow adds: 'The French wars, the abortive rebellion in Ireland, the spread of the ideals of the French Revolution to Haiti, and armed resistance to British suzerainty in India served to heighten xenophobia and validate ethnic prejudice as patriotic anti-Jacobinism' (96). Frankenstein's creature is coloured like a mummy – 'ordinarily dark brown or black' (103). While admitting that elsewhere his skin is described as yellow, Malchow asserts that the monster has been 'constructed out of a cultural tradition of the threatening "Other" – whether troll or giant, gypsy or Negro – from the dark inner recesses of xenophobic fear and loathing' (103). Malchow notes, observing the creature's diet, that 'This draws on a long European tradition which imagined wild men or natural men of the woods as (like Frankenstein's monster) colossal vegetarians, images which the eighteenth-century naturalists helped to merge with that of more primitive races of men abroad far down the ladder of racial hierarchy' (105).

With this naturalising language in mind, we should assess 'How much

---

2   See Timothy Morton, *Shelley and the Revolution in Taste: The Body and the Natural World* (Cambridge and New York: Cambridge University Press, 1994), chapter 4.

the monster's excitable character is the result of his unique physiology, and how much of his environment, is an ambiguity which exactly parallels the central conundrum of the anti-slavery debate' (105). Malchow notes the ambiguity with which Africans were represented in the novel's era as either vegetarians or as cannibals. This may account for Victor's depiction of the monster as a vampire (110), and Victor himself may be read as the guilty slave master (114–15). The essay concludes with an analysis of the novel in performance. Malchow notes the uses of the Frankenstein myth in public discourses on race, such as parliamentary debate (122). He concludes that 'The Indian Mutiny, the Jamaican rebellions of 1831 and 1865, the countless little wars fought by Victoria's armies against Maori, Ashanti, Zulus or Canadian Métis all contributed to the emotional appeal of a text which presented the Other as a rebellious and ungrateful child that owed its very existence to a white male patron' (127). Turning to literature, Malchow notes derivatives of the creature in Heathcliff (*Wuthering Heights*), the West Indian madwoman in *Jane Eyre*, and characters in William Harrison Ainsworth's *Rookwood* (1824) and H. Rider Haggard's *King Solomon's Mines* (1885) (129).

[. . .] It was not merely a case of blacks being in the public eye in Britain from time to time. Mary Godwin had certainly also been exposed at home, through both her father's writings and house guests, to the hotly contested issue of the abolition of slavery. It is reasonable to assume that this provided one source of images and buried themes in *Frankenstein*. William Godwin had covered the debates on the slave trade for the Whiggish *New Annual Register* in the 1780s and 1790s. In April 1791 he was actually present in the gallery of the Commons when Wilberforce's motion was defeated.[1] Although he accepted in *Political Justice* that there were racial differences in character as well as body, his sentiments nevertheless lay with the abolitionists, though not with Wilberforce's Tory evangelicalism. Godwin denied that differences of race or gender had any significant effect on an individual's ability to reason or to be educated. In his novel *St Leon* (1799) a prison turnkey is represented as a Negro with 'sound understanding and an excellent heart' (207). The political struggle for abolition and the potential of the freed Negro for improvement would have been common subjects of conversation in the home in which Mary Godwin was educated. Dr James Bell, an admirer of Godwin, was introduced to him there in 1799, for example. Bell was determined to go out to Jamaica 'to lighten the woes and diminish the horrors of slavery'. He died in the island shortly after arrival (234).

The prominence of the anti-slavery issue in late eighteenth-century European discourse had a direct impact on the characteristic depiction of the negro in Western art. The visual representation of the black shifted from that of an exotic, often in fancy dress, to the naked or semi-clothed victim, an object of

---

1   Peter Marshall, *Surprising Effects*, 76, 81.

pity.[2] While the intention of the evangelical abolitionists may have been to portray the black slave as 'a man and a brother', the actual effect of their propaganda – vividly rendered on canvas, medallions and chinaware, in cheap prints and ballad sheets, on mementoes of all kinds – was to reiterate an image of the Other, a special kind of childlike, suffering and degraded being, rarely heroic, that became part of the common coinage of popular culture. [. . .] Moreover abolitionist propaganda inevitably drew attention to that of the pro-slavery lobby. The apologists of Negro slavery manipulated scientific argument and injected into English popular culture, as well as into European political and intellectual discourse, the paranoid fears, sexual fantasies and, indeed, the whole range of racist stereotypes already current in Jamaican planter society. This served to create misgivings and ambiguities about race which were not unlike the challenge to Painite liberalism posed by the émigré descriptions of Jacobin ferocity in Paris. [. . .]

There is, in fact, proof that Mary Shelley did have recourse, both before and during the writing of *Frankenstein*, to a reservoir of information about the black man in Africa and the West Indies. Turning to the journal which she kept, and in which she meticulously recorded books she and Percy Shelley read, we find some interesting titles. In 1814 they both read the first two large volumes of Mungo Park's relation of the interior of western Africa, an important milestone in European 'discovery' of the continent. They read the third volume, containing the narrative of Park's death, in 1816, the year Mary began to write *Frankenstein*.[3] In the winter of 1814–15 they also read a history of the British West Indies by the wealthy merchant-planter, Bryan Edwards. Edwards was a relatively liberal Jamaican, though pro-slavery. His work, which narrated the history of the islands up to the late eighteenth century, dwelt upon differences of colour and caste and the supposed racial characteristics of West Indian slaves from different parts of Africa, as well as the horrors of slave rebellions. Mary Shelley appears to have found the work sufficiently absorbing to spend 'all evening' and 'all day' engrossed in it (34). Finally, although her journal suggests that the Shelleys finished reading John Davis's record of his travels through the American South too late (in the summer of 1817, while Murray was considering the *Frankenstein* manuscript) for it to have played a role in the construction of her novel, the themes it treats – musings about the black as natural, Rousseauian man, and the struggle of owners to retrieve fugitive slaves – indicate their continuing interest in the subject of slavery and the Negro race at just the time the novel was being written: 'Exposed to such wanton cruelty the negroes frequently run away; they flee into the woods, where they are wet with the rains of heaven, and embrace the rock for want of shelter.'[4] It remains to be seen to what extent the evidence

2 Hugh Honour, *The Image of the Black in Western Art* (Cambridge, MA: Harvard University Press, 1989), IV.1.50–7, 62–6.
3 Shelley, *Journals*, 32, 71.
4 [Malchow's note.] John Davis, *Travels of Four Years and a Half in the United States of America; During 1798, 1799, 1800, 1801 and 1802* (London: T. Ostell and T. Hurst and Bristol: R. Edwards, 1803), 92. It may also be worth mentioning that, though an apparently obscure and distant 'source', *The Arabian Nights' Entertainments* was a childhood reading which the Shelleys

of language and themes in the novel indicates a reflection at some level of the contemporary race debate in the creation and fate of Mary Shelley's monster. [. . .]

On the Victorian stage the Frankenstein story was inevitably altered to fit the melodramatic expectations of audiences of the time. On the one hand, demonic and alchemical elements were emphasised; on the other, songs and dancing were interpolated in some versions, and a comic element was occasionally introduced to lighten the story. Catastrophic storms, the burning of the cottage, and avalanches provided spectacle, while the subtler tones of the novel were sacrificed to a simplified drama of innocence versus demonic terror. Mary Shelley's ambiguities disappeared. Cooke's monster, effectively mimed, lost its articulateness and became the mute beast, tameable only by music. As Steven Forry has recently observed, the monster was 'Calibanised', though this is surely only an extension of the densely present, if buried, associations already linking Mary Shelley's monster to the Caliban-like slave.[5] By turning the creature into even more of a caricature, the Victorian stage enhanced its utility as stereotype, as image of the dark 'Other'. It may be significant, for instance, that both the popularity of a variety of burlesques on the Frankenstein story (still being played as late as the 1880s), as well as the introduction of comic song into even the more serious versions, coincides with the emergence of 'Nigger Minstrels' as an enduring entertainment in London music-halls and theatres. In any event the image of the creature swaying to the charms of music at least suggests the caricature of the 'singin' and dancin'' Old South slave. [. . .]

One would like to know more about the performances of the various stage adaptations and whether the available racial and simian associations of the creature were introduced on the stage, as they were in parliamentary debate and magazine caricature. Cooke probably darkened his skin for his performance of the satanic Samiel in an 1824 version of Die Freischütz to suggest the darkness of evil. Similarly he, like others after him, used blue greasepaint in his portrayal of the monster (Forry, 4), not with the intention of creating a racial villain, but to suggest both the lividity of a corpse and a sinister Otherness. A blue-skinned monster would inevitably, however, have suggested on the one hand an Othello, on the other a 'nigger minstrel' – Negro tragedy and Negro farce. [. . .]

Timothy Morton, *Shelley and the Revolution in Taste: the Body and the Natural World* (1994; repr. 1998) Cambridge: Cambridge University Press, 47–51

This extract explores the contemporary vegetarian contexts in which *Frankenstein* can be situated. Vegetarianism had become a viable diet for surprisingly

continued to dip into when abroad. Black slaves feature in many of the stories, sometimes with a relevant twist, as in that in which 'an ugly, tall, black slave' causes a young man to murder his wife: Shelley, *Journals*, 1.47. [. . .]

5   Steven Earl Forry, *Hideous Progenies: Dramatizations of* Frankenstein *from the 19th Century to the Present* (Philadelphia: Pennsylvania University Press, 1990), 22.

large numbers of people by the Romantic period. The justificatory language associated with it had strong connections to and resonances with women's rights, antislavery and animal rights.

[. . .] The old Prometheus gave humans language and fire for cooking. Percy Bysshe Shelley interpreted the myth as the story of the origin of flesh-eating – flesh has to be cooked to be palatable.[1] Cooking shares with language the myth of acculturation, insofar as cooking turns raw nature into culture.[2] Jonathan Parry has shown how food and eating provided the Brahmans with ways of 'conceptualising . . . the . . . circulation and transformation which maintain the cosmic and social orders', and *Frankenstein* also employs food in this way, describing the negotiation of the creature's body with the social and natural world.[3]

Frankenstein creates a monster who finds out about how good it is to cook flesh. His cooked offals supplement his diet of nuts, roots and acorns. His body is made from dismembered corpses: he shares something with the offal he eats, at any rate. But he commenced his life eating berries and drinking water (**p. 144**). Diet becomes a way of expressing the difference between natural instincts and environmental influences (nature and nurture). The creature is canny about the discourses of consumption: the dead hare which he leaves for Frankenstein to sustain him on the chase (book 3) is a rather sick deconstruction of charity: the creature writes '"eat, and be refreshed"' on the bark of a tree (**p. 162**).

The questions and anxieties which preoccupy the narrative are based around notions of organicity and faciality: the poor creature looks inhuman with his dull eyes (**p. 137**). To what extent (echoing Rousseau) can society figure the human, or will it always disfigure in its botched attempt at representation? The creature has a face, but in Frankenstein's eyes it is inhuman. The face is inhuman; the gaze is what may impart a 'subjectivity or humanity'. Signs are referred back to the passion of the face: thus, whatever the creature says, he is ruined; a particularly painful figure in a discourse that must be read rather than seen (introducing far more pathos than the numerous films of the novel. For Frankenstein, the creature deviates from a norm of faciality which is shared by the creature himself. The pathos of the creature's Eve-like self-recognition amidst nature (it is the first of the naturalised signs which he recognises spontaneously), stems from the universality of the 'humane' facial code. There is nowhere to hide:

1   Percy Shelley, *A Vindication of Natural Diet*, in *The Complete Works*, ed. R. Ingpen and W.E. Peck, 10 vols (London and New York: Ernest Benn, 1926–30), 6.6.
2   Claude Lévi-Strauss, *The Raw and the Cooked: Introduction to a Science of Mythology: 1*, tr. John and Doreen Weightman (New York and Evanston: Harper and Row, 1969 (French, 1964)), 336, 338.
3   Jonathan Parry, 'Death and Digestion: the Symbolism of Food and Eating in North Indian Mortuary Rites', *Man* 20.4 (December 1985), 612–30 (612).
4   See Deleuze and Guattari, *A Thousand Plateaus: Capitalism and Schizophrenia*, tr. Brian Massumi (Minneapolis: University of Minnesota Press, 1987), 170–1.

racism has never operated by exclusion ... Racism operates by the determination of degrees of deviance in relation to the White-Man face, which endeavours to integrate nonconformity traits into increasingly eccentric and backward waves ... there is no exterior ... There are only people who should be like us and whose crime it is not to be.[5]

In the canon of texts on the natural diet, imitation and emulation can be violent, as well as dissimulation and disguise (cookery and language, but also the face). In Ovid's *Metamorphoses* 15, Pythagoras (a founder of European vegetarian discourse) explains how human emulation of the lion caused the first carnivorous violence, through the Girardian 'mimetic violence' of the transferential gaze.[6] The attempt to naturalise is also an attempt to distinguish once and for all between simulation and dissimulation, between the despotic signifier and a natural axiom. Additionally, the politics of sympathy is 'in your face'. The creature's search for sympathetic kindness drives his narrative forward.

Faciality is a predominant figure in the rhetoric which the Shelleys associated with diet. Charity becomes institutionalised in gestures like Laon's self-mutilation in canto 5 of Percy Shelley's *Laon and Cythna*, where the whole body turns facial, something which gazes and which attracts the gaze, micrological acts of kindness that instantiate the 'natural' politics of *laissez-faire*. Percy Shelley was concerned with the face as power-mask: Ozymandias, the branded face of Leighton in *Charles I*, the face of the butcher in *Queen Mab* 8, into which the lamb gazes.

The creature's cooking lessons are part of his education in an environment where he is a Lockean blank sheet: compare the 'Peter the Wild Boy' pamphlets of 1726 (including Defoe's *Mere Nature Delineated*), or the thoughts of the linguistic researcher Lord Monboddo when he discovered Peter as a wild old man (Burnet). His education generally consists of learning to articulate in a proper way: for like Adam's Eden, the world is already there to be distinguished as classified according to the English language and western natural history (**p. 145**). However, this classification is skilfully blended into the natural sensations of the body: the creature learns to distinguish between the blackbird and the sparrow because of the felt difference between 'sweet' and 'harsh' notes (99).[7] The creature is practising the collection of empirical data and natural-historical analysis. Eighteenth-century notions of 'nature' and 'culture' turn their faces towards him spontaneously.

This figuration is part of the Shelleys' attempt to humanise radical notions of science and progress, like Percy's *A Vindication [of Natural Diet]*. It is possible to find a contradiction in *Frankenstein* between 'art' and 'science'. But such a reading cannot show how the creature is assembled potentially to be more humane than its maker, and how this Utopian 'technohumanism' is denied by the sublime

5   Ibid., 178.
6   See Jerrold Hogle, *Shelley's Process: Radical Transference and the Development of his Major Works* (Oxford: Oxford University Press, 1988), 92–3.
7   Mary Shelley, *Frankenstein; or, The Modern Prometheus (the 1818 Text)*, ed. James Rieger (Indianapolis: Bobbs-Merrill, 1974; repr. Chicago: University of Chicago Press, 1982), 99.

horrors of Frankenstein's reactions and in his text (nested questionably between Walton's and the creature's). This kind of analysis repeats a rather Frankensteinian reading of events, a dialogue between subject and object which has already alienated the abject creature.

Instead, it is necessary to show how the universalism of scientific progress is plugged into class politics through the figure of the artificial body. The creature in the state of nature is a potential *philosophe*, a 'rustic ... Newton' (*Queen Mab* 5.137–43), but environmental conditioning oppresses this potential.[8] For Percy Shelley, the oppressed working class were also suppressed *philosophes*, potential members of the new powerful class. The support of natural diet as quasi-*embourgeoisement* (along with other rituals of cleanliness) distinguishes the Shelleys' thinking from certain Marxist arguments about social change. Their program of nurtured nature is far more Rousseauist – a cultured numbers game: round off the barbarities of the aristocracy, round up the immiseration and indiscipline of the labourers. The creature is destined to become an ideal mockery of the upper-class reformist *habitus*.

As part of his continuing social degradation, the creature eats a labouring-class diet. He has a shepherd's breakfast of bread, cheese, milk and wine – he dislikes the wine (101). When he finds a kennel to hide in, he eats bread and water (102). He eats a worker's meal of cooked roots and plants from the meagre garden a little later (104, 106). He dare not show himself: his voice is like an animal's (more precisely an ass or a dog, a domesticated animal that surely deserves rights from its inclusion in a human sphere) (110). But he is not base or 'savage': he is against slaughter (125/p. **152**), and he refuses to kill Felix – ' "I could have torn him limb from limb, as the lion rends the antelope" ' (131/p. **154**). When William confronts him, the first thought that runs through the boy's head is that the monster is a cannibal (an ' "ogre" ' from the fairy tales) (139/p. **155**). This terrifying figure of otherness, however, is actually quite uncannily at home in a non-violent world.

The creature is made with a humane nature, but needs the right kind of nurture to sustain this. This was the message of upper-class reform as mediated through the discourses of diet. The creature observes the family near which he stays like a social historian whose methodology is naturalistic, based on sensations that are developed by judgment (nature and nurture again): noticing that they weep, and being 'deeply affected by it', he remarks upon their subsistence lifestyle as a cause: ' "Their nourishment consisted entirely of the vegetables of their garden, and the milk of one cow." ' (106). But the creature needs the nourishment of a radical self-image: ' "perhaps, if my first introduction to humanity had been made by a young soldier, burning for glory and slaughter, I should have been imbued with different sensations" ' (125/p. **152**).

The creature is fashioned in the image of eighteenth-century ideas about man: a re-imagined body sprung from a scientific imagination. Mary Shelley's literary thought experiment poses a question: 'Is it possible to be moral in this context?'

---

8   Percy Shelley, *Shelley: Poetical Works*, ed. Thomas Hutchinson (London and New York: Oxford University Press, 1970).

To which the answer should be: 'Yes, given the application of sympathy, or feelings of identity with other beings'. The configuration of sympathy affects the reader, through the narrative pattern of concentric facings and witnessings. The presentation of this argument is extremely sophisticated, since the narrative shows that the flashy, vitalist showman in Frankenstein the scientist cannot abide the autonomy of the life which has been created. It must be ' "destroyed as a beast of prey" ' (197). The creature is hardly a beast of prey or a 'savage'. Through this linguistic act, Frankenstein asserts what [the vegetarian John] Oswald would call his heaven-deputed despotism.[9]

A process of what may be called 'alastorisation' (or the manufacture of avenging demons) takes place; Percy Shelley explored similar themes in *Alastor* (1816). The scientist and the creature become each others' avengers. The scientist should learn the discourse of the face, see the human within the dull eyes of the creature. Instead, Frankenstein constructs a redemption narrative for his own revenge, telling of how he is miraculously fed in the desert on his pursuit of the creature (201/**pp. 161–2**). In contrast, the creature has learnt the Enlightenment's universalising rhetoric only too well. His understanding of his own physical disfigurement (or deviant faciality) generates a sense of infinite debt to his creator (which is betrayed). Before the moment of alastorisation, the creature offers the plan of natural nurture, feeding on fruits with his mate in the jungles of the New World. But the novel has advanced down the dark path of threat, debt and betrayal, and this rational, humane possibility is foreclosed. The creature speaks all the lines which the Godwin–Shelley circle would have adored, but he cannot be countenanced (faced) by Frankenstein, who has become life's impresario rather than its scientist. Like the other alastorising narratives, *The Last Man*, 'Alastor' and Coleridge's *The Rime of the Ancient Mariner*, *Frankenstein* forces attention to the cry of nature, to create a natural face in a humane landscape.

Mary Shelley remorselessly plays this thought experiment through to its conclusion. She sets up the reformist plan, deconstructs it, and finds the set of determinants which will render it hopeless, while framing the increasingly redemptive and Christianising language of Frankenstein. The novel is not about the sin of presumption, the Promethean theft of fire (though it was certainly revised later to suggest this possible reading), but about the internal failure of a Promethean project, a demonstration of the conditions necessary for the construction of Condorcet's utopian body. 'The Modern Prometheus' is laced with irony: Frankenstein is not materialist, not sympathetic, enough. He steals fire only to play God. Even the creature knows the naturalistic reformist codes better than him – the very codes by which he is condemned, but in the light of which, through figures of food and eating, he is partially vindicated.

---

9   John Oswald, *The Cry of Nature; or, an Appeal to Mercy and to Justice, on Behalf of the Persecuted Animals* (London, 1791), 77.

Gayatri Chakravorty Spivak, *A Critique of Postcolonial Reason: Towards a Theory of the Vanishing Present* (1999) Cambridge, MA: Harvard University Press, 132–40

For Spivak, the imperialism one might detect in *Frankenstein* founders on the novel's deconstruction of sexual difference. This deconstruction occurs both in Frankenstein's laboratory, a sort of male womb, and in the homoerotic creature itself, made of corpses. The unfinished *female* creature is an even more disturbing deconstruction, of the difference between death and life. Frankenstein's racism resides in his fear of what such a creature might herself produce: 'a race of devils' **(p. 158)**. Victor, Clerval and Elizabeth stand for the three parts of Kantian philosophy: the cognitive (in *The Critique of Pure Reason*), the ethical (*The Critique of Practical Reason*) and the aesthetic (*The Critique of Judgement*). Spivak sees these as part of the ideological frame of Western imperialism. (During the Romantic period, Europe had moved out of its colonial phase – exploiting the rest of the world through trade – and into its imperial phase, exerting direct political control over such countries as India.) Victor's fears about the creatures he assembles thus indicate social anxieties about the utilitarian project of world domination.

[. . .] The discourse of imperialism surfaces in a curiously powerful way in Shelley's novel, and I will later discuss the moment at which it emerges. *Frankenstein*, however, is not a battleground of male and female individualism articulated in terms of sexual reproduction (family and female) and social subject-production (race and male). That binary opposition is undone in Victor Frankenstein's laboratory – an artificial womb where both projects are undertaken simultaneously, though the terms are never openly spelled out. Frankenstein's apparent antagonist is God himself as Maker of Man, but his real competitor is also woman as the maker of children. It is not just that his dream of the death of mother and bride and the actual death of his bride are associated with the visit of his monstrous homoerotic 'corpse', unnatural because bereft of a determinable childhood: 'No father had watched my infant days, no mother had blessed me with smiles and caresses; or if they had, all my past was now a blot, a blind vacancy in which I distinguished nothing'.[1] It is Frankenstein's own ambiguous and miscued understanding of the real motive for the monster's vengefulness that reveals his competition with woman as maker: 'I created a rational creature and was bound towards him to assure, as far as was in my power, his happiness and well-being. This was my duty, but there was another still paramount to that. My duties towards the beings of my own species had greater claims to my attention because they included a greater proportion of happiness or misery. Urged by this

---

1   Mary Shelley, *Frankenstein; or, The Modern Prometheus* (New York: New American Library, 1965), 115.

view, I refused, and I did right in refusing, to create a companion for the first creature' (206).

It is impossible not to notice the accents of transgression inflecting Frankenstein's demolition of his experiment to create the future Eve. Even in the laboratory, the woman-in-the-making is not a bodied corpse but 'a human being'. The (il)logic of the metaphor bestows on her a prior existence that Frankenstein aborts, rather than an anterior death that he reembodies: 'The remains of the half-finished creature, whom I had destroyed, lay scattered on the floor, and I almost felt as if I had mangled the living flesh of a human being' (163).

In Shelley's view, man's hubris as soul maker both usurps the place of God and attempts – vainly – to sublate woman's physiological prerogative. Indeed, indulging a Freudian fantasy here, I could urge that, if to give and withhold to/ from the mother a phallus is *the* male fetish, then to give and withhold to/from the man a womb might be the female fetish in an impossible world of psychoanalytic equilibrium. The icon of the sublimated womb in man is surely his productive brain, the box in the head.

In the judgment of classical psychoanalysis, the phallic mother exists only by virtue of the castration-anxious son; in *Frankenstein*'s judgment, the hysteric father (Victor Frankenstein gifted with his laboratory – the womb of theoretical reason) cannot produce a daughter. Here the language of racism – the dark side of imperialism understood as social mission – combines with the hysteria of masculism into the idiom of (the withdrawal of) sexual reproduction rather than subject-constitution; and is judged by the text. The roles of masculine and feminine individualists are hence reversed and displaced. Frankenstein cannot produce a 'daughter' because '[. . .] a race of devils would be propagated upon the earth who might make the very existence of the species of man a condition precarious and full of terror' (158/p. 158). [. . .]

In the end, as is obvious to most readers, distinctions of human individuality seem to fall away from [*Frankenstein*]. Monster, Frankenstein and Walton seem to become each other's relays. Frankenstein's story comes to an end in death; Walton concludes his own story within the frame of his function as letter writer. In the *narrative* conclusion, he is the natural philosopher who learns from Frankenstein's example. At the end of the *text*, the monster, having confessed his guilt toward his maker and ostensibly intending to immolate himself, is borne away on an ice raft. We do not see the conflagration of his funeral pile – the self-immolation is not consummated in the text: he too cannot be contained by the text. And to stage that non-containment is, I insist, one of *Frankenstein*'s strengths. In terms of narrative logic, he is 'lost in darkness and distance' (211/ p. 166) – these are the last words of the novel – into an existential temporality that is coherent with neither the territorialising individual imagination (as in the opening of *Jane Eyre*) nor the authoritative scenario of Christian psycho-biography (as at the end of Brontë's work). The very relationship between sexual reproduction and social subject-production – the dynamic nineteenth-century topos of feminism-in-imperialism – remains problematic within the limits of Shelley's text and, paradoxically, constitutes its strength.

Earlier, I offered a reading of woman as womb holder in *Frankenstein*. I would now suggest that there is a framing woman in the book who is neither tangential, nor encircled, nor yet encircling. 'Mrs Saville', 'excellent Margaret', 'beloved Sister' are her address and kinship inscriptions (15, 17, 22). She is the occasion, though not the protagonist, of the novel. She is the feminine *subject* rather than the female individualist: she is the irreducible *recipient*-function of the letters that make up *Frankenstein*. I have commented on the singular appropriative hermeneutics of the reader reading with Jane in the opening pages of *Jane Eyre*. Here the reader must read with Margaret Saville in the crucial sense that she must *intercept* the recipient-function, read the letters *as* recipient, in order for the novel to exist. Margaret Saville does not respond to close the text as a frame. The frame is thus simultaneously not a frame, and the monster can step 'beyond the text' and be 'lost in darkness'. Within the allegory of our reading, the place of both the English lady and the unnamable monster are left open by this great flawed text. It is satisfying for a postcolonial reader to consider this a noble resolution for a nineteenth-century English novel. Shelley herself abundantly 'identifies' with Victor Frankenstein.[2]

---

2 [Spivak's note.] The most striking internal evidence is the 'Author's Introduction' that, after dreaming of the yet-unnamed Victor Frankenstein figure and being terrified (through, yet not yet quite through, him) by the monster in a scene she later reproduced in Frankenstein's story, Shelley began her tale 'on that morrow . . . with the words "It was on a dreary night of November"'' (Shelley xi/p. 171). Those are the opening words of chapter 5 of the finished book, where Frankenstein begins to recount the actual making of his monster (56/p. 137).

3

Key Passages

Introduction

Marilyn Butler's note on the Oxford edition of *Frankenstein* (lii–liii) argues for the 1818 text in the following way:

> One good reason for choosing the 1818 text is that it enables the editor to set out the substantive additions in an Appendix as an element well worth separate study . . . It is only when the relations between the two versions are expressed that readers can see how much turns on the addition of religious attitudes and judgements, and the cancellation or reinterpretations of the science . . . The Introduction [to the 1831 edition] . . . shows how much pressure, direct and indirect, was put upon the author to change the book in the way she did.
>
> (liii)

For the same reasons, I have chosen to use the first edition of the text (London: Lackington, Hughes, Harding, Mavor and Jones, 1818), as the copy text, which I have silently corrected in a very few places. For a spirited defence of the 1831 edition, see Nora Crook's essay 'In Defence of the 1831 *Frankenstein*' in Michael Eberle-Sinatra's recent collection of essays on *Frankenstein* (2000).

The later edition puts more emphasis on Frankenstein as a presumptuous imitator of God. The earlier edition makes more of the contemporary scientific debate, in which Mary and Percy Shelley were involved, between vitalist and materialist theories of life. Their friend William Lawrence was a key player in this debate, and the issue was sparking public interest around the time the original text was written. It seems appropriate, however, to include a discussion of the 1831 text, rather than simply presenting it as an alternative.

I have interspersed guiding notes within the extracts in order to make their navigation somewhat easier. It has not been possible to include everything that one would wish from the novel; but I trust that this will be a useful selection.

FRANKENSTEIN;

OR,

THE MODERN PROMETHEUS.

———

IN THREE VOLUMES.

———

Did I request thee, Maker, from my clay
To mould me man? Did I solicit thee
From darkness to promote me?———
[Paradise Lost (10.743–5)]

———

VOL. I.

———

London:

PRINTED FOR
LACKINGTON, HUGHES, HARDING, MAVOR, & JONES,
FINSBURY SQUARE.

1818.

TO

WILLIAM GODWIN,

AUTHOR OF POLITICAL JUSTICE, CALEB WILLIAMS, &C.

THESE VOLUMES

Are respectfully inscribed

BY

THE AUTHOR.

Preface[1]

The event on which this fiction is founded has been supposed, by Dr. [Erasmus] Darwin, and some of the physiological writers of Germany, as not of impossible occurrence. I shall not be supposed as according the remotest degree of serious faith in such an imagination; yet, in assuming it as the basis of a work of fancy, I have not considered myself as merely weaving a series of supernatural terrors. The event on which the interest of the story depends is exempt from the disadvantages of a mere tale of spectres or enchantment. It was recommended by the novelty of the situations which it developes; and, however impossible as a physical fact, affords a point of view to the imagination for the delineating of human passions more comprehensive and commanding than any which the ordinary relations of existing events can yield.

I have thus endeavoured to preserve the truth of the elementary principles of human nature, while I have not scrupled to innovate upon their combinations.[2] The *Iliad*, the tragic poetry of Greece, – Shakespeare, in the *Tempest* and *Midsummer Night's Dream*, – and most especially Milton, in *Paradise Lost*, conform to this rule; and the most humble novelist, who seeks to confer or receive amusement from his labours, may, without presumption, apply to prose fiction a licence, or rather a rule, from the adoption of which so many exquisite combinations of human feeling have resulted in the highest specimens of poetry.

The circumstance on which my story rests was suggested in casual conversation. It was commenced, partly as a source of amusement, and partly as an expedient for exercising any untried resources of mind. Other motives were mingled with these, as the work proceeded. I am by no means indifferent to the manner in which whatever moral tendencies exist in the sentiments or characters it contains shall affect the reader; yet my chief concern in this respect has been limited to the avoiding the enervating effects of the novels of the present day, and to the exhibition of the amiableness of domestic affection, and the excellence of universal virtue. The opinions which naturally spring from the character and situation of the hero are by no means to be conceived as existing always in my own conviction; nor is any inference justly to be drawn from the following pages as prejudicing any philosophical doctrine of whatever kind.[3]

It is a subject also of additional interest to the author, that this story was begun in the majestic region where the scene is principally laid, and in society which cannot cease to be regretted. I passed the summer of 1816 in the environs of Geneva. The season was cold and rainy, and in the evenings we crowded around a

---

1   Percy Shelley, Preface to the 1818 Edition, in E.B. Murray, ed., *The Prose Works of Percy Bysshe Shelley* (1993) Oxford: Clarendon Press, 1.177–8. '[Percy] S[helley] wrote this Preface to his wife's novel as if he were she. Mary Shelley is precise about the date of its writing, noting in her journal entry for 14 May 1817 "[w]rite Preface", which also allows her to write "Finis" to *Frankenstein*, which her husband had on the same day corrected' (Murray in Shelley, *Prose*, 408).

2   'See the antepenultimate paragraph of [Percy] S[helley]'s Preface to *Prometheus Unbound* for a restatement and expansion of this aesthetic psychology' (ibid., 408).

3   '[Percy] S[helley]'s disclaimer . . . probably springs from the social and legal reaction to the radical pronouncements of his earlier youth and is reiterated in a different form as late as the Notes to *Hellas*' (Ibid., 408).

blazing wood fire, and occasionally amused ourselves with some German stories of ghosts, which happened to fall into our hands.[4] These tales excited in us a playful desire of imitation. Two other friends (a tale from the pen of one of whom would be far more acceptable to the public than any thing I can ever hope to produce) and myself agreed to write each a story, founded on some supernatural occurrence.[5]

The weather, however, suddenly became serene; and my two friends left me on a journey among the Alps, and lost, in the magnificent scenes which they present, all memory of their ghostly visions. The following tale is the only one which has been completed.

VOLUME I

The opening of the novel establishes the intricate framing device that serves automatically to place in doubt and ironise the statements of all the narrators (Walton, Frankenstein and the creature himself). For further discussion, please see Mary A. Favret's essay, 'The Letters of *Frankenstein*' (Genre 20:1 (1987), 3–24. Favret demonstrates that the epistolary form of *Frankenstein*'s frame serves to establish the ways in which the novel undermines the idea of the linear progression of a single life. Favret reads the novel as a combination of overlapping, corresponding tales. Victor wishes to establish his authority, but this is undermined: not simply by the free play of language (as Peter Brooks has it), but by the very 'multi-dimensional' structure of the novel (8). The voice of Frankenstein becomes only one among many. Victor's insistence on his singular authority is thus challenged by the form of the text. This form finds an emblem in the monster, assembled from disparate parts (9). Walton's letters, on the other hand, depend upon the 'blind faith' validation of his silent sister. Favret uses the psychoanalytic feminist theory of Julia Kristeva to explain this: the sister stands in for the 'Other', the matrix of meaning that guarantees the significance of what Walton writes.

Letter 4 [Walton on Frankenstein]

To Mrs SAVILLE, *England.*

August 5th, 17–.

[. . .] I never saw a more interesting creature: his eyes have generally an expression of wildness, and even madness; but there are moments when, if any one performs

---

4   'Evidently an anonymously published collection entitled *Fantasmagoria, ou Receuil d'Histoires d' Apparitions de Spectres, Revenans, Fantômes. . . . .* (two vols., Paris, 1812). The work, ascribed to Jean-Baptiste-Benoît Eyries, is also referred to and epitomized in the 1831 Introduction' (ibid., 408).

5   'Actually, Byron, John William Polidori . . . Claire Clairmont, [Percy] S[helley], and Mary herself made up the ghost-story competition' (ibid., 408).

an act of kindness towards him, or does him any the most trifling service, his whole countenance is lighted up, as it were, with a beam of benevolence and sweetness that I never saw equalled. But he is generally melancholy and despairing; and sometimes he gnashes his teeth, as if impatient of the weight of woes that oppresses him. [. . .]

Such is my journal of what relates to this strange occurrence up to the present day. The stranger has gradually improved in health, but is very silent, and appears uneasy when any one except myself enters his cabin. Yet his manners are so conciliating and gentle, that the sailors are all interested in him, although they have had very little communication with him. For my own part, I begin to love him as a brother; and his constant and deep grief fills me with sympathy and compassion. He must have been a noble creature in his better days, being even now in wreck so attractive and amiable. [. . .]

Chapter I [Frankenstein's narrative begins]

[. . .] From this time, Elizabeth Lavenza became my playfellow, and, as we grew older, my friend. She was docile and good tempered, yet gay and playful as a summer insect. Although she was lively and animated, her feelings were strong and deep, and her disposition uncommonly affectionate. No one could better enjoy liberty, yet no one could submit with more grace than she did to constraint and caprice. Her imagination was luxuriant, yet her capability of application was great. Her person was the image of her mind; her hazel eyes, although as lively as a bird's, possessed an attractive softness. Her figure was light and airy; and, though capable of enduring great fatigue, she appeared the most fragile creature in the world. While I admired her understanding and fancy, I loved to tend on her, as I should on a favourite animal; and I never saw so much grace both of person and mind united to so little pretension.

> Syndy Conger discusses the significance of Shelley's strong relationship with her deceased mother, Mary Wollstonecraft. Shelley saw her mother as a Cassandra, a female prophet, even as she was a 'mythoclast' (a demolisher of myths). Conger finds the type of Shelley's mother in the character of Elizabeth Lavenza. But Conger also associates the *creature* himself with Shelley's mother. As a monstrous critic of society, the creature mimes the demonisation and vilification of Wollstonecraft's feminism in the reactionary press. See Further Reading (p. 181).

[. . .] My brothers were considerably younger than myself; but I had a friend in one of my schoolfellows, who compensated for this deficiency. Henry Clerval was the son of a merchant of Geneva, an intimate friend of my father. He was a boy of singular talent and fancy. I remember, when he was nine years old, he wrote a fairy tale, which was the delight and amazement of all his companions. His favourite study consisted in books of chivalry and romance; and when very young, I can remember, that we used to act plays composed by him out of these favourite books, the principal characters of which were Orlando, Robin Hood, Amadis, and St George. [. . .]

Natural philosophy is the genius that has regulated my fate; I desire therefore, in this narration, to state those facts which led to my predilection for that science. When I was thirteen years of age, we all went on a party of pleasure to the baths near Thonon: the inclemency of the weather obliged us to remain a day confined to the inn. In this house I chanced to find a volume of the works of Cornelius Agrippa.[1] I opened it with apathy; the theory which he attempts to demonstrate, and the wonderful facts which he relates, soon changed this feeling into enthusiasm. A new light seemed to dawn upon my mind; and, bounding with joy, I communicated my discovery to my father. I cannot help remarking here the many opportunities instructors possess of directing the attention of their pupils to useful knowledge, which they utterly neglect. My father looked carelessly at the title-page of my book, and said, 'Ah! Cornelius Agrippa! My dear Victor, do not waste your time upon this; it is sad trash.' [. . .]

When I was about fifteen years old, we had retired to our house near Belrive, when we witnessed a most violent and terrible thunder-storm. It advanced from behind the mountains of Jura; and the thunder burst at once with frightful loudness from various quarters of the heavens. I remained, while the storm lasted, watching its progress with curiosity and delight. As I stood at the door, on a sudden I beheld a stream of fire issue from an old and beautiful oak, which stood about twenty yards from our house; and so soon as the dazzling light vanished, the oak had disappeared, and nothing remained but a blasted stump. When we visited it the next morning, we found the tree shattered in a singular manner. It was not splintered by the shock, but entirely reduced to thin ribbands of wood. I never beheld any thing so utterly destroyed. [. . .]

Chapter 2

[. . .] I delivered my letters of introduction, and paid a visit to some of the principal professors, and among others to M. Krempe, professor of natural philosophy. He received me with politeness, and asked me several questions concerning my progress in the different branches of science appertaining to natural philosophy. I mentioned, it is true, with fear and trembling, the only authors I had ever read upon those subjects. The professor stared: 'Have you,' he said, 'really spent your time in studying such nonsense?'

I replied in the affirmative. 'Every minute,' continued M. Krempe with warmth, 'every instant that you have wasted on those books is utterly and entirely lost. You have burdened your memory with exploded systems, and useless names.

---

1   Henricus Cornelius Agrippa (1486–1535) was a scholar who wrote on the occult sciences and argued against the persecution of witches.

Good God! in what desert land have you lived, where no one was kind enough to inform you that these fancies, which you have so greedily imbibed, are a thousand years old, and as musty as they are ancient? I little expected in this enlightened and scientific age to find a disciple of Albertus Magnus[1] and Paracelsus.[2] My dear Sir, you must begin your studies entirely anew.' [. . .]

Partly from curiosity, and partly from idleness, I went into the lecturing room, which M. Waldman [Frankenstein's other professor] entered shortly after. This professor was very unlike his colleague. [. . .] After having made a few preparatory experiments, he concluded with a panegyric upon modern chemistry, the terms of which I shall never forget: –

'The ancient teachers of this science,' said he, 'promised impossibilities, and performed nothing. The modern masters promise very little; they know that metals cannot be transmuted, and that the elixir of life is a chimera. But these philosophers, whose hands seem only made to dabble in dirt, and their eyes to pour over the microscope or crucible, have indeed performed miracles. They penetrate into the recesses of nature, and shew how she works in her hiding places. They ascend into the heavens; they have discovered how the blood circulates, and the nature of the air we breathe. They have acquired new and almost unlimited powers; they can command the thunders of heaven, mimic the earthquake, and even mock the invisible world with its own shadows.'

Frankenstein becomes M. Waldman's disciple.

Chapter 3

[. . .] One of the phænomena which had peculiarly attracted my attention was the structure of the human frame, and, indeed, any animal endued with life. Whence, I often asked myself, did the principle of life proceed? It was a bold question, and one which has ever been considered as a mystery; yet with how many things are we upon the brink of becoming acquainted, if cowardice or carelessness did not restrain our inquiries. I revolved these circumstances in my mind, and determined thenceforth to apply myself more particularly to those branches of natural philosophy which relate to physiology. Unless I had been animated by an almost supernatural enthusiasm, my application to this study would have been irksome, and almost intolerable. To examine the causes of life, we must first have recourse to death. I became acquainted with the science of anatomy: but this was not sufficient; I must also observe the natural decay and corruption of the human body. In my education my father had taken the greatest precautions that my mind should be impressed with no supernatural horrors. I do not ever remember to

1   Albert Magnus (Albert the Great) (1206–80) was a scientist, philosopher and theologian.
2   Philippus Aureolus Paracelsus (1493–1541) was a Swiss alchemist and astrologer who was appointed to a chair of physic and surgery at Basel, though he was eventually denounced as a fraud.

have trembled at a tale of superstition, or to have feared the apparition of a spirit. Darkness had no effect upon my fancy; and a church-yard was to me merely the receptacle of bodies deprived of life, which, from being the seat of beauty and strength, had become food for the worm. Now I was led to examine the cause and progress of this decay, and forced to spend days and nights in vaults and charnel houses. My attention was fixed upon every object the most insupportable to the delicacy of the human feelings. [. . .]

No one can conceive the variety of feelings which bore me onwards, like a hurricane, in the first enthusiasm of success. Life and death appeared to me ideal bounds, which I should first break through, and pour a torrent of light into our dark world. A new species would bless me as its creator and source; many happy and excellent natures would owe their being to me. No father could claim the gratitude of his child so completely as I should deserve their's. Pursuing these reflections, I thought, that if I could bestow animation upon lifeless matter, I might in process of time (although I now found it impossible) renew life where death had apparently devoted the body to corruption. [. . .]

[. . .] Who shall conceive the horrors of my secret toil, as I dabbled among the unhallowed damps of the grave, or tortured the living animal to animate the lifeless clay? My limbs now tremble, and my eyes swim with the remembrance; but then a resistless, and almost frantic impulse, urged me forward; I seemed to have lost all soul or sensation but for this one pursuit. It was indeed but a passing trance, that only made me feel with renewed acuteness so soon as, the unnatural stimulus ceasing to operate, I had returned to my old habits. I collected bones from charnel houses; and disturbed, with profane fingers, the tremendous secrets of the human frame. In a solitary chamber, or rather cell, at the top of the house, and separated from all the other apartments by a gallery and staircase, I kept my workshop of filthy creation; my eyeballs were starting from their sockets in attending to the details of my employment. The dissecting room and the slaughter-house furnished many of my materials; and often did my human nature turn with loathing from my occupation, whilst, still urged on by an eagerness which perpetually increased, I brought my work near to a conclusion.

Frankenstein's mention of dabbling 'among the unhallowed damps of the grave' and vivisecting animals brings to mind the parodic language of Percy Shelley's 'Alastor', in which a Poet/scientist pursues a feminised nature's darker secrets. Victor's toil and sweat also renders him somewhat of an abject working-class figure, as discussed by Franco Moretti (see Modern Criticism, p. 91).

His reactions may also be compared with those of a male hysteric. In 'Reading the Symptoms: An Exploration of Repression and Hysteria in Mary Shelley's *Frankenstein*', Colleen Hobbs analyses the cultural history of hysteria, which was associated with women. (In the early modern period it was even thought that the hysterical woman's womb wandered around her body – generating the alternatives between being condemned for witchcraft or diagnosed with hysteria.) Hobbs traces the way in which the Shelleys raised their children to Rousseau's and Godwin's ideas of the need for the rational restraint of emotions. Frankenstein, likewise, resists '"unmanly" emotions' in this way (155). What Shelley depicts, through Frankenstein's outbursts (one of which is surely the creation of the creature himself), is *mute* hysteria. However, the doctor more closely resembles a 'talkative' female than a 'prideful' male hysteric (according to the traditional model expounded in the Romantic period by John Ferriar, 156). For instance, 'Victor's behavior after creating the monster … enacts a hysteric response both to the guilt of abandoning his creature and to his anxiety about hiding its existence from Clerval' (160). Hobbs comments that when Frankenstein feels like a '"love sick girl"' while making the creature, his trembling hands unwittingly express the feminine characteristics he has repressed (161). The imagery of mist provides something of a meteorological get-out clause for Frankenstein: he feels obscured by it as he goes into denial about his actions (162). His only fully erotic embraces are performed with the *lifeless* body of Elizabeth (163). He is not merely afraid of the creature, but also of uncontrollable sexuality (163). See Further Reading (**p. 179**).

[…] If the study to which you apply yourself has a tendency to weaken your affections, and to destroy your taste for those simple pleasures in which no alloy can possibly mix, then that study is certainly unlawful, that is to say, not befitting the human mind. If this rule were always observed; if no man allowed any pursuit whatsoever to interfere with the tranquillity of his domestic affections, Greece had not been enslaved; Cæsar would have spared his country; America would have been discovered more gradually; and the empires of Mexico and Peru had not been destroyed. […]

Chapter 4 [The climax of the making of the creature]

It was on a dreary night of November, that I beheld the accomplishment of my toils. With an anxiety that almost amounted to agony, I collected the instruments of life around me, that I might infuse a spark of being into the lifeless thing that lay at my feet. It was already one in the morning; the rain pattered dismally against the panes, and my candle was nearly burnt out, when, by the glimmer of the half-extinguished light, I saw the dull yellow eye of the creature open; it breathed hard, and a convulsive motion agitated its limbs.

How can I describe my emotions at this catastrophe, or how delineate the wretch whom with such infinite pains and care I had endeavoured to form? His limbs were in proportion, and I had selected his features as beautiful. Beautiful! – Great God! His yellow skin scarcely covered the work of muscles and arteries beneath; his hair was of a lustrous black, and flowing; his teeth of a pearly whiteness; but these luxuriances only formed a more horrid contrast with his watery eyes, that seemed almost of the same colour as the dun white sockets in which they were set, his shrivelled complexion, and straight black lips.

[. . .] At length [. . .] I threw myself on the bed in my clothes, endeavouring to seek a few moments of forgetfulness. But it was in vain: I slept indeed, but I was disturbed by the wildest dreams. I thought I saw Elizabeth, in the bloom of health, walking in the streets of Ingolstadt. Delighted and surprised, I embraced her; but as I imprinted the first kiss on her lips, they became livid with the hue of death; her features appeared to change, and I thought that I held the corpse of my dead mother in my arms; a shroud enveloped her form, and I saw the grave-worms crawling in the folds of the flannel. I started from my sleep with horror; a cold dew covered my forehead, my teeth chattered, and every limb became convulsed; when, by the dim and yellow light of the moon, as it forced its way through the window-shutters, I beheld the wretch – the miserable monster whom I had created. He held up the curtain of the bed; and his eyes, if eyes they may be called, were fixed on me. His jaws opened, and he muttered some inarticulate sounds, while a grin wrinkled his cheeks. He might have spoken, but I did not hear; one hand was stretched out, seemingly to detain me, but I escaped, and rushed down stairs. I took refuge in the court-yard belonging to the house which I inhabited; where I remained during the rest of the night, walking up and down in the greatest agitation, listening attentively, catching and fearing each sound as if it were to announce the approach of the demoniacal corpse to which I had so miserably given life.

Above is the first passage Shelley drafted (see her introduction to the 1831 edition). For more on the dream, please refer to Joseph's psychoanalytic reading (see Further Reading, **p. 181**). Joseph shows how Freud's notions of the 'condensation' and 'displacement' carried out by the dreaming mind are associated by Lacan with the rhetorical tropes of metaphor and metonymy, respectively. Joseph then launches into a careful reading of Frankenstein's fantasy of the folds of Elizabeth's/his mother's 'flannel'. This is a metonymy for his mother's vagina, an idea which is then associated with the vaginal enfolding of text within text in the novel.

Concerning the creature's 'inarticulate' noises: in the second volume, the creature himself makes it clear that he is aware of this very same judgement of his (non)speech. How does the creature know that he is disgusting – how can he see himself from Frankenstein's eyes? (There is a parody of this in the movie *Blade Runner*, discussed in the chapter on performance in this volume. Roy, the creature-like Replicant, tells the man who made his eyes: 'If only you could see what I have seen . . . with your eyes.') Some of the readings on race (for example, Elizabeth Bohls) in Modern Criticism attempt to explore this issue. It is as if the creature already has encoded within him white western standards of language and physical beauty: they are hard-wired, as it were.

[. . .] My heart palpitated in the sickness of fear; and I hurried on with irregular steps, not daring to look about me:

> Like one who, on a lonely road,
>   Doth walk in fear and dread,
> And, having once turn'd round, walks on,
>   And turns no more his head;
> Because he knows a frightful fiend
>   Doth close behind him tread.[1]

Chapter 5

Clerval delivers a letter from Elizabeth, describing the introduction of Justine. Victor replies; he introduces Clerval to his professors. Frankenstein is delayed from returning to Geneva; Henry and he tour around Ingolstadt in May, for a fortnight. This section is loaded with proleptic (anticipatory) irony. Shelley declares that 'A servant in Geneva does not mean the same thing as a servant in France and England. Justine, thus received in our family, learned the duties of a servant; a condition which, in our fortunate country, does not include the idea of ignorance, and a sacrifice of the dignity of a human being'. Shelley includes such republican sentiments only to question their integrity in the face of horror and tragedy. Of course, Justine's dignity *is* later sacrificed to the interests of Frankenstein himself, when he cannot bring himself to talk about his creation during Justine's trial for the murder committed by the creature.

Chapter 6

Victor receives a letter from his father, describing the murder of William. Victor and Clerval resolve to go to Geneva at once. On the outskirts of Geneva, Victor watches a storm rising. Victor returns home at dawn and resolves to stay silent. Ernest and Victor's father are convinced that Justine murdered William.

Chapter 7 [The trial of Justine]

[. . .] Concerning the picture [Justine] could give no account. [. . .]

'I commit my cause to the justice of my judges, yet I see no room for hope. I beg permission to have a few witnesses examined concerning my character; and if

---

1 [Shelley's note.] Coleridge's 'Ancient Mariner' [lines 446–51].

their testimony shall not overweigh my supposed guilt, I must be condemned, although I would pledge my salvation on my innocence.'

Several witnesses were called, who had known her for many years, and they spoke well of her; but fear, and hatred of the crime of which they supposed her guilty, rendered them timorous, and unwilling to come forward. Elizabeth saw even this last resource, her excellent dispositions and irreproachable conduct, about to fail the accused, when, although violently agitated, she desired permission to address the court.

'I am,' said she, 'the cousin of the unhappy child who was murdered, or rather his sister, for I was educated by and have lived with his parents ever since and even long before his birth. It may therefore be judged indecent in me to come forward on this occasion; but when I see a fellow-creature about to perish through the cowardice of her pretended friends, I wish to be allowed to speak, that I may say what I know of her character. I am well acquainted with the accused. I have lived in the same house with her, at one time for five, and at another for nearly two years. During all that period she appeared to me the most amiable and benevolent of human creatures. She nursed Madame Frankenstein, my aunt, in her last illness with the greatest affection and care; and afterwards attended her own mother during a tedious illness, in a manner that excited the admiration of all who knew her. After which she again lived in my uncle's house, where she was beloved by all the family. She was warmly attached to the child who is now dead, and acted towards him like a most affectionate mother. For my own part, I do not hesitate to say, that, notwithstanding all the evidence produced against her, I believe and rely on her perfect innocence. She had no temptation for such an action: as to the bauble on which the chief proof rests, if she had earnestly desired it, I should have willingly given it to her; so much do I esteem and value her.' [. . .]

> Frankenstein visits Justine in prison with Elizabeth after it is found that she has confessed. Shelley had evidently learnt from her father Godwin that the trial narrative could be the radical and/or republican novel's version of what was later called, in existentialist literature, the 'extreme situation'.

'Rise, my poor girl,' said Elizabeth, 'why do you kneel, if you are innocent? I am not one of your enemies; I believed you guiltless, notwithstanding every evidence, until I heard that you had yourself declared your guilt. That report, you say, is false; and be assured, dear Justine, that nothing can shake my confidence in you for a moment, but your own confession.'

'I did confess; but I confessed a lie. I confessed, that I might obtain absolution; but now that falsehood lies heavier at my heart than all my other sins. The God of heaven forgive me! Ever since I was condemned, my confessor has besieged me; he threatened and menaced, until I almost began to think that I was the monster that he said I was. He threatened excommunication and hell fire in my last moments, if I continued obdurate. Dear lady, I had none to support me; all looked on me as a wretch doomed to ignominy and perdition. What could I do? In an evil hour I subscribed to a lie; and now only am I truly miserable.' [. . .]

'I will try to comfort you; but this, I fear, is an evil too deep and poignant to admit of consolation, for there is no hope. Yet heaven bless thee, my dearest Justine, with resignation, and a confidence elevated beyond this world. Oh! how I hate its shews and mockeries! when one creature is murdered, another is immediately deprived of life in a slow torturing manner; then the executioners, their hands yet reeking with the blood of innocence, believe that they have done a great deed. They call this *retribution*. Hateful name! When that word is pronounced, I know greater and more horrid punishments are going to be inflicted than the gloomiest tyrant has ever invented to satiate his utmost revenge. Yet this is not consolation for you, my Justine, unless indeed that you may glory in escaping from so miserable a den. Alas! I would I were in peace with my aunt and my lovely William, escaped from a world which is hateful to me, and the visages of men which I abhor.' [. . .]

During this conversation I had retired to a corner of the prison-room, where I could conceal the horrid anguish that possessed me. Despair! Who dared talk of that? The poor victim, who on the morrow was to pass the dreary boundary between life and death, felt not as I did, such deep and bitter agony. I gnashed my teeth, and ground them together, uttering a groan that came from my inmost soul. Justine started. When she saw who it was, she approached me, and said, 'Dear Sir, you are very kind to visit me; you, I hope, do not believe that I am guilty.'

Justine, who has called herself a 'wretch' (one of the very words that Victor uses to name the creature), is an object of pity in Frankenstein's eyes. The creature, too, is similarly objectified by him: and, one might add, *abjected*, using the language of Julia Kristeva, in *Powers of Horror*. For Kristeva, the subject only becomes so when it gets rid of what it finds disgusting – the abject, that symbolises the body of the mother. It is psychically destructive to retain unresolved portions of this process. A psychoanalytic reading might assert that the abjected creature haunts Frankenstein, just as Justine does, perhaps as a result of his casual spurning of his mother. The words of Elizabeth against the idea of 'retribution' are a reminder that Shelley and Percy were both interested in the work of Basil Montagu (1770–1851), Percy's lawyer in his custody trial, who had published work opposing the death penalty. Mary Shelley's journal records her reading of Montagu and Thomas Erskine in 1816, as she was composing *Frankenstein* (Erskine was a campaigner for animal rights, among other things, in Parliament) (*Journals*, 1.94).

VOLUME 2

Chapter 1

> Victor falls into a deep depression; a tour is undertaken. Victor is joined by his father, Elizabeth and Ernest Clerval.

Chapter 2

> Victor resolves to climb to the summit of Montanvert. See the descriptions of the Alps by Shelley and Percy in Contemporary Documents, **pp. 26, 28, 30–2**.

The ascent is precipitous, but the path is cut into continual and short windings, which enable you to surmount the perpendicularity of the mountain. It is a scene terrifically desolate. In a thousand spots the traces of the winter avalanche may be perceived, where trees lie broken and strewed on the ground; some entirely destroyed, others bent, leaning upon the jutting rocks of the mountain, or transversely upon other trees. The path, as you ascend higher, is intersected by ravines of snow, down which stones continually roll from above; one of them is particularly dangerous, as the slightest sound, such as even speaking in a loud voice, produces a concussion of air sufficient to draw destruction upon the head of the speaker. The pines are not tall or luxuriant, but they are sombre, and add an air of severity to the scene. I looked on the valley beneath; vast mists were rising from the rivers which ran through it, and curling in thick wreaths around the opposite mountains, whose summits were hid in the uniform clouds, while rain poured from the dark sky, and added to the melancholy impression I received from the objects around me. Alas! why does man boast of sensibilities superior to those apparent in the brute; it only renders them more necessary beings. If our impulses were confined to hunger, thirst, and desire, we might be nearly free; but now we are moved by every wind that blows, and a chance word or scene that that word may convey to us.

> We rest; a dream has power to poison sleep.
>   We rise; one wand'ring thought pollutes the day.
> We feel, conceive, or reason; laugh, or weep,
>   Embrace fond woe, or cast our cares away;
> It is the same: for, be it joy or sorrow,
>   The path of its departure still is free.
> Man's yesterday may ne'er be like his morrow;
>   Nought may endure but mutability![1]

---

[1] Percy Shelley, 'On Mutability', from *Alastor: Or the Spirit of Solitude* (1816), lines 9–16.

[. . .] I suddenly beheld the figure of a man, at some distance, advancing towards me with superhuman speed. He bounded over the crevices in the ice, among which I had walked with caution; his stature also, as he approached, seemed to exceed that of a man. I was troubled: a mist came over my eyes, and I felt a faintness seize me; but I was quickly restored by the cold gale of the mountains. I perceived, as the shape came nearer, (sight tremendous and abhorred!) that it was the wretch whom I had created. I trembled with rage and horror, resolving to wait his approach, and then close with him in mortal combat. He approached; his countenance bespoke bitter anguish, combined with disdain and malignity, while its unearthly ugliness rendered it almost too horrible for human eyes. But I scarcely observed this; anger and hatred had at first deprived me of utterance, and I recovered only to overwhelm him with words expressive of furious detestation and contempt.

'Devil!' I exclaimed, 'do you dare approach me? and do not you fear the fierce vengeance of my arm wreaked on your miserable head? Begone, vile insect! or rather stay, that I may trample you to dust! and, oh, that I could, with the extinction of your miserable existence, restore those victims whom you have so diabolically murdered!'

'I expected this reception,' said the dæmon. 'All men hate the wretched; how then must I be hated, who am miserable beyond all living things! Yet you, my creator, detest and spurn me, thy creature, to whom thou art bound by ties only dissoluble by the annihilation of one of us. You purpose to kill me. How dare you sport thus with life? Do your duty towards me, and I will do mine towards you and the rest of mankind. If you will comply with my conditions, I will leave them and you at peace; but if you refuse, I will glut the maw of death, until it be satiated with the blood of your remaining friends.' [. . .]

'[. . .] I will not be tempted to set myself in opposition to thee. I am thy creature, and I will be even mild and docile to my natural lord and king, if thou wilt also perform thy part, the which thou owest me. Oh, Frankenstein, be not equitable to every other, and trample upon me alone, to whom thy justice, and even thy clemency and affection, is most due. Remember, that I am thy creature: I ought to be thy Adam; but I am rather the fallen angel, whom thou drivest from joy for no misdeed. Every where I see bliss, from which I alone am irrevocably excluded. I was benevolent and good; misery made me a fiend. Make me happy, and I shall again be virtuous.' [. . .]

'How can I move thee? Will no entreaties cause thee to turn a favourable eye upon thy creature, who implores thy goodness and compassion. Believe me, Frankenstein: I was benevolent; my soul glowed with love and humanity: but am I not alone, miserably alone? You, my creator, abhor me; what hope can I gather from your fellow-creatures, who owe me nothing? they spurn and hate me. The desert mountains and dreary glaciers are my refuge. I have wandered here many days; the caves of ice, which I only do not fear, are a dwelling to me, and the only one which man does not grudge. These bleak skies I hail, for they are kinder to me than your fellow-beings. If the multitude of mankind knew of my existence, they would do as you do, and arm themselves for my destruction. Shall I not then hate them who abhor me? I will keep no terms with my enemies.

I am miserable, and they shall share my wretchedness. Yet it is in your power to recompense me, and deliver them from an evil which it only remains for you to make so great, that not only you and your family, but thousands of others, shall be swallowed up in the whirlwinds of its rage. Let your compassion be moved, and do not disdain me. Listen to my tale: when you have heard that, abandon or commiserate me, as you shall judge that I deserve. But hear me. The guilty are allowed, by human laws, bloody as they may be, to speak in their own defence before they are condemned. Listen to me, Frankenstein. You accuse me of murder; and yet you would, with a satisfied conscience, destroy your own creature. Oh, praise the eternal justice of man! Yet I ask you not to spare me: listen to me; and then, if you can, and if you will, destroy the work of your hands.'

Notice how the creature's words are a circling whirlwind of passion and aggression. He has not been allowed to form a stable sense of subjectivity. The political implications of 'bloody' human laws should be noted. The image of death as a carnivore whose 'maw' the creature will 'glut' is appropriate for the interest Shelley and Percy took in vegetarianism, and it is part of their characteristic vocabulary on this topic. Moretti's remarks on the creature's promises of benevolence are useful (Modern Criticism, **p. 92**).

Chapter 3 [Frankenstein is compelled to hear the creature's story]

'It is with considerable difficulty that I remember the original æra of my being: all the events of that period appear confused and indistinct. A strange multiplicity of sensations seized me, and I saw, felt, heard, and smelt, at the same time; and it was, indeed, a long time before I learned to distinguish between the operations of my various senses. By degrees, I remember, a stronger light pressed upon my nerves, so that I was obliged to shut my eyes. Darkness then came over me, and troubled me; but hardly had I felt this, when, by opening my eyes, as I now suppose, the light poured in upon me again. I walked, and, I believe, descended; but I presently found a great alteration in my sensations. Before, dark and opaque bodies had surrounded me, impervious to my touch or sight; but I now found that I could wander on at liberty, with no obstacles which I could not either surmount or avoid. The light became more and more oppressive to me; and, the heat wearying me as I walked, I sought a place where I could receive shade. This was the forest near Ingolstadt; and here I lay by the side of a brook resting from my fatigue, until I felt tormented by hunger and thirst. This roused me from my nearly dormant state, and I ate some berries which I found hanging on the trees, or lying on the ground. I slaked my thirst at the brook; and then lying down, was overcome by sleep. [. . .]

Percy Shelley's essay 'On Life' discusses how early impressions are indistinct. For Percy, there was a link between vegetarian diet and healthy sleep. See *A Vindication of Natural Diet*, and the discussion in Morton (see Modern Criticism). As in the structural anthropology of Claude Lévi-Strauss, the creature learns through simple binary opposition, and more complex thought emerges from this basic form. In observing the 'radiant roof of light which canopied me', the creature is being both a scientist and a poet. Here the creature states: 'My eyes became accustomed to the light, and to perceive objects in their right forms; I distinguished the insect from the herb, and, by degrees, one herb from another'. That is, he learns to distinguish between metaphor and metonymy, or identity and contiguity. See the discussion of Brooks's essay in Modern Criticism (**p. 108**).

'One day, when I was oppressed by cold, I found a fire which had been left by some wandering beggars, and was overcome with delight at the warmth I experienced from it. In my joy I thrust my hand into the live embers, but quickly drew it out again with a cry of pain. How strange, I thought, that the same cause should produce such opposite effects! I examined the materials of the fire, and to my joy found it to be composed of wood. I quickly collected some branches, but they were wet, and would not burn. I was pained at this, and sat still watching the operation of the fire. The wet wood which I had placed near the heat dried, and itself became inflamed. I reflected on this; and, by touching the various branches; I discovered the cause, and busied myself in collecting a great quantity of wood, that I might dry it, and have a plentiful supply of fire. When night came on, and brought sleep with it, I was in the greatest fear lest my fire should be extinguished. I covered it carefully with dry wood and leaves, and placed wet branches upon it; and then, spreading my cloak, I lay on the ground, and sunk into sleep.

This section shows the creature acting as a kind of scientist: not the showman-scientist displayed by the Abernethy-like Victor, but an empirical, materialist scientist like Lawrence. See Marilyn Butler's and Alan Rauch's essays in Modern Criticism. The creature is also aping Prometheus (not just Victor). Cooking is his first cultural activity. What the Enlightenment period saw as phylogenetic progress (or not?) in civilisation, from hunter-gathering to agriculture, is here repeated in the creature's personal ontogeny (growth) (see Morton in Modern Criticism, **p. 117**).

'It was noon when I awoke; and, allured by the warmth of the sun, which shone brightly on the white ground, I determined to recommence my travels; and, depositing the remains of the peasant's breakfast in a wallet I found, I proceeded across the fields for several hours, until at sunset I arrived at a village. How miraculous did this appear! the huts, the neater cottages, and stately houses, engaged my admiration by turns. The vegetables in the gardens, the milk and cheese that I saw placed at the windows of some of the cottages, allured my appetite. One of the best of these I entered; but I had hardly placed my foot within the door, before the children shrieked, and one of the women fainted. The whole village was roused; some fled, some attacked me, until, grievously bruised by stones and many other kinds of missile weapons, I escaped to the open country, and fearfully took refuge in a low hovel, quite bare, and making a wretched appearance after the palaces I had beheld in the village. This hovel, however, joined a cottage of a neat and pleasant appearance; but, after my late dearly-bought experience, I dared not enter it. My place of refuge was constructed of wood, but so low, that I could with difficulty sit upright in it. No wood, however, was placed on the earth, which formed the floor, but it was dry; and although the wind entered it by innumerable chinks, I found it an agreeable asylum from the snow and rain.

Notice how the cottages and their inhabitants 'engage' the creature's 'admiration'. Surely he is acting as the innocent eye of Swift's *Gulliver's Travels*, giving the reader a naïve look at class. Notice also how Shelley refuses to turn the natural world into a Romantic idyll: it is the relative civilisation of the cottages that proves to be a paradise, not the natural state into which the creature initially escapes. The eloquence of the creature in his narrative surely adds to the pathos of his representation.

'[. . .] The young girl was occupied in arranging the cottage; but presently she took something out of a drawer, which employed her hands, and she sat down beside the old man, who, taking up an instrument, began to play, and to produce sounds, sweeter than the voice of the thrush or the nightingale. It was a lovely sight, even to me, poor wretch! who had never beheld aught beautiful before. The silver hair and benevolent countenance of the aged cottager, won my reverence; while the gentle manners of the girl enticed my love. He played a sweet mournful air, which I perceived drew tears from the eyes of his amiable companion, of which the old man took no notice, until she sobbed audibly; he then pronounced a few sounds, and the fair creature, leaving her work, knelt at his feet. He raised her, and smiled with such kindness and affection, that I felt sensations of a peculiar and overpowering nature: they were a mixture of pain and pleasure, such as I had never before experienced, either from hunger or cold, warmth or food; and I withdrew from the window, unable to bear these emotions. [. . .]

Again, the trappings of civilisation (music) are preferred to the sounds of nature; and the creature has 'never beheld aught beautiful before'. As in Rousseau, the feeling of compassion, felt by the creature at the end of this passage, unbearable as it is, is spontaneous and natural – even though this creates a paradox: how 'natural' is civilisation itself? (This is the argument pursued in Jacques Derrida's *Of Grammatology*.)

Chapter 4

The creature observes the life of the family and tries to ascertain the cause of their unhappiness. The creature helps the youths by fetching wood during the night. The young woman is astonished.

'By degrees I made a discovery of still greater moment. I found that these people possessed a method of communicating their experience and feelings to one another by articulate sounds. I perceived that the words they spoke sometimes produced pleasure or pain, smiles or sadness, in the minds and countenances of the hearers. This was indeed a godlike science, and I ardently desired to become acquainted with it. But I was baffled in every attempt I made for this purpose. Their pronunciation was quick; and the words they uttered, not having any apparent connexion with visible objects, I was unable to discover any clue by which I could unravel the mystery of their reference. By great application, however, and after having remained during the space of several revolutions of the moon in my hovel, I discovered the names that were given to some of the most familiar objects of discourse: I learned and applied the words *fire*, *milk*, *bread*, and *wood*. I learned also the names of the cottagers themselves. The youth and his companion had each of them several names, but the old man had only one, which was *father*. The girl was called *sister*, or *Agatha*; and the youth *Felix*, *brother*, or *son*. I cannot describe the delight I felt when I learned the ideas appropriated to each of these sounds, and was able to pronounce them. I distinguished several other words, without being able as yet to understand or apply them; such as *good*, *dearest*, *unhappy*.

The creature here articulates a Lockean theory of the arbitrariness of language. This was a fairly standard eighteenth-century view, that seems more radical now, perhaps because of the uses to which structuralist and post-structuralist forms of nominalism have been put. The creature spends the winter watching the family and notes their 'amiable' disposition; Felix is astonished by the creature's 'invisible hand' (surely something of a parody of Adam Smith's notion of the free market as an invisible hand in *The Wealth of Nations*, 1776). The creature watches Felix reading to Agatha and the father. The creature admires the humans' 'grace, beauty, and delicate complexions: but how was I terrified, when I viewed myself in a transparent pool! At first I started back, unable to believe that it was indeed I who was reflected in the mirror; and when I became fully convinced that I was in reality the monster that I am, I was filled with the bitterest sensations of despondence and mortification.' This is a revision of Eve's coming to consciousness by gazing into a pool in Milton's *Paradise Lost*. The winter ends; the family is less hungry; it rains frequently.

'[. . .] When I returned [from the woods], as often as it was necessary, I cleared their path from the snow, and performed those offices that I had seen done by Felix. I afterwards found that these labours, performed by an invisible hand, greatly astonished them; and once or twice I heard them, on these occasions, utter the words *good spirit, wonderful*; but I did not then understand the signification of these terms. [. . .]

The creature thinks more of communicating with the family.

Chapter 5

Spring comes; someone arrives at the door of the cottage.

'It was a lady on horseback, accompanied by a countryman as a guide. The lady was dressed in a dark suit, and covered with a thick black veil. Agatha asked a question; to which the stranger only replied by pronouncing, in a sweet accent, the name of Felix. Her voice was musical, but unlike that of either of my friends. On hearing this word, Felix came up hastily to the lady; who, when she saw him, threw up her veil, and I beheld a countenance of angelic beauty and expression. Her hair of a shining raven black, and curiously braided; her eyes were dark, but gentle, although animated; her features of a regular proportion, and her complexion wondrously fair, each cheek tinged with a lovely pink.

To what extent is the creature applying, or not, a western standard of beauty with which to judge Safie? Later the narrative identifies the creature with her, as 'she was endeavouring to learn their language; and the idea instantly occurred to me, that I should make use of the same instructions to the same end'. Note that the story of Safie occurs in the very middle of the Chinese box narrative frames. As the west gazes on the east, the novel reaches its maximum moment of simulated authenticity – surely also a rather dizzying moment of uncertainty as to the truth.

'Felix seemed ravished with delight when he saw her, every trait of sorrow vanished from his face, and it instantly expressed a degree of ecstatic joy, of which I could hardly have believed it capable; his eyes sparkled, as his cheek flushed with pleasure; and at that moment I thought him as beautiful as the stranger. She appeared affected by different feelings; wiping a few tears from her lovely eyes, she held out her hand to Felix, who kissed it rapturously, and called her, as well as I could distinguish, his sweet Arabian. [. . .]

'The book from which Felix instructed Safie was Volney's *Ruins of Empires*. I should not have understood the purport of this book, had not Felix, in reading it, given very minute explanations. He had chosen this work, he said, because the declamatory style was framed in imitation of the eastern authors. Through this work I obtained a cursory knowledge of history, and a view of the several empires at present existing in the world; it gave me an insight into the manners, governments, and religions of the different nations of the earth. I heard of the slothful Asiatics; of the stupendous genius and mental activity of the Grecians; of the wars and wonderful virtue of the early Romans – of their subsequent degeneration – of the decline of that mighty empire; of chivalry, christianity, and kings. I heard of the discovery of the American hemisphere, and wept with Safie over the hapless fate of its original inhabitants. [. . .]

In the mouth of the creature, does the use of **Volney** serve to naturalise the language of orientalism, which distinguishes between a despotic east and a civilised west? Or does it ironise stereotyped attitudes towards different nations? Notice how the indigenous 'inhabitants' of America are valued here. This echoes a theme resonant in European literature since Montaigne's essay 'Des Cannabales' and Shakespeare's *The Tempest*. For more on orientalism, see W. Joseph Lew, 'The Deceptive Other' (in Further Reading, **p. 182**). For Volney, see Contemporary Documents, **p. 33**.

'Every conversation of the cottagers now opened new wonders to me. While I listened to the instructions which Felix bestowed upon the Arabian, the strange system of human society was explained to me. I heard of the division of property, of immense wealth and squalid poverty; of rank, descent, and noble blood.

'The words induced me to turn towards myself. I learned that the possessions most esteemed by your fellow-creatures were, high and unsullied descent united with riches. A man might be respected with only one of these acquisitions; but without either he was considered, except in very rare instances, as a vagabond and a slave, doomed to waste his powers for the profit of the chosen few. And what was I? Of my creation and creator I was absolutely ignorant; but I knew that I possessed no money, no friends, no kind of property. I was, besides, endowed with a figure hideously deformed and loathsome; I was not even of the same nature as man. [. . .]

'Of what a strange nature is knowledge! It clings to the mind, when it has once seized on it, like a lichen on the rock. I wished sometimes to shake off all thought and feeling; but I learned that there was but one means to overcome the sensation of pain, and that was death – a state which I feared yet did not understand. I admired virtue and good feelings, and loved the gentle manners and amiable qualities of my cottagers; but I was shut out from intercourse with them, except through means which I obtained by stealth, when I was unseen and unknown, and which rather increased than satisfied the desire I had of becoming one among my fellows. [. . .]

The lichen metaphor is strikingly dissimilar to the Promethean language of knowledge as fire. Lichen is slow, tenacious and often overlooked, the other rapid and hard to miss, like Frankenstein's showy science. Lichen is also alive and organic, while fire is a bringer of death. The differences between the creature and Frankenstein as seekers of knowledge is again being emphasised.

'Other lessons were impressed upon me even more deeply. I heard of the difference of sexes; of the birth and growth of children; how the father doated on the smiles of the infant, and the lively sallies of the older child; how all the life and cares of the mother were wrapt up in the precious charge; how the mind of youth expanded and gained knowledge; of brother, sister, and all the various relationships which bind one human being to another in mutual bonds. [. . .]

Chapter 6

[. . .] 'The name of the old man was De Lacey. He was descended from a good family in France, where he had lived for many years in affluence, respected by his superiors, and beloved by his equals. His son was bred in the service of his country; and Agatha had ranked with ladies of the highest distinction. A few months before my arrival, they had lived in a large and luxurious city, called Paris, surrounded by friends, and possessed of every enjoyment which virtue, refinement of intellect, or taste, accompanied by a moderate fortune, could afford.

'The father of Safie had been the cause of their ruin. He was a Turkish merchant, and had inhabited Paris for many years, when, for some reason which I could not learn, he became obnoxious to the government. He was seized and cast into prison the very day that Safie arrived from Constantinople to join him. He was tried, and condemned to death. The injustice of his sentence was very flagrant; all Paris was indignant; and it was judged that his religion and wealth, rather than the crime alleged against him, had been the cause of his condemnation. [. . .]

The creature's inability to learn why the Turk has become 'obnoxious' is surely a comment upon the ideological nature of this judgement, through the satirical figure of the innocent eye, skilfully employed in Jonathan Swift's *Gulliver's Travels*, a key text for understanding *Frankenstein*. Felix helps the Turk escape from prison, and receives letters from Safie in French.

'Safie related, that her mother was a Christian Arab, seized and made a slave by the Turks; recommended by her beauty, she had won the heart of the father of Safie, who married her. The young girl spoke in high and enthusiastic terms of her mother, who, born in freedom spurned the bondage to which she was now reduced. She instructed her daughter in the tenets of her religion, and taught her to aspire to higher powers of intellect, and an independence of spirit, forbidden to the female followers of Mahomet. This lady died; but her lessons were indelibly impressed on the mind of Safie, who sickened at the prospect of again returning to Asia, and the being immured within the walls of a haram, allowed only to occupy herself with puerile amusements, ill suited to the temper of her soul, now accustomed to grand ideas and a noble emulation for virtue. The prospect of marrying a Christian, and remaining in a country where women were allowed to take a rank in society, was enchanting to her. [. . .]

To note what is forbidden to women Moslems is to make a feminist point in the period during which the novel was written. This is a point that Wollstonecraft herself could have made; indeed, the story may reflect the personal history of Shelley and her mother. The Turk escapes with Felix on the night before his execution, with papers in Felix's father's name; they travel through Lyons to Leghorn (Livorno); Felix and Safie spend some time together before her father goes east. Safie is outraged by her father's behaviour; he departs for Constantinople and she decides to rejoin Felix; though her attendant dies on the journey, she makes it safely to the De Laceys. The creature promises to furnish Victor with copies of the letters which will prove the truth of his tale. This is a typical Enlightenment form of inartificial rhetorical proof (solid empirical evidence). But surely the validity of letters is undermined by the novel's framing devices? (See the discussion of Favret's article on **p. 132**.)

Chapter 7

'One night, during my accustomed visit to the neighbouring wood, where I collected my own food, and brought home firing for my protectors, I found on the ground a leathern portmanteau, containing several articles of dress and some books. I eagerly seized the prize, and returned with it to my hovel. Fortunately the books were written in the language the elements of which I had acquired at the cottage; they consisted of *Paradise Lost*, a volume of *Plutarch's Lives*, and the *Sorrows of Werter*. The possession of these treasures gave me extreme delight; I now continually studied and exercised my mind upon these histories, whilst my friends were employed in their ordinary occupations.

Milton's poem *Paradise Lost* is a seminal work of republicanism and the sublime that inspired many of the Romantics. *Plutarch's Lives* is a classic republican text, admired in the Enlightenment by such writers as Rousseau, especially for demonstrating the split between public and private, and revealing the private lives of his subjects. **Johann Wolfgang von Goethe**'s *The Sorrows of Young Werther* is a prototypical Romantic text. The creature's literary education is radical.

'I can hardly describe to you the effect of these books. They produced in me an infinity of new images and feelings, that sometimes raised me to ecstacy, but more frequently sunk me into the lowest dejection. In the *Sorrows of Werter*, besides the interest of its simple and affecting story, so many opinions are canvassed, and so many lights thrown upon what had hitherto been to me obscure subjects, that I found in it a never-ending source of speculation and astonishment. The gentle and domestic manners it described, combined with lofty sentiments and feelings, which had for their object something out of self, accorded well with my experience among my protectors, and with the wants which were for ever alive in my own bosom. But I thought Werter himself a more divine being than I had ever beheld or imagined; his character contained no pretension, but it sunk deep. The disquisitions upon death and suicide were calculated to fill me with wonder. I did not pretend to enter into the merits of the case, yet I inclined towards the opinions of the hero, whose extinction I wept, without precisely understanding it. [. . .]

'The volume of *Plutarch's Lives* which I possessed, contained the histories of the first founders of the ancient republics. This book had a far different effect upon me from the *Sorrows of Werter*. I learned from Werter's imaginations despondency and gloom: but Plutarch taught me high thoughts; he elevated me above the wretched sphere of my own reflections, to admire and love the heroes of past ages. [. . .] I read of men concerned in public affairs governing or massacring their species. I felt the greatest ardour for virtue rise within me, and abhorrence for vice, as far as I understood the signification of those terms, relative as they were, as I applied them, to pleasure and pain alone. Induced by these feelings, I was of course led to admire peaceable law-givers, Numa, Solon, and Lycurgus, in preference to Romulus and Theseus.[1] The patriarchal lives of my protectors caused these impressions to take a firm hold on my mind; perhaps, if my first introduction to humanity had been made by a young soldier, burning for glory and slaughter, I should have been imbued with different sensations.

Notice the radical materialist theory of mind in the creature's statement at the end of this paragraph, derived in eighteenth-century British thought from the associationist David Hartley's *Observations on Man* (1749).

'But *Paradise Lost* excited different and far deeper emotions. I read it, as I had read the other volumes which had fallen into my hands, as a true history. It moved every feeling of wonder and awe, that the picture of an omnipotent God warring with his creatures was capable of exciting. I often referred the several situations, as their similarity struck me, to my own. Like Adam, I was created apparently united by no link to any other being in existence; but his state was far different from mine in every other respect. He had come forth from the hands of God a perfect creature, happy and prosperous, guarded by the especial care of his

---

1   Numa Pompilius was an early king of Rome; Lycurgus was a Spartan lawgiver; Solon, an Athenian one. Romulus was one of the mythical founders of Rome, Theseus of Athens.

Creator; he was allowed to converse with, and acquire knowledge from beings of a superior nature: but I was wretched, helpless, and alone. Many times I considered Satan as the fitter emblem of my condition; for often, like him, when I viewed the bliss of my protectors, the bitter gall of envy rose within me.

> Different characters in the novel oscillate between different characters in *Paradise Lost*, a point often made in the more recent criticism of *Frankenstein*.

'Another circumstance strengthened and confirmed these feelings. Soon after my arrival in the hovel, I discovered some papers in the pocket of the dress which I had taken from your laboratory. At first I had neglected them; but now that I was able to decypher the characters in which they were written, I began to study them with diligence. It was your journal of the four months that preceded my creation. [. . .] I sickened as I read. "Hateful day when I received life!" I exclaimed in agony. "Cursed creator! Why did you form a monster so hideous that even you turned from me in disgust? God in pity made man beautiful and alluring, after his own image; but my form is a filthy type of your's, more horrid from its very resemblance. Satan had his companions, fellow-devils, to admire and encourage him; but I am solitary and detested." [. . .]

'One day, when the sun shone on the red leaves that strewed the ground, and diffused cheerfulness, although it denied warmth, Safie, Agatha, and Felix, departed on a long country walk, and the old man, at his own desire, was left alone in the cottage. When his children had departed, he took up his guitar, and played several mournful, but sweet airs, more sweet and mournful than I had ever heard him play before. At first his countenance was illuminated with pleasure, but, as he continued, thoughtfulness and sadness succeeded; at length, laying aside the instrument, he sat absorbed in reflection.

'My heart beat quick; this was the hour and moment of trial, which would decide my hopes, or realize my fears. [. . .]

'I entered; "Pardon this intrusion," said I, "I am a traveller in want of a little rest; you would greatly oblige me, if you would allow me to remain a few minutes before the fire."

' "Enter," said De Lacey; "and I will try in what manner I can relieve your wants; but, unfortunately, my children are from home, and, as I am blind, I am afraid I shall find it difficult to procure food for you." [De Lacey continues.]

' "Do not despair. To be friendless is indeed to be unfortunate; but the hearts of men, when unprejudiced by any obvious self-interest, are full of brotherly love and charity. Rely, therefore, on your hopes; and if these friends are good and amiable, do not despair."

' "They are kind – they are the most excellent creatures in the world; but, unfortunately, they are prejudiced against me. I have good dispositions; my life has been hitherto harmless, and, in some degree, beneficial; but a fatal prejudice clouds their eyes, and where they ought to see a feeling and kind friend, they behold only a detestable monster." [. . .]

'The old man paused, and then continued, "If you will unreservedly confide to me the particulars of your tale, I perhaps may be of use in undeceiving them. I am blind, and cannot judge of your countenance, but there is something in your words which persuades me that you are sincere. I am poor, and an exile; but it will afford me true pleasure to be in any way serviceable to a human creature." [. . .]

' "How can I thank you, my best and only benefactor? from your lips first have I heard the voice of kindness directed towards me; I shall be for ever grateful; and your present humanity assures me of success with those friends whom I am on the point of meeting."

' "May I know the names and residence of those friends?"

'I paused. This, I thought, was the moment of decision, which was to rob me of, or bestow happiness on me for ever. I struggled vainly for firmness sufficient to answer him, but the effort destroyed all my remaining strength; I sank on the chair, and sobbed aloud. At that moment I heard the steps of my younger protectors. I had not a moment to lose; but, seizing the hand of the old man, I cried, "Now is the time! – save and protect me! You and your family are the friends whom I seek. Do not you desert me in the hour of trial!"

' "Great God!" exclaimed the old man, "who are you?"

'At that instant the cottage door was opened, and Felix, Safie and Agatha entered. Who can describe their horror and consternation on beholding me? Agatha fainted; and Safie, unable to attend to her friend, rushed out of the cottage. Felix darted forward, and with supernatural force tore me from his father, to whose knees I clung: in a transport of fury, he dashed me to the ground, and struck me violently with a stick. I could have torn him limb from limb, as the lion rends the antelope. But my heart sunk within me as with bitter sickness, and I refrained. I saw him on the point of repeating his blow, when, overcome by pain and anguish, I quitted the cottage, and in the general tumult escaped unperceived to my hovel.[']

Chapter 8

'Cursed, cursed creator! Why did I live? Why, in that instant, did I not extinguish the spark of existence which you had so wantonly bestowed? I know not; despair had not yet taken possession of me; my feelings were those of rage and revenge. I could with pleasure have destroyed the cottage and its inhabitants, and have glutted myself with their shrieks and misery. [. . .]

As noted above (p. 144), 'glutted' is a (Percy) Shelleyan note of cannibalism and carnivorousness. In the poem 'Alastor' it is death that gluts itself thus. The creature nears Geneva.

'At this time a slight sleep relieved me from the pain of reflection, which was disturbed by the approach of a beautiful child, who came running into the recess I had chosen with all the sportiveness of infancy. Suddenly, as I gazed on him, an idea seized me, that this little creature was unprejudiced, and had lived too short a time to have imbibed a horror of deformity. If, therefore, I could seize him, and educate him as my companion and friend, I should not be so desolate in this peopled earth.

'Urged by this impulse, I seized on the boy as he passed, and drew him towards me. As soon as he beheld my form, he placed his hands before his eyes, and uttered a shrill scream: I drew his hand forcibly from his face, and said, "Child, what is the meaning of this? I do not intend to hurt you; listen to me."

'He struggled violently; "Let me go," he cried; "monster! ugly wretch! you wish to eat me, and tear me to pieces – You are an ogre – Let me go, or I will tell my papa."

' "Boy, you will never see your father again; you must come with me."

' "Hideous monster! let me go; My papa is a Syndic[1] – he is M. Frankenstein – he would punish you. You dare not keep me."

' "Frankenstein! you belong then to my enemy – to him towards whom I have sworn eternal revenge; you shall be my first victim."

'The child still struggled, and loaded me with epithets which carried despair to my heart: I grasped his throat to silence him, and in a moment he lay dead at my feet.

'I gazed on my victim, and my heart swelled with exultation and hellish triumph: clapping my hands, I exclaimed, "I, too, can create desolation; my enemy is not impregnable; this death will carry despair to him, and a thousand other miseries shall torment and destroy him."

'As I fixed my eyes on the child, I saw something glittering on his breast. I took it; it was a portrait of a most lovely woman. In spite of my malignity, it softened and attracted me. For a few moments I gazed with delight on her dark eyes, fringed by deep lashes, and her lovely lips; but presently my rage returned: I remembered that I was for ever deprived of the delights that such beautiful creatures could bestow; and that she whose resemblance I contemplated would, in regarding me, have changed that air of divine benignity to one expressive of disgust and affright.

'Can you wonder that such thoughts transported me with rage? I only wonder that at that moment, instead of venting my sensations in exclamations and agony, I did not rush among mankind, and perish in the attempt to destroy them. [. . .]

'For some days I haunted the spot where these scenes had taken place; sometimes wishing to see you, sometimes resolved to quit the world and its miseries for ever. At length I wandered towards these mountains and have ranged through their immense recesses, consumed by a burning passion which you alone can gratify. We may not part until you have promised to comply with my requisition. I am alone, and miserable; man will not associate with me; but one as deformed and horrible as myself would not deny herself to me. My companion must be of the same species, and have the same defects. This being you must create.'

---

1 A Syndic is a chief magistrate of Geneva.

Chapter 9

[. . .] 'You must create a female for me, with whom I can live in the interchange of those sympathies necessary for my being. This you alone can do; and I demand it of you as a right which you must not refuse.' [. . .]

'I do refuse it,' I replied; 'and no torture shall ever extort a consent from me. You may render me the most miserable of men, but you shall never make me base in my own eyes. Shall I create another like yourself, whose joint wickedness might desolate the world. Begone! I have answered you; you may torture me, but I will never consent.' [. . .]

I was moved. I shuddered when I thought of the possible consequences of my consent; but I felt that there was some justice in his argument. His tale, and the feelings he now expressed, proved him to be a creature of fine sensations; and did I not, as his maker, owe him all the portion of happiness that it was in my power to bestow? He saw my change of feeling, and continued –

'If you consent, neither you nor any other human being shall ever see us again: I will go to the vast wilds of South America. My food is not that of man; I do not destroy the lamb and the kid, to glut my appetite; acorns and berries afford me sufficient nourishment. My companion will be of the same nature as myself, and will be content with the same fare. We shall make our bed of dried leaves; the sun will shine on us as on man, and will ripen our food. The picture I present to you is peaceful and human, and you must feel that you could deny it only in the wantonness of power and cruelty. Pitiless as you have been towards me, I now see compassion in your eyes; let me seize the favourable moment, and persuade you to promise what I so ardently desire.'

'You propose,' replied I, 'to fly from the habitations of man, to dwell in those wilds where the beasts of the field will be your only companions. How can you, who long for the love and sympathy of man, persevere in this exile? You will return, and again seek their kindness, and you will meet with their detestation; your evil passions will be renewed, and you will then have a companion to aid you in the task of destruction. This may not be; cease to argue the point, for I cannot consent.'

'How inconstant are your feelings! but a moment ago you were moved by my representations, and why do you again harden yourself to my complaints? I swear to you, by the earth which I inhabit, and by you that made me, that, with the companion you bestow, I will quit the neighbourhood of man, and dwell, as it may chance, in the most savage of places. My evil passions will have fled, for I shall meet with sympathy; my life will flow quietly away, and, in my dying moments, I shall not curse my maker.'

His words had a strange effect upon me. I compassionated him, and sometimes felt a wish to console him; but when I looked upon him, when I saw the filthy mass that moved and talked, my heart sickened, and my feelings were altered to those of horror and hatred. I tried to stifle these sensations; I thought, that as I could not sympathize with him, I had no right to withhold from him the small portion of happiness which was yet in my power to bestow. [. . .]

I paused some time to reflect on all he had related, and the various arguments which he had employed. I thought of the promise of virtues which he had displayed on the opening of his existence, and the subsequent blight of all kindly feeling by the loathing and scorn which his protectors had manifested towards him. His power and threats were not omitted in my calculations: a creature who could exist in the ice caves of the glaciers, and hide himself from pursuit among the ridges of inaccessible precipices, was a being possessing faculties it would be vain to cope with. After a long pause of reflection, I concluded, that the justice due both to him and my fellow-creatures demanded of me that I should comply with his request. Turning to him, therefore, I said –

'I consent to your demand, on your solemn oath to quit Europe for ever, and every other place in the neighbourhood of man, as soon as I shall deliver into your hands a female who will accompany you in your exile.'

'I swear,' he cried, 'by the sun, and by the blue sky of heaven, that if you grant my prayer, while they exist you shall never behold me again. Depart to your home, and commence your labours: I shall watch their progress with unutterable anxiety; and fear not but that when you are ready I shall appear.' [. . .]

VOLUME 3

Chapter 1

Victor's trip through Europe and up the Thames, visiting London and Oxford. Victor's republicanism seen in his admiration for the Civil War; the trip to the Orkneys.

Chapter 2

[. . .] We passed a considerable period at Oxford, rambling among its environs, and endeavouring to identify every spot which might relate to the most animating epoch of English history. Our little voyages of discovery were often prolonged by the successive objects that presented themselves. We visited the tomb of the illustrious Hampden, and the field on which that patriot fell. For a moment my soul was elevated from its debasing and miserable fears to contemplate the divine ideas of liberty and self-sacrifice, of which these sights were the monuments and the remembrancers. For an instant I dared to shake off my chains, and look around me with a free and lofty spirit; but the iron had eaten into my flesh, and I sank again, trembling and hopeless, into my miserable self. [. . .]

See Shelley's *Journal*, 1.181. Shelley visited John Hampden's monument on 17 October 1817; Hampden was a Civil War Parliamentarian whose life and work inspired the republicans and democrats of the later revolutionary (Romantic) period. Oxford was a royalist stronghold during the English Civil War; King Charles I was secured at Magdalen College.

Chapter 3

I sat one evening in my laboratory; the sun had set, and the moon was just rising from the sea; I had not sufficient light for my employment, and I remained idle, in a pause of consideration of whether I should leave my labour for the night, or hasten its conclusion by an unremitting attention to it. [. . . I was now about to form another being, of whose dispositions I was alike ignorant; she might become ten thousand times more malignant than her mate, and delight, for its own sake, in murder and wretchedness. He had sworn to quit the neighbourhood of man, and hide himself in deserts; but she had not; and she, who in all probability was to become a thinking and reasoning animal, might refuse to comply with a compact made before her creation. They might even hate each other; the creature who already lived loathed his own deformity, and might he not conceive a greater abhorrence for it when it came before his eyes in the female form? She also might turn with disgust from him to the superior beauty of man; she might quit him, and he be again alone, exasperated by the fresh provocation of being deserted by one of his own species.

Even if they were to leave Europe, and inhabit the deserts of the new world, yet one of the first results of those sympathies for which the dæmon thirsted would be children, and a race of devils would be propagated upon the earth, who might make the very existence of the species of man a condition precarious and full of terror. Had I a right, for my own benefit, to inflict this curse upon everlasting generations? I had before been moved by the sophisms of the being I had created; I had been struck senseless by his fiendish threats: but now, for the first time, the wickedness of my promise burst upon me; I shuddered to think that future ages might curse me as their pest, whose selfishness had not hesitated to buy its own peace at the price perhaps of the existence of the whole human race.

See Maureen McLane, *Romanticism and the Human Sciences* (Cambridge and New York: Cambridge University Press, 2000), 104–8. Frankenstein's creature knows 'how to speak human being if not to inhabit it'. He validates Victor's 'anthropomorphic . . . thought'. The story of the creature's possible emigration could be read as allegorical for the larger movements of populations that were so exercising the minds of contemporary thinkers, such as Thomas Malthus (please consult the Directory): 'Victor's Malthusian panic ensures that the conflict of monster and man will be imagined as a species or race conflict'. McLane concludes that 'Neither

I trembled, and my heart failed within me; when, on looking up, I saw, by the light of the moon, the dæmon at the casement. A ghastly grin wrinkled his lips as he gazed on me, where I sat fulfilling the task which he had allotted to me. Yes, he had followed me in my travels; he had loitered in forests, hid himself in caves, or taken refuge in wide and desert heaths; and now came to mark my progress, and claim the fulfilment of my promise.

As I looked on him, his countenance expressed the utmost extent of malice and treachery. I thought with a sensation of madness on my promise of creating another like to him, and, trembling with passion, tore to pieces the thing on which I was engaged. The wretch saw me destroy the creature on whose future existence he depended for happiness, and, with a howl of devilish despair and revenge, withdrew. [. . .]

Presently I heard the sound of footsteps along the passage; the door opened, and the wretch whom I dreaded appeared. Shutting the door, he approached me, and said, in a smothered voice –

'You have destroyed the work which you began; what is it that you intend? Do you dare to break your promise? I have endured toil and misery: I left Switzerland with you; I crept along the shores of the Rhine, among its willow islands, and over the summits of its hills. I have dwelt many months in the heaths of England, and among the deserts of Scotland. I have endured incalculable fatigue, and cold, and hunger; do you dare destroy my hopes?' [. . .]

Chapter 6

Elizabeth observed my agitation for some time in timid and fearful silence; at length she said, 'What is it that agitates you, my dear Victor? What is it you fear?'

'Oh! peace, peace, my love,' replied I, 'this night, and all will be safe: but this night is dreadful, very dreadful.'

I passed an hour in this state of mind, when suddenly I reflected how dreadful the combat which I momentarily expected would be to my wife, and I earnestly entreated her to retire, resolving not to join her until I had obtained some knowledge as to the situation of my enemy.

She left me, and I continued some time walking up and down the passages of the house, and inspecting every corner that might afford a retreat to my adversary. But I discovered no trace of him, and was beginning to conjecture that some fortunate chance had intervened to prevent the execution of his menaces; when suddenly I heard a shrill and dreadful scream. It came from the room into which Elizabeth had retired. As I heard it, the whole truth rushed into my mind, my arms dropped, the motion of every muscle and fibre was suspended; I could feel the blood trickling in my veins, and tingling in the extremities of my limbs. This state lasted but for an instant; the scream was repeated, and I rushed into the room.

Great God! why did I not then expire! Why am I here to relate the destruction of the best hope, and the purest creature of earth. She was there, lifeless and inanimate, thrown across the bed, her head hanging down, and her pale and distorted features half covered by her hair. Every where I turn I see the same figure – her bloodless arms and relaxed form flung by the murderer on its bridal bier. Could I behold this, and live? Alas! life is obstinate, and clings closest where it is most hated. For a moment only did I lose recollection; I fainted.

When I recovered, I found myself surrounded by the people of the inn; their countenances expressed a breathless terror: but the horror of others appeared only as a mockery, a shadow of the feelings that oppressed me. I escaped from them to the room where lay the body of Elizabeth, my love, my wife, so lately living, so dear, so worthy. She had been moved from the posture in which I had first beheld her; and now, as she lay, her head upon her arm, and a handkerchief thrown across her face and neck, I might have supposed her asleep. I rushed towards her, and embraced her with ardour; but the deathly languor and coldness of the limbs told me, that what I now held in my arms had ceased to be the Elizabeth whom I had loved and cherished. The murderous mark of the fiend's grasp was on her neck, and the breath had ceased to issue from her lips. [. . .]

The magistrate cannot believe Frankenstein's tale; the chase of creator after creature commences.

Chapter 7

[. . .] And now my wanderings began, which are to cease but with life. I have traversed a vast portion of the earth, and have endured all the hardships which travellers, in deserts and barbarous countries, are wont to meet. How I have lived I hardly know; many times have I stretched my failing limbs upon the sandy plain, and prayed for death. But revenge kept me alive; I dared not die, and leave my adversary in being. [. . .]

The deep grief which this scene had at first excited quickly gave way to rage and despair. They were dead, and I lived; their murderer also lived, and to destroy him I must drag out my weary existence. I knelt on the grass, and kissed the earth, and with quivering lips exclaimed, 'By the sacred earth on which I kneel, by the shades that wander near me, by the deep and eternal grief that I feel, I swear; and by thee, O Night, and by the spirits that preside over thee, I swear to pursue that dæmon, who caused this misery, until he or I shall perish in mortal conflict. For this purpose I will preserve my life: to execute this dear revenge, will I again behold the sun, and tread the green herbage of earth, which otherwise should vanish from my eyes for ever. And I call on you, spirits of the dead; and on you, wandering ministers of vengeance, to aid and conduct me in my work. Let the cursed and hellish monster drink deep of agony; let him feel the despair that now torments me.' [. . .]

I was answered through the stillness of night by a loud and fiendish laugh. It rung on my ears long and heavily; the mountains re-echoed it, and I felt as if all hell surrounded me with mockery and laughter. Surely in that moment I should have been possessed by phrenzy, and have destroyed my miserable existence, but that my vow was heard, and that I was reserved for vengeance. The laughter died away; when a well-known and abhorred voice, apparently close to my ear, addressed me in an audible whisper – 'I am satisfied: miserable wretch! you have determined to live, and I am satisfied.' [. . .]

The creature appears to control the terms of the chase, almost as if he were omnipresent. The plangent rhetoric of Frankenstein's prayer is designed to disturb – how does it work?

[. . .] I pursued him; and for many months this has been my task. Guided by a slight clue, I followed the windings of the Rhone, but vainly. The blue Mediterranean appeared; and, by a strange chance, I saw the fiend enter by night, and hide himself in a vessel bound for the Black Sea. I took my passage in the same ship; but he escaped, I know not how.

Amidst the wilds of Tartary and Russia, although he still evaded me, I have ever followed in his track. Sometimes the peasants, scared by this horrid apparition, informed me of his path; sometimes he himself, who feared that if I lost all trace I should despair and die, often left some mark to guide me. The snows descended on my head, and I saw the print of his huge step on the white plain. To you first entering on life, to whom care is new, and agony unknown, how can you understand what I have felt, and still feel? Cold, want, and fatigue, were the least pains which I was destined to endure; I was cursed by some devil, and carried about with me my eternal hell; yet still a spirit of good followed and directed my steps, and, when I most murmured, would suddenly extricate me from seemingly insurmountable difficulties. Sometimes, when nature, overcome by hunger, sunk under the exhaustion, a repast was prepared for me in the desert, that restored and inspirited me. The fare was indeed coarse, such as the peasants of the country ate; but I may not doubt that it was set there by the spirits that I had invoked to aid me. Often, when all was dry, the heavens cloudless, and I was parched by thirst, a slight cloud would bedim the sky, shed the few drops that revived me, and vanish. [. . .]

What his feelings were whom I pursued, I cannot know. Sometimes, indeed, he left marks in writing on the barks of the trees, or cut in stone, that guided me, and instigated my fury. 'My reign is not yet over,' (these words were legible in one of these inscriptions); 'you live, and my power is complete. Follow me; I seek the everlasting ices of the north, where you will feel the misery of cold and frost, to which I am impassive. You will find near this place, if you follow not too tardily, a dead hare; eat, and be refreshed. Come on, my enemy; we have yet to wrestle for our lives; but many hard and miserable hours must you endure, until that period shall arrive.' [. . .]

[. . .] I now gained on him; so much so, that when I first saw the ocean, he was but one day's journey in advance, and I hoped to intercept him before he should reach the beach. With new courage, therefore, I pressed on, and in two days arrived at a wretched hamlet on the seashore. I inquired of the inhabitants concerning the fiend, and gained accurate information. A gigantic monster, they said, had arrived the night before, armed with a gun and many pistols; putting to flight the inhabitants of a solitary cottage, through fear of his terrific appearance. He had carried off their store of winter food, and, placing it in a sledge, to draw which he had seized on a numerous drove of trained dogs, he had harnessed them, and the same night, to the joy of the horror-struck villagers, had pursued his journey across the sea in a direction that led to no land; and they conjectured that he must speedily be destroyed by the breaking of the ice, or frozen by the eternal frosts. [. . .]

Eve Sedgwick has commented upon the homoerotic tensions in *Frankenstein*; it is clear that this passage strikingly dramatises these tensions in the form of the chase. Tartary is central Asia, principally associated with the Mongol empire. The creature has become a hunter, replete with guns, sledge and dogs.

WALTON, *in continuation.*

August 26th, 17–.

[. . .] His tale is connected, and told with an appearance of the simplest truth; yet I own to you that the letters of Felix and Safie, which he shewed me, and the apparition of the monster, seen from our ship, brought to me a greater conviction of the truth of his narrative than his asseverations, however earnest and connected. Such a monster has then really existence; I cannot doubt it; yet I am lost in surprise and admiration. Sometimes I endeavoured to gain from Frankenstein the particulars of his creature's formation; but on this point he was impenetrable.

As we exit each framing device in turn, the truth value of each is rendered uncertain and problematic. The close of the novel is at once breathlessly present-tense, and distant in the layers of irony that have been built up by the framing devices.

September 5th.

A scene has just passed of such uncommon interest, that although it is highly probable that these papers may never reach you, yet I cannot forbear recording it. [. . .]

I mentioned in my last letter the fears I entertained of a mutiny. This morning, as I sat watching the wan countenance of my friend – his eyes half closed, and his limbs hanging listlessly, – I was roused by half a dozen of the sailors, who desired admission into the cabin. They entered; and their leader addressed me. He told me that he and his companions had been chosen by the other sailors to come in deputation to me, to make me a demand, which, in justice, I could not refuse. We were immured in ice, and should probably never escape; but they feared that if, as was possible, the ice should dissipate, and a free passage be opened, I should be rash enough to continue my voyage, and lead them into fresh dangers, after they might happily have surmounted this. They desired, therefore, that I should engage with a solemn promise, that if the vessel should be freed, I would instantly direct my course southward.

This speech troubled me. I had not despaired; nor had I yet conceived the idea of returning, if set free. Yet could I, in justice, or even in possibility, refuse this demand? I hesitated before I answered; when Frankenstein, who had at first been silent, and, indeed, appeared hardly to have force enough to attend, now roused himself; his eyes sparkled, and his cheeks flushed with momentary vigour. Turning towards the men, he said –

'What do you mean? What do you demand of your captain? Are you then so easily turned from your design? Did you not call this a glorious expedition? and wherefore was it glorious? Not because the way was smooth and placid as a southern sea, but because it was full of dangers and terror; because, at every new incident, your fortitude was to be called forth, and your courage exhibited; because danger and death surrounded, and these dangers you were to brave and overcome. For this was it a glorious, for this was it an honourable undertaking. You were hereafter to be hailed as the benefactors of your species; your name adored, as belonging to brave men who encountered death for honour and the benefit of mankind. And now, behold, with the first imagination of danger, or, if you will, the first mighty and terrific trial of your courage, you shrink away, and are content to be handed down as men who had not strength enough to endure cold and peril; and so, poor souls, they were chilly, and returned to their warm fire-sides. Why, that requires not this preparation; ye need not have come thus far, and dragged your captain to the shame of a defeat, merely to prove yourselves cowards. Oh! be men, or be more than men. Be steady to your purposes, and firm as a rock. This ice is not made of such stuff as your hearts might be; it is mutable, cannot withstand you, if you say that it shall not. Do not return to your families with the stigma of disgrace marked on your brows. Return as heroes who have fought and conquered, and who know not what it is to turn their backs on the foe.'

He spoke this with a voice so modulated to the different feelings expressed in his speech, with an eye so full of lofty design and heroism, that can you wonder that these men were moved. They looked at one another, and were unable to reply. [. . .]

Frankenstein's quelling of the mutiny speaks to his qualities as a leader, and indicates that he represents the upper rather than the lower class. In a displaced fashion, he has become the imperialist conqueror – like Coleridge's Ancient Mariner, perhaps? For further discussion of this theme, see Moretti and Spivak (Modern Criticism, **pp. 92, 122**). Throughout the novel, language and rhetoric are strong issues. Notice, for example, the number of times language is described as a natural process, for instance an avalanche: unstoppable, driving everything in its path, overwhelming (**p. 143**). There is also a strong discourse of masculinity here: 'be men, or be more than men' (**p. 163**).

September 12th.

[. . .] I am interrupted. What do these sounds portend? It is midnight; the breeze blows fairly, and the watch on deck scarcely stir. Again; there is a sound as of a human voice, but hoarser; it comes from the cabin where the remains of Frankenstein still lie. I must arise, and examine. Good night, my sister.

Great God! what a scene has just taken place! I am yet dizzy with the remembrance of it. I hardly know whether I shall have the power to detail it; yet the tale which I have recorded would be incomplete without this final and wonderful catastrophe.

I entered the cabin, where lay the remains of my ill-fated and admirable friend. Over him hung a form which I cannot find words to describe; gigantic in stature, yet uncouth and distorted in its proportions. As he hung over the coffin, his face was concealed by long locks of ragged hair; but one vast hand was extended, in colour and apparent texture like that of a mummy. When he heard the sound of my approach, he ceased to utter exclamations of grief and horror, and sprung towards the window. Never did I behold a vision so horrible as his face, of such loathsome, yet appalling hideousness. I shut my eyes involuntarily, and endeavoured to recollect what were my duties with regard to this destroyer. I called on him to stay.

He paused, looking on me with wonder; and, again turning towards the lifeless form of his creator, he seemed to forget my presence, and every feature and gesture seemed instigated by the wildest rage of some uncontrollable passion.

'That is also my victim!' he exclaimed; 'in his murder my crimes are consummated; the miserable series of my being is wound to its close! Oh, Frankenstein! generous and self-devoted being! what does it avail that I now ask thee to pardon me? I, who irretrievably destroyed thee by destroying all thou lovedst. Alas! he is cold; he may not answer me.'

[. . .] The monster continued to utter wild and incoherent self-reproaches. At length I gathered resolution to address him, in a pause of the tempest of his passion: 'Your repentance,' I said, 'is now superfluous. If you had listened to the voice of conscience, and heeded the stings of remorse, before you had urged your diabolical vengeance to this extremity, Frankenstein would yet have lived.'

'And do you dream?' said the dæmon; 'do you think that I was then dead to agony and remorse? – He,' he continued, pointing to the corpse, 'he suffered not more in the consummation of the deed; – oh! not the ten-thousandth portion of the anguish that was mine during the lingering detail of its execution. A frightful selfishness hurried me on, while my heart was poisoned with remorse. Think ye that the groans of Clerval were music to my ears? My heart was fashioned to be susceptible of love and sympathy; and, when wrenched by misery to vice and hatred, it did not endure the violence of the change without torture, such as you cannot even imagine. [. . .]

I was at first touched by the expressions of his misery; yet when I called to mind what Frankenstein had said of his powers of eloquence and persuasion, and when I again cast my eyes on the lifeless form of my friend, indignation was re-kindled within me. 'Wretch!' I said, 'it is well that you come here to whine over the desolation that you have made. You throw a torch into a pile of buildings, and when they are consumed you sit among the ruins, and lament the fall. Hypocritical fiend! if he whom you mourn still lived, still would he be the object, again would he become the prey of your accursed vengeance. It is not pity that you feel; you lament only because the victim of your malignity is withdrawn from your power.'

When Walton calls the creature 'wretch' he is using Frankenstein's language. See the discussion in Duyfhuizen's essay (Modern Criticism, pp. 108–9).

'Oh, it is not thus – not thus,' interrupted the being; 'yet such must be the impression conveyed to you by what appears to be the purport of my actions. Yet I seek not a fellow-feeling in my misery. No sympathy may I ever find. When I first sought it, it was the love of virtue, the feelings of happiness and affection with which my whole being overflowed, that I wished to be participated. But now, that virtue has become to me a shadow, and that happiness and affection are turned into bitter and loathing despair, in what should I seek for sympathy? I am content to suffer alone, while my sufferings shall endure: when I die, I am well satisfied that abhorrence and opprobrium should load my memory. Once my fancy was soothed with dreams of virtue, of fame, and of enjoyment. Once I falsely hoped to meet with beings, who, pardoning my outward form, would love me for the excellent qualities which I was capable of bringing forth. I was nourished with high thoughts of honour and devotion. But now vice has degraded me beneath the meanest animal. No crime, no mischief, no malignity, no misery, can be found comparable to mine. [. . .]

The creature's many references to his sense of 'loathing' serve to naturalise a form of aesthetic judgement. Please refer to the essays by Gigante (Further Reading) and Youngquist (Modern Criticism).

'But it is true that I am a wretch. I have murdered the lovely and the helpless; I have strangled the innocent as they slept, and grasped to death his throat who never injured me or any other living thing. I have devoted my creator, the select specimen of all that is worthy of love and admiration among men, to misery; I have pursued him even to that irremediable ruin. There he lies, white and cold in death. You hate me; but your abhorrence cannot equal that with which I regard myself. I look on the hands which executed the deed; I think on the heart in which the imagination of it was conceived, and long for the moment when they will meet my eyes, when it will haunt my thoughts, no more. [. . .]

'Farewell! I leave you, and in you the last of human kind whom these eyes will ever behold. Farewell, Frankenstein! If thou wert yet alive, and yet cherished a desire of revenge against me, it would be better satiated in my life than in my destruction. But it was not so; thou didst seek my extinction, that I might not cause greater wretchedness; and if yet, in some mode unknown to me, thou hast not yet ceased to think and feel, thou desirest not my life for my own misery. Blasted as thou wert, my agony was still superior to thine; for the bitter sting of remorse may not cease to rankle in my wounds until death shall close them for ever.

'But soon,' he cried, with sad and solemn enthusiasm, 'I shall die, and what I now feel be no longer felt. Soon these burning miseries will be extinct. I shall ascend my funeral pile triumphantly, and exult in the agony of the torturing flames. The light of that conflagration will fade away; my ashes will be swept into the sea by the winds. My spirit will sleep in peace; or if it thinks, it will not surely think this. Farewell.'

He sprung from the cabin-window, as he said this, upon the ice-raft which lay close to the vessel. He was soon borne away by the waves, and lost in darkness and distance.

THE END.

Changes to the 1831 Edition: A Selection

Mary Wollstonecraft Shelley, Introduction to the Third (Standard Novels) Edition of *Frankenstein* (1831) London: Henry Colburn and Richard Bentley.[1]

In the third edition, Shelley enhances the interiority of the characters, especially at the beginning. She amplifies Frankenstein's sense of (religiously induced) guilt, and makes his education more a matter of his own private self-teaching: it is somewhat removed from the family environment and thus Ingolstadt University's professors look worse. (Marilyn Butler comments that it was 'notoriously unorthodox' anyway (*Frankentein*, ed. Butler, 198).) Some descriptions of science are cut (volume 1, chapter 1) or, as Butler puts it, 'transvalued' (199): natural history and alchemical magic are somewhat conflated. The possibly incestuous implication of Elizabeth being Frankenstein's cousin is resolved as she now becomes a stranger and Ernest's childhood sickness is removed (volume 1.5): 'Taken together with the improved health of Alphonse, these changes remove the theme of an aristocratic family's degenerative state which was originally so notable in the first and third volumes' and thus played into Shelley's republican sympathies (200). Butler adds that Shelley cut 'Two emphatic pronouncements by Elizabeth' which promoted Godwin's criticism of justice; and Shelley added Clerval's proposed career as a 'colonial administrator' (1.5), despite the fact that 'several remarks in 1818, and the Safie theme, imply disapproval of colonialism' (200). For further discussion, see Butler's edition, 198–200. In addition to these changes, the creature's cruelty towards Justine becomes motivated less by masochistic, more by sadistic frenzy: she must be punished because she is, in the view of the sadist, 'asking for it'.

The publishers of the Standard Novels, in selecting *Frankenstein* for one of their series, expressed a wish that I should furnish them with some account of the origin of the story. I am the more willing to comply, because I shall thus give a general answer to the question, so very frequently asked me – 'How I, then a young girl, came to think of and to dilate upon so very hideous an idea?' It is true that I am very averse to bringing myself forward in print; but as my account will only appear as an appendage to a former production, and as it will be confined to such topics as have connexion with my authorship alone, I can scarcely accuse myself of a personal intrusion.

It is not singular that, as the daughter of two persons of distinguished literary celebrity, I should very early in life have thought of writing. As a child I scribbled; and my favourite pastime during the hours given me for recreation was to 'write stories'. Still, I had a dearer pleasure than this, which was the formation of castles

---

1 The differences between this and Percy's introduction to the 1818 edition are evident. Note the way in which Shelley casts herself as a builder of castles in the air – a literary trope of modesty in the face of success, but also an echo of Frankenstein's description of Elizabeth (**p. 133**).

in the air – the indulging in waking dreams – the following up trains of thought, which had for their subject the formation of a succession of imaginary incidents. My dreams were at once more fantastic and agreeable than my writings. In the latter I was a close imitator – rather doing as others had done than putting down the suggestions of my own mind. What I wrote was intended at least for one other eye – my childhood's companion and friend,[2] but my dreams were all my own; I accounted for them to nobody; they were my refuge when annoyed – my dearest pleasure when free.

I lived principally in the country as a girl, and passed a considerable time in Scotland. I made occasional visits to the more picturesque parts; but my habitual residence was on the blank and dreary northern shores of the Tay, near Dundee. Blank and dreary on retrospection I call them; they were not so to me then. They were the eyry[3] of freedom, and the pleasant region where unheeded I could commune with the creatures of my fancy. I wrote then – but in a most common-place style. It was beneath the trees of the grounds belonging to our house, or on the bleak sides of the woodless mountains near, that my true compositions, the airy flights of my imagination, were born and fostered. I did not make myself the heroine of my tales. Life appeared to me too common-place an affair as regarded myself. I could not figure to myself that romantic woes or wonderful events would ever be my lot; but I was not confined to my own identity, and I could people the hours with creations far more interesting to me at that age than my own sensations.

After this my life became busier, and reality stood in place of fiction. My husband, however, was from the first, very anxious that I should prove myself worthy of my parentage, and enrol myself on the page of fame. He was for ever inciting me to obtain literary reputation, which even on my own part I cared for then, though since I have become infinitely indifferent to it. At this time he desired that I should write, not so much with the idea that I could produce any thing worthy of notice, but, that he might himself judge how far I possessed the promise of better things hereafter. Still I did nothing. Travelling, and the cares of a family, occupied my time; and study, in the way of reading or improving my ideas in communication with his far more cultivated mind, was all of literary employment that engaged my attention.

In the summer of 1816, we visited Switzerland, and became the neighbours of Lord Byron. At first we spent our pleasant hours on the lake, or wandering on its shores; and Lord Byron, who was writing the third canto of *Childe Harold*, was the only one among us who put his thoughts upon paper. These, as he brought them successively to us, clothed in all the light and harmony of poetry, seemed to stamp as divine the glories of heaven and earth, whose influences we partook with him.

But it proved a wet, ungenial summer, and incessant rain often confined us for days to the house. Some volumes of ghost stories, translated from German into

2   Butler speculates that this might be Isabel Baxter of Dundee, 'with whom MWS stayed for much of 1812 and 1813–14. But MWS hardly "lived principally in the country as a girl"' (*Frankenstin*, ed. Butler, 260).
3   '([R]emote) nest of a bird of prey' (ibid., 260).

French, fell into our hands. There was the *History of the Inconstant Lover*, who, when he thought to clasp the bride to whom he had pledged his vows, found himself in the arms of the pale ghost of her whom he had deserted. There was the tale of the sinful founder[4] of his race whose miserable doom it was to bestow the kiss of death on all the younger sons of his fated house, just when they reached the age of promise. His gigantic, shadowy form, clothed like the ghost in *Hamlet*, in complete armour, but with the beaver up, was seen at midnight, by the moon's fitful beams, to advance slowly along the gloomy avenue. The shape was lost beneath the shadow of the castle walls; but soon a gate swung back, a step was heard, the door of the chamber opened, and he advanced to the couch of the blooming youths, cradled in healthy sleep. Eternal sorrow sat upon his face as he bent down and kissed the forehead[s] of the boys, who from that hour withered like flowers snapt from the stalk. I have not seen these stories since then; but their incidents are as fresh in my mind as if I had read them yesterday.

'We will each write a ghost story', said Lord Byron; and his proposition was acceded to. There were four of us. The noble author began a tale, a fragment of which he printed at the end of his poem of *Mazeppa*. Shelley, more apt to embody ideas and sentiments in the radiance of brilliant imagery, and in the music of the most melodious verse that adorns our language, than to invent the machinery of a story, commenced one founded in the experiences of his early life. Poor Polidori had some terrible idea about a skull-headed lady who was so punished for peeping through a keyhole – what to see I forget – something very shocking and wrong of course; but when she was reduced to a worse condition than the renowned Tom of Coventry,[5] he did not know what to do with her and was obliged to dispatch her to the tomb of the Capulets,[6] the only place for which she was fitted. The illustrious poets also, annoyed by the platitude of prose, speedily relinquished their uncongenial task.

I busied myself *to think of a story*, – a story to rival those which had excited us to this task. One which would speak to the mysterious fears of our nature and awaken thrilling horror – one to make the reader dread to look round, to curdle the blood, and quicken the beatings of the heart. If I did not accomplish these things, my ghost story would be unworthy of its name. I thought and pondered – vainly. I felt that blank incapability of invention which is the greatest misery of authorship, when dull Nothing replies to our anxious invocations. 'Have you thought of a story?' I was asked each morning, and each morning I was forced to reply with a mortifying negative.

Every thing must have a beginning, to speak in Sanchean phrase;[7] and that beginning must be linked to something that went before. The Hindoos give the world an elephant to support it, but they make the elephant stand upon a tortoise.

---

4 'The second, unnamed story, about a vampire, appears to have partly prompted both Byron and MWS. [. . .] Rieger [in his edition of the 1818 text, 1974] comments that MWS does not recollect the two stories accurately' (ibid., 260).
5 'Spied on Lady Godiva, and is supposed to have been struck blind. But Polidori claims that the story he really told at Cologny was a first attempt at his novel *Ernestus Berchtold: or the Modern Oedipus* (1819)' (ibid., 260).
6 One of the duelling families in *Romeo and Juliet*.
7 Sancho Panza from Cervantes's *Don Quixote* 2.33.

Invention, it must be humbly admitted, does not consist in creating out of void, but out of chaos;[8] the materials must, in the first place, be afforded: it can give form to dark, shapeless substances, but cannot bring into being the substance itself. In all matters of discovery and invention, even of those that appertain to the imagination, we are continually reminded of the story of Columbus and his egg.[9] Invention consists in the capacity of seizing on the capabilities of a subject; and in the power of moulding and fashioning ideas suggested to it.

Many and long were the conversations between Lord Byron and Shelley, to which I was a devout but nearly silent listener.[10] During one of these, various philosophical doctrines were discussed, and among others the nature of the principle of life, and whether there was any probability of its ever being discovered and communicated. They talked of the experiments of Dr Darwin (I speak not of what the Doctor really did, or said that he did, but, as more to my purpose, of what was then spoken of as having been done by him), who preserved a piece of vermicelli in a glass case, till by some extraordinary means it began to move with voluntary motion.[11] Not thus, after all, would life be given. Perhaps a corpse would be reanimated; galvanism had given token of such things: perhaps the component parts of a creature might be manufactured, brought together, and endued with vital warmth.

Night waned upon this talk, and even the witching hour had gone by, before we retired to rest. When I placed my head on my pillow, I did not sleep, nor could I be said to think. My imagination, unbidden, possessed and guided me, gifting the successive images that arose in my mind with a vividness far beyond the usual bounds of reverie. I saw – with shut eyes, but acute mental vision – I saw the pale student of unhallowed arts kneeling beside the thing he had put together. I saw the hideous phantasm of a man stretched out, and then, on the working of some powerful engine, show signs of life, and stir with an uneasy, half-vital motion.[12] Frightful it must be; for supremely frightful would be the effect of any human endeavour to mock the stupendous mechanism of the Creator of the world. His success would terrify the artist; he would rush away from his odious handywork, horror-stricken. He would hope that, left to itself, the slight spark of life which he had communicated would fade; that this thing, which had received such imperfect animation would subside into dead matter; and he might sleep in the belief that the silence of the grave would quench forever the transient existence of the hideous corpse which he had looked upon as the cradle of life. He sleeps; but he is awakened; he opens his eyes; behold, the horrid thing stands at his bedside, opening his curtains and looking on him with yellow, watery, but speculative eyes.

---

8 A distinction also made in Milton's *Paradise Lost*, one of the creature's texts.
9 'When Columbus was told by a courtier that anyone might have discovered the Indies, he allegedly challenged all present to stand an egg on end. After everyone failed, he did it himself by crushing the end' (*Frankenstein*, ed. Butler, 260).
10 'Polidori's *Diary* indicates a conversation at which he was himself present' (ibid., 260).
11 This is based on a general discussion in Erasmus Darwin's *The Temple of Nature* (see Contemporary Documents, p. 32).
12 An allusion, as often in *Frankenstein*, to one of Shelley's favourite poems, Coleridge's *The Rime of the Ancient Mariner* 5.387–8. That part of the poem itself features animated corpses.

I opened mine in terror. The idea so possessed my mind, that a thrill of fear ran through me, and I wished to exchange the ghastly image of my fancy for the realities around. I see them still; the very room, the dark *parquet*, the closed shutters, with the moonlight struggling through, and the sense I had that the glassy lake and white high Alps were beyond. I could not so easily get rid of my hideous phantom; still it haunted me. I must try to think of something else. I recurred to my ghost story – my tiresome, unlucky ghost story! O! if I could only contrive one which would frighten my reader as I myself had been frightened that night!

Swift as light and as cheering was the idea that broke in upon me. 'I have found it! What terrified me will terrify others; and I need only describe the spectre which had haunted my midnight pillow.' On that morrow I announced that I had *thought of a story*. I began that day with the words, 'It was on a dreary night of November,'[13] making only a transcript of the grim terrors of my waking dream.

At first I thought but a few pages – of a short tale; but Shelley urged me to develope the idea at greater length. I certainly did not owe the suggestion of one incident, nor scarcely of one train of feeling, to my husband, and yet but for his incitement it would never have taken the form in which it was presented to the world. From this declaration I must except the preface. As far as I can recollect, it was entirely written by him.

And now, once again, I bid my hideous progeny go forth and prosper. I have affection for it, for it was the offspring of happy days, when death and grief were but words, which found no true echo in my heart. Its several pages speak of many a walk, many a drive, and many a conversation, when I was not alone; and my companion was one who, in this world, I shall never see more. But this is for myself; my readers have nothing to do with these associations.

I will add but one word as to the alterations I have made. They are principally those of style. I have changed no portion of the story nor introduced any new ideas or circumstances. I have mended the language when it was so bald as to interfere with the interest of the narrative; and these changes occur almost exclusively in the beginning of the first volume. Throughout they are entirely confined to such parts as mere adjuncts to the story, leaving the core and substance of it untouched.

M.W.S.

London,
October 15th, 1831.

Volume I, chapter I

[. . .] I have often attributed my attachment to, my passionate enthusiasm for, the dangerous mysteries of ocean, to that production of the most imaginative of modern poets. There is something at work in my soul, which I do not under-stand. I am practically industrious – pains-taking; a workman to execute with

---

13 The beginning of the fourth chapter of the first volume.

perseverance and labour: – but besides this, there is a love for the marvellous, a belief in the marvellous, intertwined in all my projects, which hurries me out of the common pathways of men, even to the wild sea and unvisited regions I am about to explore.

But to return to my dearer considerations. [. . .]

When my father returned from Milan, he found playing with me in the hall of our villa, a child fairer than pictured cherub – a creature who seemed to shed radiance from her looks, and whose form and motions were lighter than the chamois of the hills. The apparition was soon explained. With his permission my mother prevailed on her rustic guardians to yield their charge to her. They were fond of the sweet orphan. Her presence had seemed a blessing to them; but it would be unfair to her to keep her in poverty and want, when Providence afforded her such powerful protection. They consulted their village priest, and the result was, that Elizabeth Lavenza became the inmate of my parents' house – my more than sister – the beautiful and adored companion of all my occupations and pleasures.

Volume 1, chapter 2 [added chapter; a selection]

My temper was sometimes violent, and my passions vehement; but by some law in my temperature they were turned, not towards childish pursuits, but to an eager desire to learn, and not to learn all things indiscriminately. I confess that neither the structure of languages, nor the code of governments, nor the politics of various states, possessed attractions for me. It was the secrets of heaven and earth that I desired to learn; and whether it was the outward substance of things, or the inner spirit of nature and the mysterious soul of man that occupied me, still my enquiries were directed to the metaphysical, or, in its highest sense, the physical secrets of the world.

Before this I was not unacquainted with the more obvious laws of electricity. On this occasion a man of great research in natural philosophy was with us, and, excited by this catastrophe, he entered on the explanation of a theory which he had formed on the subject of electricity and galvanism, which was at once new and astonishing to me. All that he said threw greatly into the shade Cornelius Agrippa, Albertus Magnus, and Paracelsus, the lords of my imagination; but by some fatality the overthrow of these men disinclined me to pursue my accustomed studies. It seemed to me as if nothing would or could ever be known. All that had so long engaged my attention suddenly grew despicable. By one of those caprices of the mind, which we are perhaps most subject to in early youth, I at once gave up my former occupations; set down natural history and all its progeny as a deformed and abortive creation; and entertained the greatest disdain for a would-be science, which could never even step within the threshold of real knowledge [. . .]

Volume 1, chapter 3 [previously 1.2; substituted for 'professors . . . upon those subjects' (p. 134)]

Chance – or rather the evil influence, the Angel of Destruction, which asserted omnipotent sway over me from the moment I turned my reluctant steps from my father's door – led me first to Mr Krempe, professor of natural philosophy. He was an uncouth man, but deeply embued in the secrets of his science. He asked me several questions concerning my progress in the different branches of science pertaining to natural philosophy. I replied carelessly; and, partly in contempt, mentioned the names of my alchymists as the principal authors I had studied.

[. . .] In rather too philosophical and connected a strain, perhaps, I have given an account of the conclusions I had come to concerning them in my early years. As a child, I had not been content with the results promised by the modern professors of natural science. With a confusion of ideas only to be accounted for by my extreme youth, and my want of a guide on such matters, I had retrod the steps of knowledge along the paths of time, and exchanged the discoveries of recent enquirers for the dreams of forgotten alchymists.

Volume 1, chapter 6 [previously 1.5; a description of Clerval]

[He] had never sympathised in my tastes for natural science; and his literary pursuits differed wholly from those which had occupied me. He came to the university with the design of making himself complete master of the oriental languages, as thus he should open a field for the plan of life had marked out for himself. Resolved to pursue no inglorious career, he turned his eyes toward the East, as affording scope for his spirit of enterprise [. . .]

Volume 2, chapter 16 [previously 2.8; the creature encounters Justine, who is now asleep rather than 'passing near me']

'And then I bent over her, and whispered "Awake, fairest, thy lover is near – he who would give his life but to obtain one look of affection from thine eyes; my beloved, awake!"

'The sleeper stirred; a thrill of terror ran through me. Should she indeed awake, and see me, and curse me, and denounce the murderer? Thus would she assuredly act, if her darkened eyes opened, and she beheld me. The thought was madness; it stirred the fiend within me – not I, but she shall suffer: the murder I have committed because I am for ever robbed of all that she could give me, she shall atone. The crime had its source in her: be hers the punishment!

4

Further Reading

Further Reading

Recommended Editions

Shelley, Mary Wollstonecraft. *Frankenstein or, The Modern Prometheus (The 1818 Text)*. Ed. Marilyn Butler. Oxford and New York: Oxford University Press, 1994, 1998.
   A very helpful and scholarly introduction to the novel which points out Shelley's relationships with science.

Frankenstein; or, the Modern Prometheus. Ed. D.L. Macdonald and Kathleen Scherf. Peterborough, Ontario: Broadview Press, 1994.
   Contains helpful selections from the creature's reading list (such as Volney and Plutarch), and other materials such as Humphry Davy and Erasmus Darwin.

Frankenstein: Or, the Modern Prometheus; the 1818 Text. Ed. James Rieger. Chicago and London: University of Chicago Press, 1974, 1982.
   This is a copiously annotated edition which usefully incorporates the 1823 autograph variants and 1831 revisions into the main body of the text.

Robinson, Charles E., ed. *The Frankenstein Notebooks*. New York: Garland, 1996.
   This is an essential source for understanding in greater detail the formation of Shelley's novel, and contains everything from revisions of the novel to speculations about the dates involved in the story (lxv–lxvi).

Further Reading

Shelley's life

Mellor, Anne K., *Mary Shelley: Her Life, Her Fiction, Her Monsters* (New York: Methuen, 1988).
Poovey, Mary, *The Proper Lady and the Woman Writer: Ideology as Style in the*

Works of Mary Wollstonecraft, Mary Shelley, and Jane Austen (Chicago and London: University of Chicago Press, 1984).

On the web, a good source general source is the Romantic Chronology: http://english.ucsb.edu:591/rchrono/

General, essay collections

For further information on readings of the novel, please refer to the excellent website developed by the *Keats–Shelley Journal* as part of Romantic circles: http://www.rc.umd.edu/reference/ksjbib/mwshelley/ShellMW99.html

Botting, Fred, ed. *Frankenstein: Mary Shelley*. New Casebooks Series. New York: St Martin's Press, 1995. A collection of recent essays.

Smith, Johanna M., ed. *Frankenstein*. Case Studies in Contemporary Criticism (Bedford Books). Boston and New York: St Martin's Press and London: Macmillan, 1992. Helpful for elucidating different kinds of theoretical approach.

Studies in Romanticism 38.3 (Fall 1999). A special edition of readings of Mary Shelley.

Monstrosity and the body

Bann, Stephen, ed. *Frankenstein: Creation and Monstrosity*. London: Reaktion Books, 1994. A study of ideas about monstrosity in visual culture, with the novel as its main focus.

Bewell, Alan. 'An Issue of Monstrous Desire: *Frankenstein* and Obstetrics'. *Yale Journal of Criticism* 2.1 (1988): 105–28. Bewell elucidates some of the recent strands in feminist readings of *Frankenstein*. He recalls Ellen Moers's argument that the novel should be read as a ' "birth myth" '. Critics such as Mary Jacobus have challenged the reduction of *Frankenstein* to biology (105). Barbara Johnson, on the other hand, edits Shelley's literal body out of her reading of the text as monstrous autobiography. Meanwhile, as Homans has observed, Moers's universalism leaves the reader unclear about the actual Shelley and the cultural determinants of her pregnancy (106). Bewell suggests that *Frankenstein* contemplates the long history of the representation of monstrosity and birth, and that it is also an 'attempt to introduce an ambiguously female-based theory of creation in the Romantic discourse on the imagination' (107). Books on midwifery stressed the influence of the pregnant woman's imagination on the foetus (109). On the one hand, this idea was a way of subjecting women to control over the contents of their minds. On the other, it opened a realm of female creativity (115). Bewell notes that in the 1831 preface, Shelley plays upon the obstetric and mental senses of 'dilate', wondering ' "How I . . . came . . . to dilate upon[,] so very hideous an idea?" ' (120). Unlike Erasmus Darwin, Shelley's view of the female creative imagination is active (121–3).

Gigante, Denise. 'Facing the Ugly: the Case of Frankenstein'. *New Literary His-*

tory 67 (June, 2000): 565–88. A helpful elucidation of the ways in which the physiognomy of the creature falls into and out of eighteenth-century theories of the sublime and the beautiful, such as those of Edmund Burke and Immanuel Kant.

Hansen, Mark. ' "Not Thus, After All, Would Life be Given": Technesis, Technology and the Parody of Romantic Poetics in *Frankenstein*'. *Studies in Romanticism* 36.4 (1997), 303–14. This is a hard but worthwhile read. Hansen uses Donna Haraway's essay 'A Cyborg Manifesto' to explain how the creature lacks anything organic (the crucial Romantic aesthetic term). This leads to a discussion of the aesthetics of monstrosity, based on Aristotle's theory of machines.

Hobbs, Colleen. 'Reading the Symptoms: An Exploration of Repression and Hysteria in Mary Shelley's *Frankenstein*'. *Studies in the Novel* 25.2 (1993): 152–69. See the discussion in Key Passages (**pp. 136–7**).

Language and literary form

Cantor, Paul A. 'The Nightmare of Romantic Idealism'. In *Creature and Creator: Myth-Making and English Romanticism*. Cambridge and New York: Cambridge University Press, 1984, 103–32. A simple introduction to the ways in which the novel could be read as a variation on a Romantic theme: the work of art that is 'about' art.

Crook, Nora. 'In Defence of the 1831 *Frankenstein*'. In Michael Eberle-Sinatra, ed. *Mary Shelley's Fictions: From Frankenstein to Falkner*. Basingstoke, Hampshire: Macmillan, 2000 and New York: St Martin's Press, 2000. This is a strongly argued case for regarding the 1831 edition as not very ideologically different from that of 1818. Frankenstein warns of the dangers of 'presumption' in the first edition (8); his behaviour at Justine's trial is only developed and shaded in the 1831 edition (8–9). Frankenstein feels that he does not possess free will even in the first edition (10–13). The essay closes with a powerful analysis of the role of necessity in the novel, dramatised in the ways in which the characters feel compelled to action (13–17). The developments of the second edition allow Crook to conclude that 'if the Creature was ultimately to win, there should at least be a contest' (17).

Cross, Ashley, ' "Indelible Impressions": Gender and Language in Mary Shelley's *Frankenstein*'. *Women's Studies* 27.6 (1998): 547–80. Why do the supposedly arbitrary language and accepting politics the creature has learnt not actually accept but actively reject him (559)? Eighteenth-century thought, argues Cross, developed Locke's theory of language as arbitrary towards the stronger notion that language could actually *constitute* thought (rather than being determined by it (560–1)).

Kiely, Robert. *The Romantic Novel in England*. Cambridge, MA: Harvard University Press, 1972, chapter 8. An old, straightforward introduction to the novel. Kiely is particularly strong on the religious overtones of Frankenstein's ostensibly scientific language (161–2).

Lau, Beth. '*Frankenstein, The Rime of the Ancient Mariner* and *Kubla Khan.*' In Nicholas Roe, ed. *Samuel Taylor Coleridge and the Sciences of Life*, 207–23. Oxford and New York: Oxford University Press, forthcoming. An analysis of an allusive thread that runs throughout the novel. Lau argues that 'far from being a target of disapproval, Coleridge was a profoundly sympathetic and congenial figure to Mary Shelley, and his ideas and literary themes resonated with and helped shape her own' (**p. 209**). Both texts appear to 'condemn selfish ambition and advocate a loving, harmonious co-existence with people and other living things' (**p. 210**). Both the Ancient Mariner and Victor Frankenstein exhibit a remorseful passive aggression, beholding in horror the events that they themselves have precipitated (**p. 216–17**).

Young, Arlene, 'The Monster Within: The Alien Self in Jane Eyre and *Frankenstein*'. *Studies in the Novel* 23.3 (1991): 325–38. Young points out that Jane Eyre's wanderings resemble nothing so much as the flight of Frankenstein's creature. Both *Jane Eyre* and *Frankenstein* contain a doppelgänger theme: the relationship of the creature to Victor, and of Jane to Bertha Mason (327). Both Jane and the creature flee their 'only home' (328), are guided by the moon (329), and 'Each develops an overwhelming sense of self-hatred and becomes isolated from society' (330). Both are reduced to abject scavenging (332). But the principal point of comparison is between the Moor House and the De Lacey residence. Both characters are fascinated by, and simultaneously excluded from, these domestic scenes. This reinforces the novels' theme of alienation. Shelley's novel provides the symbolic subtext for Charlotte Brontë's *Bildungsroman* (novel of individuation).

Biographical approaches

Gilbert, Sandra M. and Susan Gubar. 'Horror's Twin: Mary Shelley's Monstrous Eve.' In *The Madwoman in the Attic: The Woman Writer and the Nineteenth-Century Literary Imagination*. New Haven: Yale University Press, 1979, chapter 7. A feminist interpretation in a book that has become a classic.

Hill-Miller, Katherine C. '*My Hideous Progeny*': *Mary Shelley, William Godwin, and the Father–Daughter Relationship*. Newark: University of Delaware Press and London: Associated University Presses, 1995, 88–93. Hill-Miller points out that Mary Shelley conflates Elizabeth and the creature. Both are figures not only for the dead mother (Mary Wollstonecraft) but also for the daughter. In this feminist psychoanalytic reading, the creature's violent rage finds it basis, behind anger towards the father, in the absence of the mother.

Moers, Ellen. *Literary Women*. New York: Doubleday, 1977, 90–9. This is one of the classic feminist readings.

Todd, Janet. 'Frankenstein's Daughter: Mary Shelley and Mary Wollstonecraft'. *Women and Literature* 4.2 (1976): 18–27. Todd analyses the influence of Shelley's mother, Mary Wollstonecraft, on *Frankenstein*. For example, Wollstonecraft often pointed out 'the blighting effect of trade' and 'the effect of ignorance and poverty on the mind', as did her daughter (19). The centrality of the first person narrative, moreover, that of a slighted or condemned being, is another similarity. Jemima in Wollstonecraft's novel *The Wrongs of Woman* and the creature in *Frankenstein* share this centrality. Jemima 'represents the specific horror of being a woman deprived of family', like the creature (21). Both the creature and Jemima exhibit the social theory propounded by Wollstonecraft's husband, the philosophical anarchist William Godwin. Briefly, this theory states that innate natural goodness is distorted or even checked by inadequate social structures (23).

Gender issues

Conger, Syndy M. 'Prophecy and Sensibility: Mary Wollstonecraft in *Franken-stein*'. *1650–1850* 3 (1997): 301–28. See the discussion in Key Passages (**p. 133**).

Hurley, Kelly. 'Marginal Subjects in *Frankenstein*'. In Alfred David, Kelly Hurley and Philip Schwyzer. *Teaching with the 'Norton Anthology of English Litera-ture,' Seventh Edition: A Guide for Instructors*. New York: W.W. Norton, 2000. A helpful brief guide to ways of teaching issues of class and race in the novel.

Joseph, Gerhard. 'Virginal Sex, Vaginal Text: The "Folds" of *Frankenstein*'. In Lloyd Davis, ed. *Virginal Sexuality and Textuality in Victorian Literature*. Albany: State University of New York Press, 1993, 25–32. See the discussion in Key Passages (**p. 138**).

Mellor, Anne K. 'Possessing Nature: The Female in *Frankenstein*.' In Anne K. Mellor, ed. *Romanticism and Feminism*. Bloomington: Indiana University Press, 1988, 220–32.

Michel, Frann. 'Lesbian Panic and Mary Shelley's *Frankenstein*'. *GLQ* 2.3 (1995): 237–52. Michel starts by noting that there is an absence of 'erotic bonds between women' in *Frankenstein* (238). Feminist readings of the novel, such as Homans's, 'have tended to interpret the creature as both female and maternal' (242). Thus the denial by Frankenstein of a female mate for the creature asserts what Michel calls 'lesbian panic' (243). At another stage, Jus-tine forms her 'primary attachment . . . to other women' (244). Though evi-dence is slim that she bonds erotically with Elizabeth before her death, Michel speculates that representations of same-sex relationships between women in the eighteenth and nineteenth centuries often involved relationships between higher and lower social orders such as that between Agatha and Safie, or Eliza-beth and Justine (245–6). Michel sees the pressure against lesbian desire in *Frankenstein* as stemming from the novel's resistance to direct homosexual male desire. Percy's essay on Greek homosexuality ('A Discourse on the Man-ners of the Ancient Greeks Relative to the Subject of Love'), written when the novel was first published, points out that male homosexuality could be predi-cated on the oppression of women (248). Michel reads this as part of the history of *heterosexual* prejudices about homosexuality that demean female desire in general, and lesbian desire in particular (249–50).

Randel, Fred V. '*Frankenstein*, Feminism, and the Intertextuality of Mountains'. *Studies in Romanticism* 23.4 (1984): 515–32. Still useful. Randel notices that *Frankenstein* attempts to reconcile two opposing spheres: the mountainous (empty of human culture) and the domestic. Beyond this, he observes the clash between patriarchal and non-patriarchal conceptions of mountains in general; and between masculine and feminine spaces of creation.

Orientalism

W. Joseph Lew, 'The Deceptive Other: Mary Shelley's Critique of Orientalism in *Frankenstein*'. *Studies in Romanticism* 30 (Summer, 1991): 255–83. One of the (as yet) few essays devoted to the study of what Edward Said has named 'orientalism': the ways in which western forms of knowledge construct the 'east' as an object of fascination and control.

Directory of Figures

For reasons of space, some names have been omitted; please consult Contexts for further details of the period. The names in this chapter appear in bold on their first occurance in the sourcebook.

Aldini, Giovanni (1762–1834) Grandson of Luigi Galvani, an Italian physicist and physician, who publicised his grandfather's discoveries and promoted the research of electricity in the medical field.

Bentham, Jeremy (1748–1832) Political philosopher and writer on jurisprudence who promoted utilitarianism as the test for morality.

Bichat, Marie-François-Xavier (1771–1802) His work in physiology and anatomy led to the science of histology, the study of bodily tissues. Bichat studied the diseased tissue of organs and was the first to observe, without a microscope, that the organs of the body were composed of smaller units, or tissues, identifying twenty-one types.

Birch, John (c. 1745–1815) Surgeon who promoted the use of electricity as a health aid and founded a hospital department devoted to its study.

Blake, William (1757–1827) Engraver, painter, poet and radical (both political and religious), author of *Songs of Innocence* (1789) and *Songs of Experience* (1794), and the larger prophetic works *Milton* (1804) and *Jerusalem* (1804). He was part of the London circle that included Mary Wollstonecraft, Mary Shelley's mother.

Blumenbach, Johann Friedrich (1752–1840) Considered by many to be the father of modern anthropology, Blumenbach was one of the first to classify mankind in terms of race. As a professor at the University of Göttingen, Germany, his research involved physiology and comparative anatomy and their further application to the natural-historical study of humankind. Investigations resulted in his dividing man into five races: Caucasian, American, Ethiopian, Mongolian and Malayan.

Brough, R.B. [Robert Barnabas] (1828–60) Writer. A composer of popular burlesques played at theatres such as the Adelphi, Lyceum, and Olympic, and a popular journalist.

Brough, William (1826–70) Writer. William, like his younger, yet more famous, brother Robert Barnabas Brough, wrote plays, mainly burlesques, and articles for a number of publications.

Buffon, Comte de [Georges-Louis Leclerc] (1707–88) French naturalist. Author of *Histoire naturelle* (1749–88).

Burke, Edmund (1729–97) An Irish member of the British Parliament. Author of *Reflections on the Revolution in France* (1790), which denounces the French Revolution, and a treatise on the sublime (1757), an influence on *Frankenstein*'s characterisation of Switzerland and the creature.

Byron, Lord [George Gordon] (1788–1824) The sixth Lord Byron, notorious author of *Don Juan*. Accompanied by his physician and secretary John William Polidori, Byron joined the Shelleys and Claire Clairmont, with whom he had begun an affair, in Geneva, Switzerland, in 1816. The events of that summer inspired Mary Shelley's *Frankenstein* and Polidori's *Vampyre*, and Byron began his drama *Manfred*.

Cabanis, Pierre-Jean-Georges (1757–1808) French Materialist philosopher. Cabanis believed that the body's chemical processes controlled all physical function in man, including that of behaviour. The soul was nonexistent, and emotion and intelligence the mere result of neurological impulse.

Canning, George (1770–1827) A British statesman who served as Foreign Secretary from 1822–7. He had previously contributed to the reactionary *Anti-Jacobin*, a journal that attacked Wordsworth and Coleridge, among others, during the hysteria of the 1790s.

Charlotte, Princess (1796–1817) Died in childbirth at twenty-one; the subject of a stirring political essay by Percy Shelley.

Coleridge, Samuel Taylor (1772–1834) Poet and philosopher. Collaborated with Robert Southey in the planning of a propertyless Pantisocratic society in America ('Pantisocracy' is 'the equal rule of all'), but it was never realised. His work with William Wordsworth on *Lyrical Ballads* (1798, 1800) established his career. Coleridge wrote 'Kubla Khan' and *The Rime of the Ancient Mariner*, essential to the text of *Frankenstein*, and many other poetic, dramatic and prose works.

Condorcet, Marie-Jean-Antoine-Nicolas de Caritat, Marquis de (1743–94) Progressive French Enlightenment philosopher and educational reformer who was one of the first to promote the notion of progress, or of mankind's gradual perfection. An ardent supporter of the French Revolution, Condorcet was eventually imprisoned as a Girondin, and while in prison was found dead one morning, a result of either exhaustion or poisoning.

Cooke, Thomas Potter (1786–1864) The first actor to portray Frankenstein's creature. He performed the part in London (in *Presumption*) and Paris (*Le*

Monstre) when the novel was first adapted as a play, and continued, according to sources, to play it for another seven years.

Cooper, Sir Astley Paston (1768–1841) Surgeon and lecturer on anatomy and eventual president of the Royal Academy of Surgeons.

Croker, John Wilson (1780–1857) Politician and essayist who did not favour the poetic school of which Leigh Hunt, Percy Shelley and John Keats were a part, calling it the 'Cockney School'. Wrote a critique of Keats's *Endymion* (*Quarterly Review* 32, September 1818).

Darwin, Erasmus (1731–1802) Poet and physician whose expertise in general medicine was known to George III, who unsuccessfully invited Darwin to be court physician. Darwin revealed his theories of generation and evolution in *Zoonomia*. The poem *The Botanic Garden* is concerned with plant physiology and allegorises the reproduction of plants.

Davy, Sir Humphry (1778–1829) Natural philosopher and poet who gave immensely popular lectures on galvanism and chemistry at the Royal Institution, attended by men of letters, people of rank, and the highly fashionable. A promoter of electrochemical science, Davy presented his experiments and discoveries in electricity in 1807 and later won the Napoleon Prize for his work with galvanic fluids.

Ferriar, John (1761–1815) Physician and writer who helped to relieve detrimental working-class conditions in the town of Manchester by fighting for sanitary working and living environments, public baths and decreased child labour. Ferriar investigated hysteria and was highly praised for his insight into the problem of mental hallucination.

George III [George William Frederick] (1738–1820) Successor to the throne on 25 October 1760 upon the death of George II. Lost the American War of Independence and fought against the Whigs. Suffered a series of bouts with dementia between 1765 and 1810, during which he forced Frances Burney to listen to his ravings and was often straight-waistcoated. George III eventually succumbed to insanity and blindness during the last years of his life.[1] It is now thought that his madness was a product of a physical condition called 'porphyria', a metabolic imbalance. The eventual diagnosis led his son George to be declared Prince Regent.

George IV (1762–1830) Prince Regent during George III's madness and eventual King. He was notorious (and vilified in the radical press) for his ostentation and habits of consumption. Brighton Pavilion, an orientalist palace, was built for him.

Goethe, Johann Wolfgang von (1749–1832) Literary and scientific writer, author of the dramatic poem *Faust* (begun in 1770 and completed in 1832, the first

---

1 Porter, Roy. *A Social History of Madness: The World Through the Eyes of the Insane*. New York: Weidenfeld & Nicolson, 1987, 42.

part published in 1808), *The Sorrows of Young Werther* (1774) and the 'Wilhelm Meister' novels (1777–1829).

Godwin, William (1756–1836) Philosophical anarchist; Shelley's father. See Contexts (**pp. 7, 9**).

Hazlitt, William (1778–1830) Literary critic and essayist, a close friend of Coleridge and Lamb and a member of the circles to which Lamb and Godwin belonged.

Herschel, Sir John Frederick William (1792–1871) Astronomer who advanced the study of stellar and nebular science, chemistry, physics and mathematics; inventor of photography on sensitised paper in 1839.

Holbach, Paul-Henri Dietrich, Baron d' (1723–89) French encyclopedist and philosopher who espoused a materialist view of nature, hedonist ethics and strict atheism.

Hunt, James Henry Leigh (1784–1859) Born in England to American parents, remembered largely for his contributions to theatrical, literary and political criticism. As editor of the *Examiner*, he discovered and published the work of new writers such as Robert Browning, Alfred, Lord Tennyson, John Keats and Percy Bysshe Shelley.

Hunter, John (1728–93) Surgeon, founder of pathological anatomy in England. Promoted investigation and experimentation. Hunter taught anatomy at Surgeon's Hall, performed surgery at St George's Hospital, became an army surgeon and in 1776 became King George III's personal physician.

Johnson, Dr James (1777–1845) Physician and author of popular medical works, aiding in the advancement of medicine. Creator and author of many articles in the popularly received journal, the *Medico-Chirurgical Review*.

Johnson, Joseph (1738–1807) Radical bookseller and publisher of works by such writers as Anna Letitia Aikin Barbauld, Joseph Priestley, Cowper, Erasmus Darwin, Fuseli, Maria Edgeworth and Mary Wollstonecraft among others. He was a member of the London circle that included Mary Wollstonecraft and William Blake.

Keats, John (1795–1821) Poet, dramatist, prolific writer of letters and member of the Shelley circle; died of tuberculosis ('consumption'); author of 'To a Nightingale', 'On a Grecian Urn', *Endymion* and two poems on Hyperion.

Laplace, Pierre-Simon, Marquis de [also Comte de Laplace (1806–17)] (1749–1827) French mathematician, astronomer and physicist. The first to successfully apply the Newtonian theory of gravitation to the solar system (1773). Laid foundations for the scientific study of heat, magnetism and electricity, and aided in the creation of the metric system and the founding of the scientific Society of Arcueil.

Lewis, 'Monk' [Matthew Gregory] (1775–1818) Author of *Ambrosio, or The*

Monk, the popular and controversial Gothic romance. The codicil to his will was witnessed by Lord Byron, Percy Shelley and John Polidori.

Malthus, Thomas (1766–1834) Political economist. *Essay on the Principle of Population as it Affects the Future Improvement of Society* (1798) argues that population grows geometrically, is maintained arithmetically and is 'checked' by 'vice and misery'. The essay went through six editions in his lifetime.

Monboddo, James Burnett, Lord (1714–99) Scottish jurist and anthropologist who, in his work *Of the Origin and Progress of Language* (1773–92), explores the origins and development of language and society through proto-Darwinian investigations into the cultures of primitive societies, comparisons between man and primate, and discussions of the progress of society.

More, Hannah (1745–1833) Poet and religious writer who wrote on a number of political-social issues. Acquainted with writers such as Ann Yearsley (1756–1806) and the Bluestocking Elizabeth Montagu (1720–1800), and Samuel Johnson.

Paine, Thomas (1737–1809) English political writer, author of *Common Sense* (1776), a pamphlet expressing the need for the American colonies to gain political and economic independence from Britain; *The Rights of Man* (1790, a bestseller), in opposition to Burke's *Reflections on the Revolution in France*. *The Age of Reason* (1794) questioned Christian dogma and argued against organised religion.

Peacock, Thomas Love (1785–1866) Novelist, poet and official of the East India Company. Wrote *Headlong Hall* (1816) and *Nightmare Abbey* (1818).

Peake, Richard Brinsley (1792–1847) Treasurer for the Drury Lane Theatre for forty years. Had more than twenty plays produced, principally at Drury Lane and at the Adelphi, mostly farces, melodramatic romances and comedies.

Polidori, John William (1795–1821) Personal physician and secretary to Lord Byron. While in Geneva with the Shelleys, he began composition of his novel fragment *The Vampyre*, which influenced the creation of a French play and Marshner's opera.

Polito, Mr (fl. *c.* 1770) (birth and death dates unknown) An exhibitor of exotic, wild and disfigured animals and persons at Bartholomew Fair, a late-summer carnival popular for its presentation of curiosities, drama, novelty acts, song and dance.

Radcliffe, Ann (1764–1823) Novelist. Author of the Gothic romances *The Mysteries of Udolpho* and *The Italian, or The Confessional of the Black Penitents*.

Rousseau, Jean-Jacques (1712–78) French composer, philosopher, writer and political theorist whose writings became cornerstones of the French Revolution and the Romantic age. *Discours sur l'origine de l'inegalité* (*Discourse on the Origin of Inequality*), 1755, argues that mankind is essentially good, but is corrupted by society, and that inequality, a symptom of society, is unjust to the poor. Beginning with the famous lines 'Man was born free, but he is everywhere in chains', *Du Contrat social* (*The Social Contract*, 1762) proposes liberation for mankind through the creation of a just social contract. *Emile* (1762) is a novel about education, and *Julie: ou, la nouvelle Héloïse* (1761) about the achievement of domestic happiness. Rousseau's books were burned in Paris and Geneva; orders existed for his arrest. He escaped and continued to write, living in exile for the remainder of his life.

Scott, Sir Walter (1771–1832) Poet and novelist. Author of the Waverley novels (1814), *Guy Mannering* (1815), *Rob Roy* (1817), *Ivanhoe* (1819) and others.

Shelley, Percy Bysshe (1792–1822) Poet, dramatist, novelist and writer of political and philosophical prose. Died a premature death by drowning when his boat became caught in a squall off the Gulf of Spezia in Italy. Author of the poems *Queen Mab*, *Alastor* (an influence on *Frankenstein*), *The Mask of Anarchy* and 'The Triumph of Life', *The Cenci* and *Prometheus Unbound* (plays), 'A Defence of Poetry' and 'A Philosophical View of Reform'.

Smith, Adam (1723–90) Political economist who wrote the *Theory of Moral Sentiments* (1759), which was highly praised by Hume. His *Inquiry into the Nature and Causes of the Wealth of Nations* (1776) established political economy as a separate field of scientific study.

Smith, Horace [Horatio Smith] (1779–1849) Poet and author. Composed *Rejected Addresses* (1812) with his brother James, a parody of poets such as Wordsworth, Cobbett, Crabbe, Byron, Scott, and Southey. He was acquainted with Leigh Hunt and Percy Shelley, with whom he stayed as a guest in 1817.

Swift, Jonathan (1667–1745) Dean of St Patrick's, Dublin, and author of *The Battle of the Books*, *Tale of a Tub* (1704), and many satirical and serious pamphlets on political issues. 'A Modest Proposal' ironically suggests eating babies to solve overpopulation and malnourishment in Ireland. *Gulliver's Travels* (1726) is the satirical story of Lemuel Gulliver, a shipwrecked surgeon who visits various different societies, including that of the Houyhnhnms, intelligent and noble horses plagued by the brutal humanoid Yahoos.

Thelwall, John (1764–1834) One of the principal English supporters of the French Revolution; enjoyed a brief moment of fame in the 1790s until political and cultural reaction forced him to retreat from active political life. In 1794 he was imprisoned in the Tower of London and Newgate, awaiting trial for Treason.

Trelawny, Edward John (1792–1881) Author, adventurer and friend of Thomas Medwin. Through Medwin, he befriended Percy Shelley and Lord Byron. Travelled with Byron to aid in the Greek War of Independence, but was shot to death soon after Lord Byron died in battle.

Volney, Constantin-François de Chasseboeuf, Comte de (1757–1820) Historian and philosopher, traveller and Girondist politician who was acquainted with figures such as Benjamin Franklin and Baron d'Holbach. Author of *Les Ruines, ou méditations sur les révolutions des empires* ('The Ruins: or a Survey of the Revolutions of Empires') (1791), an investigation of the rise and fall of civilisations, significant for its condemnation of tyranny, and a favourite of Percy Shelley's.

Walker, Adam (1731–1821) Author, inventor and itinerant teacher of Percy Shelley from his preparatory school days at Syon House.

Wallack, James William (*c.* 1791–1864) Actor and stage manager.

Wilberforce, William (1759–1833) A wealthy Cambridge graduate and popular British politician and philanthropist, who campaigned for the abolition of the slave trade.

William IV (1765–1837) An admiral of the Navy and Duke of Clarence, William IV became the King of Great Britain and Ireland in 1830. The death of Princess Charlotte, daughter and heir of George IV, would have caused William's daughters from his marriage to Adelaide of Saxe-Coburg Meinengein to succeed to the throne. Because his two daughters died in early childhood, Princess Victoria actually succeeded to the throne. While William was king, the Reform Act of 1832 was passed, an act supported and encouraged by the king that allowed voting rights to middle-class land owners.

Wollstonecraft, Mary (1759–97) Feminist writer and political philosopher who promoted equal treatment and education for women. Wollstonecraft died two weeks after giving birth to Mary (Shelley). See Contexts (**p. 7**).

Wordsworth, William (1770–1850) Poet who collaborated with Samuel Taylor Coleridge in the creation of *Lyrical Ballads* (1798), and the author of the autobiographical *The Prelude* (1850), a poem revised several times during his life. Wordsworth was known to the Shelley circle principally for *Lyrical Ballads* and *The Excursion* (1814), which with *The Prelude* was to have formed part of the unfinished *magnum opus*, the philosophical and autobiographical work *The Recluse*.

Works Consulted

Dictionary of National Biography, ed. Sir Leslie Stephen and Sir Sidney Lee. Oxford: Oxford University Press, 1973.

Enciclopedia Italiana: di scienze, lettere ed arti. Vol. 2. Milano, Roma: Instituto Giovanni Treccani, 1929.

Highfill, Philip H., Jr, Kalman A. Burnim and Edward A. Langhans, eds. *A Biographical Dictionary, of Actors, Actresses, Musicians, Dancers, Managers and Other Stage Personnel in London, 1660–1800*. Vol. 12. Carbondale and Edwardsville: Southern Illinois University Press, 1987.

Mellor, Anne K. and Richard E. Matlak. *British Literature 1780–1830*. New York and London: Harcourt Brace, 1996.

The New Encyclopaedia Britannica, 15th edn. London and Chicago: Encyclopaedia Britannica, 1998.

Porter, Roy. *A Social History of Madness: The World Through the Eyes of the Insane*. New York: Weidenfeld & Nicolson, 1987.

Serafin, Steven, ed. *Dictionary of Literary Biography*. Vol. 144. Detroit, Washington, DC and London: Gale Research, 1994.

Shelley, Mary. *Frankenstein: Or the Modern Prometheus; the 1818 Text*, ed. Marilyn Butler. Oxford and New York: Oxford University Press, 1994.

Index

NOTE: Page numbers in bold indicate an extract by an author or from a particular work; page numbers in italic indicate information is in a figure or its caption; page numbers followed by *n* indicate information is in a footnote.

Cobham, Billy 79
'Cockney School' of poetry 185
Coleridge, Samuel Taylor 19*n* 184; *Ancient Mariner* 120, 139, 170*n*, 180; *Lyrical Ballads* 8, 11
Collins, William 40, 41
colonialism 81, 112–13, 121, 167
Columbus, Christopher 170
comedy films 67, 71–3
comics 79
commodity culture 9–10, 80, 81, 90–2, 149
compassion 105, 146
computer games 79
Condon, Bill 77
Condorcet, Marie Jean Antoine Nicolas de Caritat, Marquis de 82, 120, 184
Conger, Syndy 133, 181
consilience 22*n*
Cooke, Thomas Potter 29–30, 38–9, 48, *52*, 60, 116, 184
cooking traditions 117, 118, 145
Cooper, Sir Astley Paston 88, 185
corpses: constitute creature 91–2, 97, 117; supply for medical studies 86–8
creation myth 99–100, 101–2; *see also* birth myth; *Paradise Lost*
creature 1; appearance 137–8; awareness of appearance 110, 113, 120, 138, 147, 153; condemned to solitude 92, 180; corpses constitute 91–2, 97, 117; creation of 53–5, 137–9, 152–3; as cultural image 3, 30, 45, 65, 66; deconstructed 121; diet of 113, 116–20, 144–5, 156; dumbed down 65, 66; education of 40, 42, 94–5, 105, 107, 118, 147, 151–3; eloquence of 104, 108, 113, 116, 138, 143–4, 146, 165; female companion *see* female creature; and Frankenstein 91–2, 103, 108, 117, 118–19, 120; and Frankenstein's death 44, 164–6; Frankenstein's denial of female companion 92, 99–100, 101–2, 108, 111, 121–2, 155–60; Frankenstein's pursuit of 76, 142–4, 160–6; humanity of 46–7; as 'innocent eye' 146, 150; Marxist interpretation 90–2; as materialist 17, 145; murderous rages 154–5, 164–5, 180; namelessness 38, 39, 91, 108–9; as narrator 37–8, 109–11, **144–55**; as Other

55, 113–14, 116, 119; portrayal as Caliban figure 116; portrayal on film *64*, 65, 66, 69, 70, 97; portrayal on stage 29–30, 38–9, 48, *52*, 116, 184; Rousseauean nature 94–5, 105, 117, 119, 144–6; as self-made being 40, 46, 107; skin colour 113, 116, 137; social formation 42–4, 94–5, 108, 117, 118, 119, 145–6, 149; and women 99–101; 'wretch' designation 109, 137, 138, 141, 143–4, 165
Crick, Francis Harry Compton 99
Crime of Dr Frankenstein, The (multimedia rhapsody) 63
Croker, John Wilson 185
Cronenberg, David 77
Crook, Nora 179
Cross, Ashley 179
cultural studies 81
culture 145–6
Cunha, Richard E. 67
Curse of Frankenstein, The (film) 71

Darwin, Erasmus 32, 93, 131, 170, 178, 185
Davis, John 115
Davis, Mannie 67
Davy, Sir Humphrey 19, 27, 84, 185
Dawley, J. Searle 64
De Lacey family 44, 146–54
Dean, James Byron 61
Deane, Hamilton 61
deconstruction 81, 109–11, 121
Defoe, Daniel 65, 118
Deleuze, Gilles 118
Derrida, Jacques 81, 146
Descartes, René 47
desire 94, 99, 181
despotism 120; and education 93, 94
Devil Among the Players, The (play) 61
Dick, Philip K. 46, 59
diet 113, 116–20, 144–5, 156
disciplinary society 87
dissection 85–8, 135–6
DNA discovery 99
Do Androids Dream of Electric Sheep? (Dick) 46, 59
Dr Jeykll and Mr Hyde (Stevenson) 91
domestic fiction 94
doppelgänger theme 180